HUMANITIES
Self, Society & Culture

Caspar D. Friedrich, *On a Sailing Ship*, c. 1818–19; oil on canvas;
Hermitage Museum, Leningrad.

HUMANITIES

Self, Society & Culture

THIRD EDITION

General Editors:
William R. Hanna and Clive Cockerton

Contributors:
Michael Badyk, Kathy Casey, Melanie Chaparian, Wayson Choy,
Clive Cockerton, R. Chris Coleman, Toby Fletcher, Jay Haddad,
William R. Hanna, Don Holmes, Jill Le Clair, Mitchell Lerner, John Maxwell,
Tom Olien, Barbara Ritchie, Antanas Sileika, Linda Smithies, John Steckley

Editorial Committee:
Michael Badyk, Gary Berman, George Byrnes, Kathy Casey, Melanie Chaparian,
Wayson Choy, Clive Cockerton, R. Chris Coleman, Mo Farge, Jay Haddad,
William R. Hanna, Don Holmes, Joe Kertes, Mitchell Lerner, John Maxwell,
Barbara Ritchie, Antanas Sileika, John Steckley, Herman Suligoj,
Donna Williamson

THOMPSON EDUCATIONAL PUBLISHING, INC.
Toronto

Canadian Cataloguing in Publication Data

Main entry under entry:
Humanities : self, society & culture

3rd ed.
Previous eds. published under title:
Humanites: a course in general education.
ISBN 1-55077-033-0

1. Humanities. I. Hanna, William R. II. Cockerton, Clive.
III. Title: Humanities : a course in general education.

H85.H85 1991   001.3   C91-094989-1

Credits
W.H. Auden, "The Unknown Citizen," *Collected Shorter Poems, 1927-57 by W.H.Auden*, Random House. Earl Babbie, "Determinism Versus Freedom" from *Observing Ourselves: Essays in Social Research* © 1986 by Wadsworth, Inc., reprinted by permission of the publisher. Paul Chance, "Your Child's Self-Esteem," *Parents*, January 1982. Dona Lee Davis, *Blood and Nerves*, Institute of Social and Economic Research, Memorial University of Newfoundland, 1983. Doris Lessing, "Group Minds," taken from *Prisons We Choose to Live Inside*, Harper Collins. Cheryl Merser, "Men, Women, Equality and Love," in *"Grown-Ups": A Generation in Search of Adulthood*, G.P. Putnam's Sons, 1987. John Rockwell, "Leftist Causes? Rock Seconds Those Emotions," and Douglas Shenson*, "Limits of the Possible,"* copyright © 1988 by The New York Times Company, reprinted by permission. Susan Sontag, excerpt from *On Photography*, copyright © 1973, 1974, 1977 by Susan Sontag, reprinted by permission of Farrar, Straus and Giroux.

Photographs by Gary Gellert, Humber College: pp. x, 30, 32, 50, 90, 121, 122, 146, 148, 165, 166, 182, 184, 200, 221, 222, 245, 246; Photograph by Keith Thompson, p. 87; Family sculpture by Gustave Vigeland, Norway, p. 224.

Printed in Canada.
  2 3 4 5   94 93 92 91

Contents

~ UNIT 5 ~
ARTS AND CULTURE / 223

HUMANITIES

Self, Society & Culture

THINKING AND WRITING SKILLS

… to be possessed of a vigorous mind is not enough; the prime requisite is rightly to apply it. The greatest minds, as they are capable of the highest excellences, are open likewise to the greatest aberrations; and those who travel very slowly may yet make far greater progress, provided they keep always to the straight road, than those who, while they run, forsake·it.

René
Descartes

Humanities is concerned with the issues and topics that have preoccupied humankind throughout history. Because of the complexity of the issues with which we will be dealing, clarity of thought and expression are essential. It is obvious that certain thoughts require high levels of skill in language. The development of these high-level skills is achieved more efficiently when we attempt to grapple with challenging content. It is the purpose of this course to offer such content and to help the student develop the skills necessary to express his or her own thoughts about the content.

The following skills section will help you be more precise in your use of terminology and assist you in performing the essential thinking and writing tasks such as summary, comparison and contrast, and evaluation.

Definition of Terms Used in Essay Examinations

Compiled and edited by Don Holmes

The seven most often used.

*COMPARE When you are asked to compare, you should examine qualities, or characteristics, in order to discover resemblance. The term *compare* is usually stated as *compare with*, and it implies that you are to emphasize similarities, although differences may be mentioned.

*CONTRAST When you are instructed to contrast, dissimilarities, differences, or unlikenesses of associated things, qualities, events or problems should be stressed.

*CRITICIZE In a criticism you should express your judgment with respect to the correctness or merit of the factors under consideration. You are expected to give the results of your own analysis and to discuss the limitations as well as the good points or contributions of the plan or work in question.

*DEFINE   Definitions call for concise, clear, authoritative meanings. In such statements details are not required, but boundaries or limitations of the definition should be briefly cited. You must keep in mind the class to which a thing belongs and whatever differentiates the particular object from all others in the class.

*DESCRIBE   In a descriptive answer, you should recount, characterize, sketch, or relate in narrative form.

DIAGRAM   For a question which specifies a diagram, you should present a drawing, chart, plan, or graphic representation in your answer. Generally the student is also expected to label the diagram and in some cases to add a brief explanation or description.

*DISCUSS   The term *discuss*, which appears often in essay questions, directs you to examine, analyze carefully, and present considerations pro and con regarding the problems or items involved. This type of question calls for a complete and detailed answer.

ENUMERATE   The word *enumerate* specifies a list or outline form of reply. In such questions, you should recount, one by one, in concise form, the points required.

EVALUATE   In an evaluation question, you are expected to present a careful appraisal of the problem, stressing both advantages and limitations. Evaluation implies authoritative and, to a lesser degree, personal appraisal of both contributions and limitations.

EXPLAIN   In explanatory answers, it is imperative that you clarify, elucidate, and interpret the material you present. In such an answer, it is best to state the "how" or "why," reconcile any differences in opinion or experimental results, and where possible, state causes. The aim is to make plain the conditions which give rise to whatever you are examining.

ILLUSTRATE A question which asks you to illustrate usually requires you to explain or clarify your answer to the problem by presenting a figure, picture, or concrete example.

INTERPRET An interpretation question is similar to one requiring explanation. You are expected to translate, exemplify, solve, or comment upon the subject and usually to give your judgment or reaction to the problem.

JUSTIFY When you are instructed to justify your answer, you must prove or show grounds for decisions. In such an answer, evidence should be presented in convincing form.

*LIST Listing is similar to enumeration. You are expected in such questions to present an itemized series or a tabulation. Such answers should always be given in concise form.

OUTLINE An outlined answer is organized description. You should give main points and essential supplementary materials, omitting minor details, and present the information in a systematic arrangement or classification.

PROVE A question which requires proof is one which demands confirmation or verification. In such discussions, you should establish something with certainty by evaluating and citing experimental evidence or by logical reasoning.

RELATE In a question which asks you to show the relationship or to *relate,* your answer would emphasize connections and associations in descriptive form.

REVIEW A review specifies a critical examination. You should analyze and comment briefly in organized sequence upon the major points of the problem.

STATE In questions which direct you to specify, give, state, or present, you are called upon to express the high points in brief, clear narrative form. Details, and usually illustrations or examples, may be omitted.

SUMMARIZE When you are asked to summarize or present a summary, you should give in condensed form the main points or facts. All details, illustrations, and elaborations are to be omitted.

TRACE When a question asks you to trace a course of events, you are to give a description of progress, historical sequence, or development from the point of origin. Such narratives may call for probing or for deductions.

ANALYZE To analyze means to find the main ideas and show how they are related and why they are important.

COMMENT ON To comment on a problem or topic means to discuss, criticize, or explain its meaning as completely as possible.

Reading the Humanities Text

Barbara Ritchie

You're probably wondering about the title of this article. Why is there a section on reading? You know how to read; you've been doing it since you were six or seven. So what's so special about reading the *Humanities* text?

Well, as you have no doubt discovered by now, reading a college text is very different from the reading you did in high school or the reading you do when you are relaxing with a favourite novel or the sports page. The articles in your *Humanities* text (and in virtually all your other college courses) are more challenging, more factually dense, and yes, more difficult than the kinds of articles you have probably encountered before. If you are like the majority of students, you will benefit by using specific study reading strategies to improve your comprehension and retention skills.

Keep in mind that the selections in your *Humanities* text cover a wide range of topics and are written in a variety of styles. Naturally you will be more interested in some than others, and just as naturally you will probably find you have little or no difficulty comprehending those articles that deal with topics you are interested in and already know something about. For example, students interested in children will enjoy Paul Chance's article "Your Child's Self-esteem" while those whose interest is of a more scientific or technological bent will no doubt be intrigued with "Acid Raid" by Michael Badyk. We think the selections in the *Humanities* text are of high interest and, for the most part, are highly readable. However, we would like to present some strategies you can use to make your reading more effective and efficient.

Before you begin your first *Humanities* reading assignment, take a few minutes to preview the entire text. This will give you a sense of the purpose and organization not only of the text, but of the course. By glancing at the table of contents, you will see that the first chapter of the *Humanities* text is devoted to the skills you will need to demonstrate in order to be successful in the course. This is a good chapter to refer to before you write a test or an essay since it not only provides definitions of terms commonly used in testing situations, but it also includes specific examples of how to set up essay type questions.

Further perusal of the table of contents will show you that the *Humanities* text is divided into five units and each unit is subdivided into two or three issues. Each of the units has an introduction; make a mental note always to read these since everything else in the unit follows from them. Flipping through the pages at random will also aid you in your endeavour to get a general sense of the organization of the text—you will note, for example, that some of the articles are followed by questions helpful to you in your studying.

Once you have previewed the text, you are ready to begin your first reading assignment. When you are reading for studying purposes (and basically most of the reading you do in college is of this kind: reading you will be tested on), it is often helpful to approach the assignment with specific steps to take *before you read, while you are reading*, and *after you have completed your reading*.

BEFORE YOU READ

You would not attempt to run a marathon or play a championship game of tennis without first warming up your body; if you were a good enough athlete you might be able to complete these tasks, but it stands to reason you would not be as effective at either if you did not properly prepare your body for the task at hand. In the same way, it is necessary to warmup your brain for the equally challenging mental task of reading. Just as the athlete's warm-up makes him or her a more effective competitor, so your mental warmup will make you a more effective reader and student. Here's what you do before you read.

Preview the chapter.

> **(a) Read the title asking yourself specific questions about the title.** What does the article seem to be about? What do you already know about the topic? Based on the title and what you already know about the topic, what kind of predictions can you make about the article you are about to read?
>
> **(b) Read the introductory paragraph.** The main idea of the article is often found in the introductory paragraph.
>
> **(c) Read the last paragraph or summary.** The concluding paragraph often reiterates the main points and the conclusions.
>
> **(d) Read the questions that follow.**

BEFORE YOU READ

- Read the title asking yourself specific questions about the title.
- Read the introductory paragraph.
- Read the last paragraph or summary.
- Read the questions that follow.

WHILE YOU READ

Have you ever finished reading an assigned chapter in a textbook and found that at the end of the chapter you had not understood one word of what was written? Or have you ever found yourself in the middle of an assigned chapter and realized that although you have been "reading" the text, in fact, you have been thinking about your part-time job or your date for Saturday night or any other of a hundred things more interesting to you at that particular moment than the textbook?

Most of us have been in these situations. Sometimes what we are reading has too many unfamiliar words for us to make much sense of the content without spending half our time looking up meanings in the dictionary. At other times, we are not really concentrating on our reading and we let ourselves be distracted. The problem, however, is that the reading must be completed and understood and hence, we must reread the chapter. Inefficient reading wastes valuable time.

In order to make the time you spend reading your *Humanities* text (or any college text) as effective as possible you must learn to concentrate on your reading and to become actively involved in it. Here are some suggestions on how to do just that.

- **Make sure your study environment is conducive to studying.**
  Despite what many students claim, it is impossible to read effectively in a noisy environment. This means you turn off the stereo and the television while you are reading.

- **Take an active part in the reading process.**
  This means developing strategies to help you make sure you understand what you are reading and to help you concentrate on the material at hand. For example, you could do the following.

  (a) Mark significant ideas and details. The important word here is *significant.* Don't mark everything you read! After all, the purpose of marking is to set off important points so that you can come back to them later when you are studying. Marking most of the text won't be much help to you if you want to scan the text quickly for the salient points before a quiz. How do you know what to mark? Well, the following list should give you some idea of what to underline or highlight when you are reading:

  i. *Main ideas in paragraphs.*

  ii. *Vocabulary words* that are unfamiliar to you so that you can look them up later.

  iii. *Definitions and examples.*

  iv. *Signal words*—words that signal the direction of the writer's thought. Such words are commonly used by writers to indicate emphasis, illustration, cause and effect, comparison and contrast, sequencing and conclusions.

  Here are a few examples of ***signal words.*** (Your Communications instructor may refer to these words as *transition words* and give you a more complete list.)

  Words which signal **EMPHASIS**
  the main value
  should be noted
  the primary concern

Words which signal **ILLUSTRATION**
    for example
    for instance
    to illustrate
Words which signal **CAUSE AND EFFECT**
    therefore
    as a result
    thus
Words which signal **COMPARISON**
    in the same way
    like
    similarly
Words which signal **CONTRAST**
    however
    in contrast
    on the other hand
Words which signal **SEQUENCING**
    first of all
    next
    then
Words which signal **CONCLUSIONS**
    finally
    in conclusion
    last of all

WHILE YOU READ

- Make sure your study environment is conducive to studying.
- Take an active part in the reading process.
- Mark significant ideas and details.
- Ask questions as you read.

(b) Ask questions as you read. Since reading is an act of communication, in order to ensure that you understand everything the writer is trying to tell you, approach the assigned article with specific questions in mind. For example, you could ask yourself the following questions as you read

   i. what is the main purpose of the article? (to inform, to instruct, to analyse, to criticize, to entertain?)

  ii. what is the main idea of each paragraph, section, or complete article?

 iii. what specific details (examples, statistics, facts) does the author use to develop his main ideas?

  iv. what conclusions can I draw from this article?

AFTER YOU READ

- Recite to yourself the important points in the article immediately after you have finished reading it.

AFTER YOU READ

In order to ensure that you have fully comprehended your assigned article, it is imperative that you recite to yourself the important points in the article immediately after you have finished reading it. A written paraphrase of a short article or a summary of a lengthy article are good indicators of how well you have understood the assigned reading.

* * *

We think you will find the selections in the *Humanities* text interesting as well as informative. The preceding strategies will be especially helpful if you come across an article that you find a little more challenging than the others, but the basic premise that you should read your college texts actively applies to all the selections. And remember: if there is something in the text that you don't understand even after applying the strategies, ask your instructor for help. After all, that's what he or she is there for.

Writing A Summary

Linda Smithies

sum·ma·ry *n* : a condensed statement—
adj brief; concise

Summarizing is something we do all the time without really being aware of it. After watching a good movie or television show, a friend may ask, "What was it about?" Generally we answer with details about the plot, the main characters, the special effects, and so on. But most of us will probably embellish these objective details with our own subjective impressions, too—which actor or actress we thought was the most convincing, which special effects were the most spectacular, which part of the plot didn't make sense, and so on. These embellishments certainly add spice to our conversation, but they probably reveal as much about us, particularly our thoughts and feelings, as they do about the movie or show.

However, when you are asked to summarize, either in writing or orally, an article in this book or one of the *Humanities* lectures, you should make sure you don't include these thoughts and impressions. These will become important later when it comes time to evaluate what you have read or heard, but you can't evaluate until you know the content well, so doing a summary is the best way to get started.

What you must do, though, is identify the main points of the article or lecture. But, sometimes finding the main points can be a daunting task, especially when they are mixed in with lots of minor points, such as examples, case studies, colourful language, repetition, and comparisons. In fact, most good writers or lecturers strive to use lots of these minor points to make the main points more interesting and less abstract or theoretical. So your job of separating the main points from the minor ones can be a difficult one.

To help you accomplish this task, ask yourself a few questions when reading an article or listening to a lecture:

1. What is the specific *topic* or *issue* under discussion? Just like the rest of us in our everyday conversations, writers and lecturers often get side-tracked and may ramble on about concepts that are very interesting, but not really on the main point. By constantly reminding yourself about the topic or issue under discussion, you will be better able to separate the "relevant" from the "ramble."

2. What is the *main purpose* of the article or lecture? Is the writer or lecturer trying to persuade us to see the issue or topic from his or her point of view? Give us the historical background? Provide us with detailed statistical or factual information to increase our knowledge about the topic or issue? Often, writers and lecturers will address all these questions, but generally there is one all-important purpose which has guided their selection of material to talk or write about. Since knowing this all-important purpose helps you to select the main points, listen carefully to a lecturer's opening comments and read carefully the introductions to the articles—these are the places where you will find "statements of purpose."

3. What *clues* has the lecturer or writer provided to help you separate the main points from the not-so-important points. Phrases like "First of all…," "We must consider as well…," "Furthermore…," "What is also important…" tell us the writer or lecturer is moving from one main point to another. In contrast, phrases like "For example…" and "Take the case of…" tell us that we are now going to read or hear an embellishment of the main point, not the main point itself.

4. Finally, once you feel you have found all the main points, *review your notes*. Fill in any gaps you may have missed the first time through, eliminate any repetition or irrelevant information, and make sure you know the definitions of all the words and concepts. Once you know the content and can summarize it effectively, you are ready for the next stage—evaluation.

Comparison and Contrast

Clive Cockerton

This course, like many other courses, will frequently ask you to compare and contrast two or more thinkers, issues and situations. When you are asked to compare and contrast, you are being asked to do more than just *describe* two things. You are being asked to do the work of finding the most significant points of similarity and difference. It is a complex task involving both analysis in detail (breaking up whatever is being compared into smaller parts) and synthesis (bringing the parts together in the new light shed by your comparison).

Many people, when asked to compare, for example, Freud and Skinner, would launch into an essay that would list everything about Freud followed by everything about Skinner and would look something like this:

INTRODUCTORY PARAGRAPH:
Identify topic. Name elements of comparison; fundamental views of
human nature, therapeutic strategies, free will.

PART A: Fundamental Views of Human Nature

PART B: Therapeutic Strategies

PART C: Free Will

PART D: Conclusion

While this essay format can *describe* the ideas of the two men in a very sophisticated way, it doesn't really bring them together and compare them on the basis of some element (their attitude to the question of free will, for instance). A much better format would look like the diagram opposite.

It should be clear from this format that the elements (the fundamental views of human nature, therapeutic strategies, and free will) are the main organizing elements of your comparison and must be carefully chosen to make an effective comparison.

Of course, we use this comparison technique outside of school all the time, whenever we need to make a choice, whether it be what car we are going to buy or in which restaurant to have dinner. In both cases, we look for the most significant elements in our choice. In the instance of the car, the first step is to analyze the decision into its elements such as cost, technological innovation, space, comfort, and safety. There may be many more elements but usually there are only one or two dominant ones such as cost and safety upon which we naturally concentrate most of our time. Similarly, the example of restaurants yields a number of factors such as cost, quality of food, decor and service. Again, these elements organize themselves along the lines of our priorities. Although decor and service may form a minor part of our decision, most often the choice will be made based on value and quality. When comparing thinkers and their ideas we analyze or breakdown the subject into elements as well. This is a critical phase and many writers like to use a grid, such as that on the following page, so that they can chart their comparison in a more graphic way. As well you may wish to include space for your conclusion or decision on the relative merits of the competing theories.

As in the case of cars and restaurants, you may quickly decide that one or two elements are the dominant ones with the others playing supporting but minor roles. You may wish to group all the minor elements into one paragraph, and plan to spend at least one paragraph on each of the major elements. As you are putting together your paragraph, it is useful to think about the rhetorical structures that can be helpful in comparison. Such structures might include:

1. *While* Freud emphasizes X, Skinner, *on the other hand,* suggests Y.

2. *Although* Freud and Skinner disagree about A, there seems to be some common ground on the subject of B.

COMPARISON AND CONTRAST

When you are asked to compare and contrast, you are being asked to do more than just *describe* two things. You are being asked to do the work of finding the most significant points of similarity and difference.

Theories of Human Personality

ELEMENTS	FREUD	SKINNER	MY CONCLUSION
Nature of personality	We are largely unconscious of the interplay of powerful urges (eros and thanatos). Psyche divided into three areas: id, ego, superego.	We are extremely flexible beings whose behaviours are controlled and shaped by the environment and the effect of rewards and punishments.	
Free will	No free will	No free will	
Therapeutic strategies	Talking with analyst attempts to make patients conscious of the forces that motivate them.	Behaviour modification. Change the behaviour by changing the consequences.	

In many cases, your consideration of the elements will lead you to decide that a particular thinker has an advantage in his explanation of the various elements, and you may wish to provide the reader with a sense of where you stand on the issue and which thinker you support.

When you have read the first selection in Unit Three, you might like to try filling out the following grid on the views of human nature of Hobbes, Locke, and Marx. Be sure to come to your own conclusion on each element. Ask yourself if there are any important elements of comparison left out of this grid. After completing the grid, think about how you would turn the elements into paragraphs.

Theories of Human Nature			
THINKERS **ELEMENTS**	**HOBBES**	**LOCKE**	**MARX**	**MY CONCLUSION**
The nature of the individual				
Relationship of the individual to society				
The role of authority				
Importance of a fair contract				
Self-interest *vs.* altruism				

Evaluation

Wayson Choy

"What's my life worth?" "What do I mean when I say 'I want to be happy'?" "What can I do about changing my life?"

These are questions every intelligent person comes to ask. There are, of course, no easy answers. However, in the *Humanities* course, the same questions are raised in challenging ways—and you are asked to take on the adventure of coming to some possible conclusions. You are asked to *evaluate* the knowledge presented to you in your readings, in the lectures and in the give-and-take of the seminar classes.

You are asked to *evaluate* ideas, theories, concepts, and feelings—to begin to understand how to take information and discover the differences between opinion and knowledge. If you're fortunate, you may also discover the differences between knowledge and wisdom, feelings and insights.

For example, most people assume that "one opinion is as good as another." In fact, most opinions are not to be trusted, however sincere the opinion-maker may be.

Naturally, if our life does not depend on the opinion, we may simply ignore it or politely nod our head. But, if your life depended on the opinion, "It's hot outside!" — because your rare blood disease will kill you at any temperature over 30 degrees—you would probably need to evaluate that opinion. You would depend, not on the opinion, "It's hot outside!"—but more wisely on the statement, "The official Canada Weather Thermometer Report reads 25 degrees Celsius…"

People's lives have actually depended upon these opinions:

"The bottom line is that you can't fight City Hall!"

"Russia is the Evil Empire."

"Only Homosexuals get AIDS. That's God's punishment."
"That grenade is not defective."
"John knows a scientist who says smoking is harmless."
"Tell you the truth, all you need is money to be happy."
"You can't do anything about poor single mothers."
"If you fail this test, you're just stupid."
"People should have the right to carry guns."
"Any one gets raped, they asked for it!"
"You just have to work hard to succeed in life."
"Foreigners shouldn't take work away from Canadians."
"Women should stay home; it's more natural."
"A man should always stand and fight!"

Imagine accepting all of these opinions as if they were true; as if, indeed, we need only hear them and nod our heads and live our lives accordingly. Many people do just that regardless of how disturbed they may be when they hear the words spoken.

The process of education begins with that feeling of being disturbed: Education of any personal worth is often a process of disturbance—first, disturbance; then, evaluation.

You will hear startling things, discover that your world may be more complex than you ever realized. You will test modern social and psychological theories, use new ideas and new language to begin to understand your own life. You will refer to authorities, artists, writers, facts and figures, make judgments, use logic in your debate, think in new ways, and—perhaps reluctantly at first—you may even throw out some ideas you thought were true. There will be fresh ways to test your most sacred ideas, and, if you work hard, you will learn how to communicate your new insights more clearly to others.

You will begin to *evaluate*: It is, finally, your own life that you will evaluate.

EXERCISE

Take any *one* of the opinions above that disturbs you, explain why you think it is "only an opinion" and *not* knowledge. Begin by defining what you mean by "opinion" and "knowledge." Finally, discuss the steps which would help you logically challenge that particular opinion—and perhaps change the mind of those who believe the opinion to be true.

Worksheet 1

DEFINE:

1. _____

_____

_____

_____

_____

_____

_____

_____

_____

Worksheet 2

SUMMARIZE:

1. _____

_____

_____

_____

_____

_____

_____

_____

_____

_____

_____

_____

_____

_____

_____

_____

Worksheet 3

COMPARE AND CONTRAST:

1. _____ **WITH** _____

_____
_____
_____
_____
_____
_____
_____
_____
_____
_____

Worksheet 4

EVALUATE:

1._____
_____
_____
_____
_____
_____
_____
_____
_____
_____
_____
_____
_____
_____
_____
_____
_____

Tips on Writing An Essay Exam in *Humanities*

R. Chris Coleman

Here is an actual question taken from a previous essay exam in Humanities. The answer had to be a minimum of 250 words and was worth 70 points. Fifty percent (35 points) was given for content and 50% for how well the sentences communicated ideas. How would you go about answering this question?

> **QUESTION:**
> How does ONE of the four schools of personality explain human nature? For instance: Why are we frequently in conflict with ourselves? How does our personality develop? Can we change our basic personality behaviour? Explain.

In answering an essay type question, it's important not to make the task any more difficult than it is already. Your instructor wants you to show *(a)* that you took notes during lectures, *(b)* that you read the assigned sections in the text, *(c)* that you understood and remember what was said, and *(d)* that you appreciate its relevance and significance.

Also, it is especially important to realize you are not expected to explore just your own thoughts, feelings and opinions. In the example above, for instance, it would be a mistake to write something like:

In my opinion, our basic personality is already formed at birth as a result of our past-life experiences before we were born.

While some people may believe this theory, it is not one of the four schools of personality theory dealt with directly in the Humanities course material.

On an essay exam, you are expected to recall as much as you can of the course material. So, of course, it's a major advantage to know the material well before you write.

One of the challenges in writing an essay exam is that time is limited. Because of the lack of time to rewrite, planning and preparing become more important than usual.

One helpful tip is, *before you start actually composing your essay*, jot down in point form everything you can think of related to the question. Don't worry yet whether or not you will include every point in your final answer. Just make the list as long as you can. Having such a list helps you organize your material and keeps you on topic.

To illustrate, suppose in answering the question above that you chose to explain the psychoanalytic school of personality theory. Somewhere in your list of points you would include these points, though probably not in this order:

SIGMUND FREUD (turn of century)
3 Aspects Of Personality:
1) **ID** = unconscious
       - ***Eros*** = instinct for life
       - ***Thanatos*** = death wish
       - Child-like

2) **EGO** = awareness of self
       - thinks, deals with react
       - mediates between id & superego
       - Adult

3) **SUPEREGO** = conscience, shoulds
       - *Socialization* = internalize values
       - Parental

(etc.)

Of course, to be complete for the above question, your actual list would be much longer.

USEFUL TIP ~

Before you start actually composing your essay, jot down in point form everything you can think of related to the question.

USEFUL TIP ~

Usually the question itself not only will tell you what your instructor expects, but also will hint at how you should arrange the material.

Your list might even include a quotation or two that you've memorized during study for the exam. Including memorized passages in an essay type answer is fine, providing you fully understand what they mean and can explain them in your own words. Here's a quotation that would be useful in formulating a line of argument for the answer to the above question:

> "Human personality emerges ... by the interactive functions between ego, superego, and id." (*Humanities*, p.39)

Once your list is more or less complete, you are ready to *organize* the material. Usually the question itself not only will tell you what your instructor expects, but also will hint at how you should arrange the material.

Generally speaking, key words in the question like "**DEFINE, SUMMARIZE, COMPARE, CONTRAST, EVALUATE**" are cues as to how your instructor expects you to organize your answer. The introductory sections in your Humanities text show you how to organize material for each of these types of answers. In the example we're working on, there are two key words, very closely related"*explain* and *how*. You must explain how human personality emerges and develops, according to Freudian psychoanalytic theory.

Any essay is basically an *argument*. First you make a definite statement, called a **THESIS STATEMENT**. Then you *support* or back up your thesis statement using specific points taken directly from the course material. Try to show, prove or demonstrate that there is sufficient evidence to support your thesis statement.

For many questions on *Humanities* exams, there is no single, absolutely right answer—just those answers that are adequately supported with specific points, and those answers which, unfortunately, are not. Therefore, it is advisable to use as much material from the text and lectures as you can.

In organizing your answer, you might find it helpful to construct an outline. Some people actually jot their outline down on paper. Others, to save time, merely keep their outline in their heads. It doesn't really matter, as long as you proceed according to some definite plan or strategy.

Don't make the mistake of just starting to write hoping something positive will magically happen.

For the question above, your outline might look something like this:

1. Thesis statement.: Define 3 parts of personality: id, ego, superego.
2. Explain how they interact with each other.
3. Why we are frequently in conflict with ourselves.
4. How our personality develops.
5. How we can change.

Notice how similar the outline is to the question itself? It should be. Otherwise you may not be covering everything the question is asking for.

The average sentence in college level writing is about 15–20 words. Therefore, if you plan to write a short paragraph for each of the 5 points on your outline, with each paragraph containing 3–5 sentences, you should have no trouble meeting the requirement of a minimum of 250 words: (5 paragraphs) X (4 sentences) X (15 words) = 300 words. Of course, this is a very rough guide.

With your list of points and your outline complete, you are ready to start composing your answer. One difference between an essay exam and a regular essay is that you already know that your audience is your own instructor. So imagine your instructor sitting directly opposite you, and proceed to talk to that person on paper the way you would if you were face to face.

Do not try to impress your instructor by using "big" words. On the other hand, you should avoid street language as well. Use precise vocabulary. *Write to express what you mean, clearly.*

Another difference between and essay exam and a normal essay is that you are not expected to write a striking introduction, or a thoughtful conclusion. Simply start with your thesis statement. Very often the wording of your thesis statement will be quite similar to the question itself. For example, using the quotation you memorized, you might write something like this as a thesis statement:

> Sigmund Freud, who originated psychoanalytic theory at the turn of the century, suggested that "human personality emerges by the interactive functions between ego, superego, and id." (26 words)

The next step is to define terms. Compose sentences incorporating the points you jotted down on your list of points. *Try to be concise by combining as many specific points as you can into each sentence*

USEFUL TIP ~

Don't make the mistake of just starting to write hoping something positive will magically happen.

USEFUL TIP ~

Compose sentences
incorporating the points you
jotted down on your list of
points. Try to be concise by
combining as many specific
points as you can into each
sentence you write without
being verbose.

you write without being verbose. It would be ridiculous to write
something like:

> In my opinion at this point in time it seems like what Freud
> was saying was that the id is the same as what we in this day
> and age in our society call the unconscious. *(36 words)*

Although this sentence is 36 words long, it would get only one or
two marks for content. In fact, it might even lose a mark or two
because it communicates the ideas so poorly. Think about it this way.
If somebody were to write just seven such sentences, although they
would be well over the 250 word minimum, their mark for content
would be only 14 out of 35, or 40%.

A much better sentence might look something like this:

> The id or unconscious, the most important aspect of person-
> ality, contains eros and thanatos, two instincts that govern
> all behaviour. *(20 words)*

This sentence is only twenty words long, yet it contains about
seven valid points.

> The id or unconscious *(point)* the most important *(point)*
> aspect of personality *(point)* contains eros *(point)* and
> thanatos *(point)* two instincts *(point)* that govern all behavi-
> our *(point)*.

Now, if you could write 20 sentences, with each sentence containing only two valid points, you would have 40 points, well over the
35 points offered for content for this question. Of course, not all
instructors will mark answers exactly this way, but this can be a
useful guide for constructing your answers.

The next sentence in your answer might define eros and thanatos:

> Eros is our drive for life, sex and pleasure, while thanatos is
> for death, aggression, hostility and destruction. (18 words)

Notice that there are more points included in this sentence than
appeared on the original list of points. Obviously, it's a good idea to
incorporate more points if they occur to you as you're writing.

Following these three sentences might come a sentence defining
ego, then another defining superego. Then you would have a five
sentence paragraph defining the parts of personality according to
psychoanalytic theory.

In the next paragraph, you might discuss how these parts interact
with each other and what happens if one part gets repressed or has

too much expression. This paragraph would naturally lead into a third paragraph that explains why we are frequently in conflict with ourselves. And so on.

As you go, you might want to give examples from your personal experience to illustrate your points. This is often a good idea, providing you have enough room to include all the course material as well, and providing your illustrations are very brief and concise:

> For example, when I want a donut, my id says, "Go for it!";
> my superego says, "Don't. You're on a diet!"; and my adult
> ego says, "Let's have carrot sticks instead."

Often you can be more persuasive if you consider opposing views. Anticipate what someone might say, or already has said, to argue against you. Then show why you think your argument is more logical, consistent, justified or valid. In answering the question above, it might be useful to mention the other three theories of personality. In no more than a sentence for each, you might indicate how each differs from the theory you have chosen to explain more fully.

Some final tips. Although you will be trying to write fast, be careful not to write so quickly that your writing becomes illegible.

Also, try to give yourself enough time at the end of the exam to read your answer over a couple of times. Read first for your ideas. Then read to correct grammar, spelling and punctuation.

Good luck.

USEFUL TIP ~

Try to give yourself enough time at the end of the exam to read your answer over a couple of times. Read first for your ideas. Then read to correct grammar, spelling and punctuation.

UNIT 1

THE INDIVIDUAL

■ **ISSUE 1:**
Why Are We the Way We Are?

■ **ISSUE 2:**
Freedom and Constraint

Why Are We the Way We Are?

We believe that civilization has been built up, *under the pressure of the struggle for existence*, by sacrifices in the gratification of the primitive impulses.

Sigmund Freud

Introduction

Jay Haddad

In the first issue, we are going to examine human personality in all its complexities. This section will deal with the insightful, controversial, and contradictory schools of thought about the way human personality evolves. We will be challenged not only to understand and appreciate the contribution of each theory to personality development but also to compare and contrast what each school has to say. It's fine to accept or reject a particular school of thought—as long as we understand what it is we are accepting or rejecting!

The next article lays out four main schools of psychology as they relate to personality development; as well, the article emphasizes the assumptions each school makes about human behaviour and the potential we have for changing or correcting any unwanted or negative personality traits.

Personality

Jay Haddad

How much of our personality is learned and how much of our personality is part of our genetic endowment? How much of your personality is changeable and how much is not?

Think about yourself for a minute—would you consider yourself moody? Or shy?

If you feel that you are a moody person, from where does such a trait come? Could it have been genetically passed on to you in the DNA which you inherited from your parents? Is it perhaps an integral part of your body chemistry? Could your "moodiness" be caused by psychological tensions, by anxieties that are stored in your unconscious? Could "moodiness" be a stage you are going through? Or is it a permanent fact of your personality? Will it change? Can it change? You can ponder the same questions with regard to shyness, in fact, to any aggressive or passive behaviours you are aware of as being part of who you are.

As we begin Unit I, you will see that there are several schools of thought with respect to the nature and origin of personality; at times, the schools are not in conflict with one another but quite often there is a fundamental difference in the way in which the human personality is viewed.

A great deal of conflict often exists in the *basic assumptions* made by each school about the *nature of personality*. Your task, depending on the trait or situation you are attempting to examine, will be to evaluate critically the relative merits of each school's attempt to explain the root causes of human personality.

Schools of Thought

SCHOOLS OF THOUGHT	MAJOR THINKERS	BASIC ASSUMPTIONS ABOUT THE NATURE OF HUMANITY
Biological	Biologists	*Human beings have no free will.* Humans are animals whose behaviours are controlled by inherited instincts, in-born physical capacities and individual physical handicaps. Humans are genetically "programmed" at birth.
Psychoanalytic	Freud	*Human beings have no free will.* Humans are not just physical beings, but complex psychological beings, controlled by powerful biological urges from within which are largely unconscious. Humans are in constant conflict between strong sexual and aggressive drives and the controls of conscience and the laws and morals of society.
Behavioural	Watson Skinner Pavlov	*Human beings have no free will.* Humans are infinitely flexible and their behaviours are controlled and shaped by the environment and the effects of its rewards and punishments.
Humanistic Existential	Rogers Maslow	*Human beings have free will.* Humans are humane and caring, motivated from within to grow and develop towards "self-actualization" or the fullest blossoming of their potential.

SCHOOLS OF THOUGHT

Biological School

The assumption here is that humans have very little choice or free will because our biology determines personality. This "anatomy is destiny" view points to a strong causality between genetic programming and human personality. This view assumes that the 23 chromosomes you inherit from your father and the similar number you inherit from your mother will determine the person you will be. The assumption is a little like Darwin's "natural selection" where strong breeders, that is, people with "good genes," will have strong offspring. Perhaps "good genes" mean that particular gene combinations give some individuals a headstart on a successful life. In short, the biological view assumes humans are controlled by instincts and inborn physical capacities: you are born with your strong points and weak points and there's nothing you can really do about it.

Be aware that what one person may define as "good genes" may be totally offensive to another person. Because chromosomes may now be technically manipulated and altered by "gene engineers," many unspoken social, ethical, legal, political, racial and gender questions, etc., need to be raised and openly examined.

Some might argue that the biological view absolves the individual from taking any responsibility for behaviour because "I was born this way."

One could also assume that gifted or delinquent or athletic children are exempt from their parents' input because their genetic programming was with them at birth. The parents only carried the genes: the genetic inheritance caused the child's intelligence, delinquency or athletic abilities. This is referred to as the "nature" argument in the *nature vs. nurture* debate. The biological school would assume that personality is basically an inherited phenomenon, and that humans have genes which map out traits like moodiness, shyness, dominance, passivity, and so on.

Psychoanalytic School

Sigmund Freud (1856–1939) devised an interesting way to examine the dynamics of human personality. There are, he assumed, three distinct aspects of human personality:

THE BIOLOGICAL SCHOOL

The biological view assumes humans are controlled by instincts and in-born physical capacities: you are born with your strong points and weak points and there's nothing you can really do about it.

First, there is the self we think we are, the self which attempts to deal with reality. This Freud called the *ego*. *Ego* is who we are; it's our awareness of self. It's the person we think we are and the person we display to the outside world. But *ego*, theorized Freud, is never in control of self; *id* comes first!

The *id* is our unconscious, the largest and most important part of personality. The *id* must contain the two biological instincts which govern, dominate and motivate *all* human behaviour—*eros* and *thanatos*. *Eros* is referred to as our "life" instinct, but is more generally thought of as the sex, lust, or "pleasure drive." *Thanatos* relates to our "death" instinct but more commonly it is viewed as the human drive toward aggression, hostility and destruction.

As children, the unconscious *(id)* instincts (sex and aggression) surface freely into *ego* or into behavioural action. Children can exhibit anger, rage, destruction and hatred as well as lust, pleasure, arousal and sensuality.

Soon, though, the third aspect of personality emerges: *superego*. *Superego* is, very simply, our conscience; *superego* is our *moral* sense of personality, the part of us that knows (or is supposed to know) right from wrong.

As a person grows up, psychoanalysis assumes, the biological, unconscious, real urges from the *id*, *eros* and *thanatos*, are no longer freely displayed. This is called socialization or internalization which is really the *superego's* attempt to influence *ego* into becoming the personality you are "supposed" to be. As you mature, you also internalize the values and ideals of your society—certainly of your family, your surrounding culture, etc.

> *(Note that as Freud was developing his concepts, he himself was greatly influenced by his own family history and by the values and pressures of his own society. For this reason, many of his pioneering ideas are often challenged today as being sexist or culturally biased.)*

On the next page is a graphic presentation of the psychoanalytic view of personality:

The urges or impulses from our unconscious put great pressure on *ego* because *ego* often cannot deal with them or will not deal with them. *Ego's* function is to "think" and *ego* must handle the conflicting demands of *id* and *superego*. *Id* is the primitive, unconscious, childish part of self, saying, "*Do it!* Go for it! I want it!" *Superego*, our moral arbitrator, jumps in and says, "*No!* Don't do it! It's not right! You know

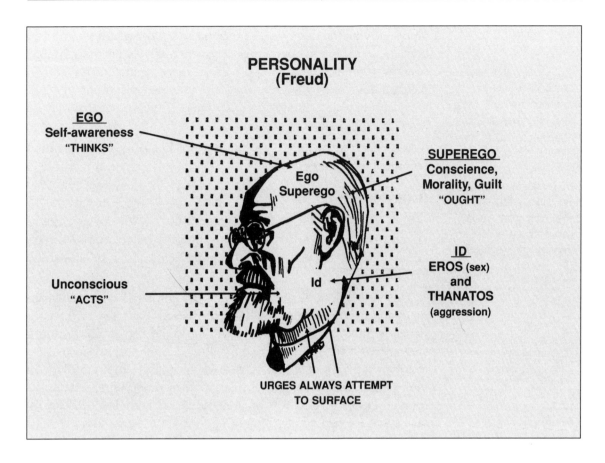

PERSONALITY
(Freud)

EGO
Self-awareness
"THINKS"

Ego
Superego

SUPEREGO
Conscience,
Morality, Guilt
"OUGHT"

ID
EROS (sex)
and
THANATOS
(aggression)

Unconscious
"ACTS"

Id

URGES ALWAYS ATTEMPT
TO SURFACE

better than that!" *Ego* must weigh the nagging voice of parents and society (morality) against the urges of our unconscious (sex and aggression). Human personality emerges, Freud suggests, by the interactive functions between *ego, superego,* and *id.* Too much *ego* repression or denial caused by anxiety or guilt (*superego*) could leave a personality in a disturbed, frustrated or highly dependant state. However, if there is too much *ego* expression, then the *id* surfaces freely, especially if there is insufficient internalization of values by the *superego.* If the *id* is allowed to dominate, one's aggression or delinquency will necessitate society's intervention.

The assumptions of the Freudian school are simple: in order to gain insight into the causes of personality, one must delve into the world of *id*—the human unconscious which contains all hidden memories, childhood experiences, early life traumas and forbidden fantasies. Freud and his followers initiated the "talking" cures, intended to give patients insight into their own unconscious minds. Imagine a patient lying on a couch, talking freely of his fears and

THE FREUDIAN SCHOOL

The assumptions of the Freudian school are simple: in order to gain insight into the causes of personality, one must delve into the world of *id*—the human unconscious which contains all hidden memories, childhood experiences, early life traumas and forbidden fantasies.

THE BEHAVIOURAL SCHOOL

The behavioural school views behaviours as learned phenomena. Our society merely exerts reinforcers on each individual to shape personality. The assumption here is that delinquent behaviours, addictive behaviours or anti-social behaviours are all *learned inappropriate responses.*

fantasies, with the therapist sitting at his side, taking notes—and you have the stereotyped beginnings of psychoanalysis. From such talks, from both random and guided conversations, pioneering Freudian psychologists attempted to unlock the unconscious, go deeply into the *id,* and bring to the *ego* an awareness of the causes that may be troubling the patient.

With such knowledge, we can at least begin to understand the complexities of personality.

Behavioural School

Now we arrive at the "nurture" component of the nature-nurture debate. This school makes three assumptions: behaviour is learned; behaviour is reinforced, and that which is learned can be unlearned and relearned.

This view about personality places the emphasis on the environment and the manner in which you are raised. Your input from your genes is minimal; you can be anything in life, if you are nurtured (rewarded) toward achieving that goal. Star athletes, musicians and academicians, for example, have been nourished and reinforced in their personality development with increased and enriched opportunities. Deprived children, on the other hand, learn low self-esteem and may receive encouragement or a payoff for breaking the rules or breaking the law. Human personality is "shaped," according to behavioural theory.

The cause (*stimulus*) seems unimportant; people emit behaviours, that is, people just do things and don't concern themselves with the "why" (the *cause*) of the behaviour. We are interested in the *payoff!* If whatever you do (and let's not care about "why" you did it) is positively or negatively reinforced, the likelihood of you doing it again *increases.* Similarly, if whatever you do is punished or ignored (no reinforcement), the likelihood of you doing it again *decreases.* This is the *Law of Effect,* the most important equation in all of behavioural science.

B.F. Skinner (1904–90) in his books and articles (*Walden Two, Beyond Freedom and Dignity,* etc.) attempts to explain the importance of "shaping" behaviours by their consequences. He discusses how personality is relatively neutral and becomes dominant only in the way behaviours are rewarded or not rewarded. For example, a three-year-old child, standing in a checkout line with her mother may ask for some candy two feet away from her. Mother says, "No." The

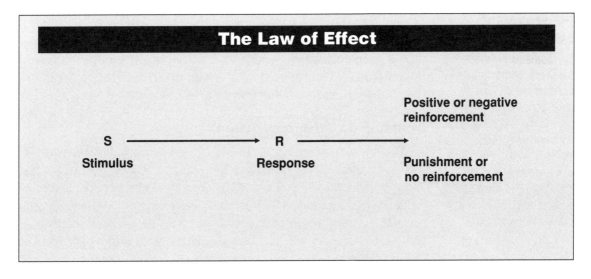

child throws a tantrum, screams, cries and jumps up and down. Mother relents; the child gets the candy and stops crying. The Law of Effect explains what has happened from a behavioural point of view. The response of the child (the tantrum) led to a reward (positive consequences) in that the child received the candy (payoff). Is the tantrum behaviour, according to the Law of Effect, likely to *increase* or *decrease* in this child's personality repertoire?

The behavioural school views behaviours as learned phenomena. Our society merely exerts reinforcers on each individual to shape personality. The assumption here is that delinquent behaviours, addictive behaviours or anti-social behaviours are all *learned inappropriate responses*.

If you assume, as behaviourists do, that anything that is learned can be unlearned and relearned, there is great optimism for changing behaviour (through therapy or intervention techniques). Simply change the reinforcers so that tantrum behaviour (as in the 3-year-old) is no longer rewarded and the child will learn a new behaviour. (Hopefully, a more appropriate behaviour will take its place.) Therapeutically, this is called *behaviour modification*, with no references to "unconscious" impulses or to genetic predispositions at all! One may simply change the behaviour by changing the *consequences* which modify each response.

The important question to ask is not why any person does something inappropriate (Why are some men abusive? Why do some women drink all day? Why is crime increasing among 14-year-olds?)—but rather, in what way is the inappropriate behaviour

THE HUMANISTIC-EXISTENTIAL SCHOOL

The *humanists* assume that we all are fundamentally *free* to make choices at each and every turning point in our lives. We have "free will" irrespective of our biology (*genes*), our past (*unconscious*), or our conditioning (*Law of Effect*).

leading to a payoff? That is, in what way is the behaviour of drinking or sexual abuse being rewarded or reinforced? In what way does crime (anti-social behaviour) lead to payoff in groups of young people today? The Law of Effect, in summary, allows us to examine personality based on behaviour and reinforcers.

Humanistic-Existential School

The previous three schools share one important dimension in common: they assume that the individual is *not* in control of self. Your personality, in other words, is motivated by genetic factors of which you are unaware *(biological school),* or by unconscious forces from the past of which you are unaware *(psychoanalytic school),* or, finally, by learned, inappropriate social responses of which you are unaware *(behavioural school).* All of these theories assume a lack of choice or *free will* on the part of the individual. Personality, they emphasize, is *determined* by forces outside of your control!

The *humanists* assume that we all are fundamentally *free* to make choices at each and every turning point in our lives. We have "free will" irrespective of our biology (genes), our past (unconscious), or our conditioning (Law of Effect). This is the newest of the schools of thought and, because of its emphasis on *choice* and *free will,* probably the most popular theory today.

There is an apparent optimism but a heavy responsibility in assuming that despite your biology, your past or your previous learning, you are free to be whatever you want to be—you are *limitless* in exercising the potential you have within yourself for growth or change! For example, if you were moody or shy as a teenager, you can enjoy the thrill and challenge and excitement of making new choices that will change you. If you were terribly repressed sexually or behaviourally (perhaps due to your parents' hangups), *you* don't have to be—you are free to change (if only you realize it)! If you learned delinquent patterns in your youth and were rewarded for anti-social behaviours, "today is the first day of the rest of your life." Change! Grow! Recognize your incredible potential! The choice is yours!

This tone of optimism for personal growth and change strongly inspired the "School of the '60s," giving rise to the Human Potential Movement. Walk into most bookstores in North America today and you will discover that the majority of modern books on psychology (at least 80% of them) have been influenced by the humanist-

existential school. Authors from Rogers to Maslow, Dyer to Busca-
glia, Harris to Gordon, clearly support the humanistic message:
control is yours, no one else's!

Human personality is capable of changing; humans are motivated
from within to grow and develop. This view holds that personality
is not static but rather dynamic, always changing. If a person is
moody, it is the individual's choice to be moody; the control or
responsibility lies with the individual. Thus, "hope springs eternal,"
for one's past, one's biology and one's learning, are not as important
as the present "now" for doing something about yourself, for making
choices that will allow you to change and grow.

Abraham Maslow, one of the pioneers of the Human Potential
Movement, wrote "the bible" for humanistic psychology (*Toward A
Psychology Of Being*). Prior to Maslow, psychological theory was
always oriented toward balance (equilibrium, homeostasis); that is,
when human needs arise, the individual is in an "unbalanced" state
(disequilibrium) and therefore seeks "balance" (homeostasis) by
satisfying that need. For example, if your stomach is growling and
you are preoccupied with satisfying your hunger needs, then you
are in an "unbalanced" (disequilibrium) state. In order for your body
to return to homeostasis (balance) you must satisfy your hunger
needs by eating.

Maslow, however, rejected this quest for seeking balance in his
new psychology (he actually called his humanism the "third force"
in contrast to both psychoanalysis and behaviourism). Maslow stated
that the "unbalanced" state is the *normal* state. According to Maslow,
we are always in a state of "need" (i.e., unbalanced); we are always,
therefore, "unbalanced"!

In attempting to seek equilibrium or balance we are not aware of
the fact that the satisfaction of one need only leads to the creation of
yet another need; it's our needs that are in a continual pattern of
change. From this, Maslow developed his famous pyramid where he
demonstrated the existence of our needs in a hierarchical manner:

We start off with basic biological needs: hunger, thirst, sex, sleep,
elimination. When our basic needs are met, new needs arise—but
needs of a higher level. For example, following our basic PHYSIO-
LOGICAL needs comes the need for safety and security: having a place
to sleep, the security of territoriality and so on. When SAFETY needs
are met, LOVE needs arise—our need for bonding, belonging as
strong social needs. Following love comes the need for ESTEEM, the

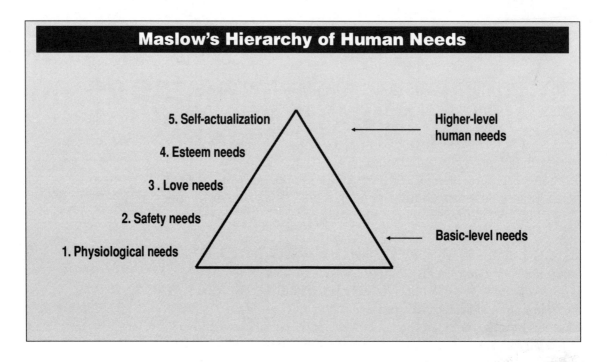

sense of self-worth, the ability to feel good about yourself. Ultimately, our never-ending need is the peak of the hierarchy—the need for SELF-ACTUALIZATION or the fulfilment of all of our human potential. This lofty need obviously never gets fully satisfied; thus, we are in a constant state of evolving, growing, becoming … yet we are always "unbalanced"! One need satisfied simply gives rise to another need—perhaps one of a higher level, as the pyramid shows.

Maslow's theory evolved after years of studying "healthy" individuals (as opposed to people who have severe psychological problems). The important thing to remember about Maslow (and humanism) is the fact that he wanted humanistic psychology to be a prescription toward health, toward a better quality of life and toward a more complete understanding of the "wholeness" of being human as we seek growth and fulfilment throughout our lifetime.

Conclusion

It must sound fairly confusing to lay down the assumptions made by personality theories and discover that they are quite opposite and contradictory!

If the humanists believe that we are essentially "free," while the behaviourists believe that we are essentially "controlled," which

~ Review ~

Personality: Four Schools of Thought

This section discusses four reasoned approaches to the question, "Why are we the way we are?"

According to the biological model of human nature associated with 19th-century naturalist Charles Darwin, personality is inherited and cannot be altered through human choice or behaviour. We are determined by heredity, not environment. We must play the cards nature has dealt us because we will pick up no others along the way.

A late 19th- and early 20th-century Viennese doctor named Sigmund Freud revolutionized our perception of human personality by proposing an intricate psychoanalytic model involving components that he called the *ego*, *id*, and *superego*, which interact with each other to determine personality. The id, our unconscious, is comprised of our pleasure drives (*eros*) and our drives towards aggres-sion, hostility and destruction (*thanatos*). The superego is our moral sense; the ego is our self-awareness or consciousness which negotiates between demands of the id and the expectations of the superego. According to Freud and the psychoanalytic school, the degree to which the ego and superego repress, alter, or fulfill biological drives determines personality.

The third school of thought is the behavioural school. Behaviourists minimize the role of heredity and heighten the role of environment in determining why we are the way we are. According to the behaviourists, behaviour is learned, is reinforced through positive or negative rewards, and can be changed through conditioning. B.F. Skinner is a major proponent of the behavioural school.

The biological, psychoanalytic, and behavioural schools maintain that we are shaped by outside forces and we do not possess free will. The fourth and most recent school of thought, known as the humanist-existential school, suggests that we possess free will and the power to change ourselves and the outside world. Humanists contend that we hold all the cards in the game of life and are free to deal them as we wish. The multitude of self-help books and personal growth manuals in bookstores suggests the prevalence of this view in contemporary western society.

These four schools of thought contain many differences, even contradictions. Which one is right? Or does each reflect some part of the whole make-up of personality? Collectively, these four schools of personality theory provide a universe of insight into the dynamic phenomenon of human personality.

school is more correct? Carl Rogers says this is a unique paradox with which we all must live: both schools are correct; we are at the same time helpless souls conditioned and shaped by the reinforcers in our environment AND supreme masters of our own destiny, making free choices throughout every phase of our lives.

Can we understand this paradox? Søren Kierkegaard, a famous Danish philosopher, said: "The paradox is the source of the thinker's passion and the thinker without paradox is like a lover without feeling."

This paradox is uniquely human and allows us to discover the complexity of the human psyche. We *are* influenced, programmed,

~ Review ~

Personality: Four Schools of Thought:
Fill in the Blanks

This section discusses four reasoned approaches to the question, "Why are we the way we are?" According to the _____ model of human nature associated with 19th-century naturalists, personality is inherited and cannot be altered through human choice or behaviour. We are determined by heredity, not environment. We must play the cards nature has dealt us because we will pick up no others along the way.

A late 19th- and early 20th-century Viennese doctor named _____ revolutionized our perception of human personality by proposing an intricate model, referred to as the _____ model of personality, involving components which interact to determine personality.

The _____, our unconscious, is comprised of our pleasure drive (_____) and our drive towards aggression, hostility and destruction (_____). The _____ is our moral sense; the_____ is our self-awareness or consciousness, which negotiates between demands of the _____ and the expectations of the _____.

According to this school, the degree to which the _____ and _____ repress, alter, or fulfil biological drives determines personality.

or controlled by forces totally external to us. Yet, we are also capable at any time of making spontaneous decisions, decisions for which we are wholly responsible.

Psychologists use tests (personality tests with no right or wrong answers) to determine the degree of control that an individual believes he or she may have over his or her own life. There are those individuals that psychologists label "internally controlled" and those categorized as "externally controlled." Internally controlled people believe they are in total command of their lives; they believe that what they do matters and they assume responsibility for their success or failure. Externally controlled individuals feel that they have no real personal control of their lives. It is always the fault of someone else or some other agency when things go wrong. Parents, employers, boyfriends/girlfriends, etc., all make great scapegoats. Their destiny (happiness or unhappiness, success or failure) is perceived to lie in the hands of "others." They feel powerless insofar as they *believe* that what they do has little or no impact on anyone or anything.

Perhaps when viewed from this perspective, our paradox makes more sense. Those individuals who are "internally controlled" clearly fall into the humanist camp, while the "externally controlled" individuals belong in the behaviourist camp. Internally controlled people would probably vote and engage in other activities which would indicate their degree of *perceived* control over their own lives. Externally controlled people, predictably, wouldn't vote and might say: "What difference does my vote make anyway?"

Examine the paradox and you will probably find that our attitudes and beliefs are full of contradictions. In this case, perhaps, there is a continuum, ranging from "absolutely no control over my life" to "absolute control over my life." Maybe the behaviourist vs. humanist debate is better understood by first understanding our complex range of perceptions about how much of our lives we *believe* we actually control!

QUESTIONS

1. State what basic assumption is made about the nature of personality with the biological school.
2. State the problems that exist with respect to the genetic engineering of so-called "good genes."
3. Relate the thinking of this school to: (a) taking personal responsibility for behaviour; and (b) parental input for gifted, delinquent or athletic children.
4. List and define in a short sentence each of the three distinct aspects of human personality according to Sigmund Freud.
5. List and define in a short sentence each of the two biological instincts contained with the *id*.
6. Define socialization/internalization using the terms *ego* and *superego*.

7. State what, according to Freud, are the psychological problems associated with: (a) too much *ego* repression; and (b) too much *ego* expression.

8. List the specific aspects of the "world of *id* " that give the Freudian school insights into the causes of personality.

9. Explain how the "talking" cures of Freudian psychoanalysis are supposed to work.

10. List the three assumptions that are made by the behavioural school.

11. State where emphasis is placed in this view of personality.

12. State what the Law of Effect is, using the term *reinforcement*. Illustrate your answer with the example of the child throwing a tantrum in order to receive candy.

13. State what assumption is made concerning behaviours that are delinquent, addictive or anti-social.

14. Define behaviour modification.

15. State the question behaviourists ask concerning inappropriate behaviour.

16. State the assumption that the first three schools share and contrast that with the thinking of the humanistic-existential school.

17. State the view this school holds with respect to the ability of the human personality to change.

EXERCISE

Remember, your task is to assess the relative impact or importance or merits of each school of thought.

Choose a behaviour and examine the analysis and assumptions made by each school with respect to the causes and treatments of the behaviour. For example, you can look at alcohol addiction and assume—

a. It is *biologically* based, caused by a genetic weakness or predisposition. Alcoholism is not the person's fault, and, therefore, treatment lies in understanding and correcting the biological imbalance. Any "talking" cures (psychoanalysis) would be totally useless and irrelevant to this view.

b. Alcohol addiction is *unconsciously* motivated, caused by misdirected *eros* or *thanatos* energy surfacing to *ego* in the form of an addiction to drinking. The person is consciously unaware of the cause of this "oral" dependency, and therapy would involve many hours of exposing the unconscious *(id)*, that is, of talking out one's feelings, anxieties and early life experiences.

c. Alcohol addiction, to the behaviourist, is a bad habit! It is a behaviour which has obviously been reinforced, in that the behaviour (response) of drinking has led to good things happening (reward). The consequences (reinforcement) of alcohol dependency must be altered so that abstinence leads to reward. Therefore, sessions of behaviour modification might be used to slowly change the reinforcers. (A drastic method of intervention, called "aversive conditioning," was illustrated in the movie, *A Clockwork Orange*.) In short, "bad" behaviours can be unlearned and relearned through appropriate conditioning (reinforcement) methods.

d. The humanist would assume you have chosen alcohol dependency as an escape; this is understandable in a world filled with stress and anxiety. Do you want to change? If you do, you have the power and control within you to make that choice. As one anti-drug campaign put it, "Say NO to drugs!" It's that simple— or is it?

•

The above theories and examples are presented in an oversimplified and non-technical way. In reality, of course, these theories and therapies do overlap and are more complex. However, we have presented them to you as separate and independent schools to promote analysis, insight and comparison.

Is one theory better than another? Should certain concepts from one theory be married to another theory? Do you yourself have some new clues about personality and human behaviour?

The adventure is to know more about yourself, for such insights often help you to understand how you relate to others, and how you may enrich your own life. Self knowledge, understanding some of the potential causes that make you a personality, also enables you to understand others.

We share with humankind that quality called "personality." It is an exciting, lifetime adventure to discover who we are—and why.

ISSUE 2

Freedom and Constraint

… if some day they truly discover a formula for all our desires and caprices—that is an explanation of what they depend upon, by what laws they arise, just how they develop, what they are aiming at in one case or another and so on, and so on, that is a real mathematical formula—then, after all, man would most likely at once stop to feel desire, indeed, he will be certain to. For who would want to choose by rule? … for what is a man without desire, without free will and without choice …

Dostoyevsky

I share genes with people in Japan; our physical resemblance is therefore striking. But the enormous psychological and behavioural gulf that separates me from those people is obvious the moment we open our mouths—environment has been the most important factor shaping our personalities.
The question of how much nature and nurture determine our personalities is rather trivial scientifically, but the social implications can be staggering, as victims of the Nazi concentration camps can attest.

David Suzuki

Introduction

Clive Cockerton

The first three articles in this section examine the question of freedom vs. determinism. By showing *how* we are free or determined, each article adds a useful perspective on our understanding of who we are.

The Paul Chance article ("Your Child's Self-Esteem") should be required reading for anyone who has children now or who will some day raise children. Chance develops the theme that self-esteem is the most significant ingredient contributing to success in life. Furthermore, self-esteem is directly related to how we have been raised from early childhood.

Determinism Versus Freedom

Earl Babbie

Determinism is an embarrassment for social scientists. It is a fundamental paradigm for nearly all of our research, yet none of us wants to speak out on its behalf. Closer to the bone, our livelihoods depend on determinism, and yet we hope it isn't true. Crudely put, social research assumes a deterministic paradigm that fundamentally denies the existence of free will. Here's an example of how it works.

A standard research question for social researchers would be something like, "What causes prejudice?" Most people would recognize this as a worthwhile subject for research: if we knew what caused prejudice, we might be able to eliminate it.

Millions of dollars have been invested in research aimed at discovering various aspects of what causes prejudice, and a great deal has been learned. For example, prejudice and education are largely incompatible; fundamentalist Christian beliefs seem to promote anti-Semitism; associating with minority group members tends to reduce prejudice toward them. In fact, laws that make discrimination illegal seem to have the long-term effect of reducing prejudice, suggesting that you can legislate morality.

But every time we discover that prejudice (or tolerance) is *caused* by something, we drive another nail in the coffin of individual choice and freedom. To see what I mean, imagine the following research report.

> We've studied prejudice exhaustively, and we conclude that some people are prejudiced because they want to be and others aren't prejudiced because they don't want to be.

DETERMINISM

Much of modern social research assumes a deterministic paradigm (a model or outlook) that fundamentally denies the existence of free will. The clear implication of the model that explanatory science is based on is that our lives are completely determined by outside forces. Whenever we look for causes, we imply that we are *caused.*

A researcher submitting that report would not continue to receive funding very long. When we ask for reasons for prejudice, we expect reasons. How can you prevent prejudice if you don't know what causes it?

Here's the rub. If people's prejudice is caused by such things as their level of education, their religion, and where they grew up, they didn't have anything to say about it. They were the victims of circumstances beyond their control. It's as though they were machines or robots, not human beings exercising free will. We don't normally put the matter quite so crudely, but that's the implication of the model social science is based on.

Notice the implications of this model for crime and punishment. If I robbed the bank because of social forces beyond my control, is it really appropriate to punish me? Don't the forces that are controlling me constitute "extenuating circumstances"? If someone stuck a gun to my head and made me cooperate in a bank robbery, you probably wouldn't think I should be punished. This argument has been an important theme in the American criminal justice system in recent decades, in part because researchers have been able to explain criminal behavior on the basis of social determinism.

What I've said about prejudice and crime applies equally to all other human characteristics—to tolerance as much as to prejudice, for example. Observing that some people are more religious than others, social researchers seek to find the factors responsible. There's no room in the model for people simply choosing to be religious.

What's your political preference? Republican? Democrat? Independent? Whatever it is, you probably feel that you made a personal and well-reasoned choice. But social researchers assume that your choice was made for you by factors beyond your control, and they're pretty effective at finding out what those factors are. In the end, this model implicitly assumes that everything you are and do is determined by forces you cannot control and may not be aware of. The implication is that you have no freedom.

Be clear that I am not saying you *are* totally determined, but that's the clear implication of the model explanatory science is based on. Whenever we look for causes, we imply that we are caused.

This basic model is the same one used in the natural sciences. When we boil a pot of water, we say that the heat causes the water to turn to steam. We never ask whether the water chose to become steam any more than we ask whether a rock wants to fall when we throw it off a cliff. Gravity causes the rock to fall.

The model is more threatening when we apply it to human beings, although there are some limits to this. We don't mind saying that a virus causes us to cough and have a runny nose or that a bump on the head causes us to lose consciousness. We don't protest our loss of freedom in situations like those.

Sometimes we are willing to let external social forces cause our failures in life. We may blame losing our jobs on the economy, greedy bosses, or cheap foreign labor. We hold our spouses to be the cause of our unhappy marriages. Still, we are unwilling to consider ourselves to be totally determined. Let's see why.

For one thing, the idea of being totally determined contradicts our experience of life. The deterministic model suggests that whether you go to college and how well you do in your studies are caused by forces beyond your control. And yet you have the experience of deciding whether to go to college. You do whatever is necessary to get admitted. Once enrolled, you study, do your assignments, and generally feel responsible for how it all turns out. If someone were to tell you that your success in college was actually being determined by forces beyond your control, you might laugh at the notion. Your good grades were caused by your hard work, and you decide to study rather than to go to the movies. Right?

Don't answer too quickly. Social research confirms that studying is an important factor in the determination of grades, but let's look a little more deeply into who decided you should study hard. Let's assume you're the student in question, and I'll try to discover who's really responsible for your good grades.

Me: Why did you get good grades?

You: Because I studied hard.

Me: Okay, Why did you study hard?

You: Because I wanted to get good grades.

Me: Makes sense. Why did you want to get good grades?

You: What do you mean? Everybody wants to get good grades.

Me: Maybe, but if everyone wanted good grades as much as you did, then they all would have studied as hard as you, and they all would have gotten good grades.

You: Okay, so maybe I wanted good grades more than other students. In part, I knew it would mean a lot to my family. Just about everyone in our family has gone to college for generations—and most of them seem to have done well.

Me: I understand.

You: But there's more to it than that. Both my parents are physicians, running a medical clinic together. For as long as I can remember, they have talked about me going to medical school and then joining them in their practice. It would break their hearts if I didn't do well in college and couldn't get into medical school.

Me: As I listen to what you say, it sounds more and more to me as though your good grades were not the result of your free choice. Consider this. A student comes from a family in which just about everyone had gone to college for generations and had gotten good grades. The student's parents are both physicians and have always wanted their child to attend medical school and join them in their practice. I'd wager that just about anyone with that background would study hard and do well.

You: Well, those circumstances have obviously had something to do with my studying hard, but that's not the whole story. It was still my choice. I didn't have to study. I could have goofed off.

Me: I'm not so sure.

You: Okay, here's proof. I have an older brother who obviously had the same background as me in the ways we've discussed, and I know my parents wanted him to join them in the practice. However, he spent all his time in college partying and he flunked out. So that disproves the argument that free choice doesn't matter.

Me: Perhaps. If that's the case, let's find out more about how your free choice operated in the matter. Why do you suppose you make your free choice to study whereas your brother didn't? Why did your brother make a free choice to spend his time partying rather than studying?

You: Well, I've always had the feeling that my parents pushed him too hard. I think his failure in college was his way of resisting their pressure. It's ironic that this comes up in our discussion of determinism and free choice. I guess he felt our parents were trying to determine his future, and he wanted to prove he had a choice in the matter.

Me: And if your parents had pushed you like that, do you think you might have goofed off and flunked out?

You: I think there would be a good chance of that.

Me: So the reason for your success and your brother's failure is that your parents pushed him too hard but didn't do that to you. I'm not sure I see where your free choice was in that. In fact, it sounds a little like your brother's attempt to show he had free choice was actually caused by your parents' pressure.

You: Well, maybe that's a bad example. Besides, we've only scratched the surface of why I got good grades. For example, you yourself said that studying hard had some impact on grades. But that's not the whole picture. I didn't want to say this before, but I'm simply smarter than my brother.

Me: Is that something you chose, or is it more of your circumstances?

This discussion could continue almost endlessly, but the end result would be the same. Every time I asked you for a reason why you got good grades, you'd have one. The problem is that you are trapped by your reasons. Every reason you give for your good grades takes away from your free choice in the matter. Even when the reason looks like an example of free choice (studying hard, for example), that reason turns out to have reasons behind it that undermine your freedom.

If this point is not clear to you, try the following exercise.

1. Select some action you've taken or some characteristic that describes you.

2. Write down the 10 most important reasons why you took that action or have that characteristic.

3. For each of those 10 reasons, write the 5 most important reasons why those first-level reasons are true for you.

4. Now write the 3 most important reasons why each of the 50 second-level reasons is true for you.

5. Now ask yourself how likely it is that anyone with those [150] reasons would have taken the action or had the characteristic you started the exercise with.

6. If you can honestly say that someone with all those reasons might have turned out differently, ask yourself how that could possibly be. The reason you now give should be added to your list of reasons. Now repeat this step.

There's simply no way out. The paradigm we operate within demands this outcome. And remember, the same paradigm is used by social researchers studying human behavior.

If you find this discussion disconcerting, you should take a moment to consider why you are reading this book. The deterministic model suggests that you have to be reading it right now. I certainly can't know all the reasons that forced you to be reading the book, but I can guess at some. Perhaps you've been assigned the book for a college course. Perhaps a close friend urged you to read it, and you feel you owe it to that friendship to read the book. Perhaps you've gotten hooked by the discussion, and you can't put it down until you know how it turns out. Whatever your reasons, the deterministic model suggests that you have no choice but to be reading this book right now.

Before you assert your independence by closing the book, consider two more points. First, if you stop reading the book right now, the deterministic model suggests that you were forced to do so. Perhaps your discomfort made you quit. Maybe it was something I said. If you had to quit because you were late for class, that's a perfect example of your quitting having been determined.

Second, no matter what you do, I'll still be here saying these things about determinism, social science, and freedom. You can slam the book shut, chop it up into little pieces, and burn the shredded paper. Then, twenty years from now, you'll be in a used-book store, see a worn out, dog-eared copy of this book. You'll pick it up, open to this page, and I'll still be here saying the same things. Worse yet, I'll know that you've come back to the book, just as I know you're reading now. (Realize that if you quit reading, you'll never know if I *think* you're still reading. You'll have to peek back in here to find out and Zap!—I'll get you again. You're hopelessly trapped. I'm like the light inside your refrigerator.)

The real problem we have with the deterministic model, I think, lies not so much in what it says about our past and present as in what it says about our future. Just as the model says you didn't have any freedom in the past, it also says you have none from now on. In fact, the model suggests that how you turn out, whether you will succeed or fail in various ventures, whether you will be basically satisfied or dissatisfied during the remainder of your life, is already determined. Given the trillions of pieces making up your current circumstances, what happens in your life seems inevitable, and you seem to lack the freedom to change them. That's the implication of the model.

It's worth noting that millions of people around the world accept fatalistic world views essentially like this. Many Moslems, for example, consider life merely the unfolding of Allah's will and consider themselves merely players in the predetermined drama.

In talking to hundreds of students about this topic, I have found that their greatest discomfort about determinism involves fears about what they would be like if they accepted it as true. Let's resume our previous fictitious dialogue and look at some of those fears.

Me: So how do you think you'd behave if you accepted the notion that you have no free choice?

You: I'd simply give up. Why on earth should I study hard and try to get good grades if I really believed that I had no control over how things would turn out? Do you think I'd keep trying to be a good student?

Me: Okay, so you're afraid that you might quit school if you accepted a totally deterministic image of human life. How else would you behave?

You: It's not just a matter of quitting school, damn it! I mean really quit: just drop out, stop caring about anything. Like, for example, I spend a lot of time and energy working for social justice. I see a lot of things around me that just aren't right, and I devote a lot of myself to making them better. Now, do you think I'd keep working for social justice if I really believed that my every thought, word, and deed—not to mention the future of the world—was already determined, that I couldn't really change anything? Do you think I'd even care? Do you think anyone would, if they believed that? If I believed in determinism, I would be a totally different person. Do you understand what I am saying?

Me: I understand that you are concerned that you'd be a different kind of person if you accepted that you were totally determined, but I want to hear some more about how you'd change.

You: I've already told you. I wouldn't care about things that mean a lot to me now. I'd stop trying to make a contribution to others. I wouldn't try to get ahead.

Me: I appreciate your concerns that you might give up trying to succeed personally and might give up trying to make a difference in the world, but my question is this: how would you change if you truly accepted a totally deterministic view of life?

You: I've told you! I'd change totally. I'd become a totally different person. It wouldn't be a pretty sight. I'd just sit in a corner and not do anything. Or maybe I'd watch television all day and night. No. I know what, I'd just devote myself to having a good time. I wouldn't care about the future since it's already taken care of. Right?

Me: Again, I hear the fears you have about what you might be like, but I still want to know how you'd change if you truly accepted a totally deterministic view of life.

You: There you go again. I've already told you how I'd change.

Me: You've told me what you might look like afterward. I want to know how you'd change.

You: But I told you how I'd change....Wait a minute. When you say how, do you mean, like, how?

Me: That's it exactly.

You: You mean if I truly accepted the view that everything I think, say, do, and am is totally caused by forces over which I have no personal control, how would I change? How could I?

Me: And what would you be like if you accepted that view?

You: Well, if life really was totally determined, and I came from a family who all went to college and wanted me to join their medical practice, I guess I'd study hard and get good grades.

Me: Would you feel bad about things being that way?

You: Not unless I was determined to feel bad.

You and I are so deeply embedded in the view that we have free choice that our greatest fears about determinism refer to the irresponsible free choices we think we'd make if we found out we didn't have any freedom. Ironic, isn't it? If it turned out that you didn't have any freedom, you couldn't make any free choices—irresponsible or otherwise.

We don't know whether you have free choice or are completely determined, but we do know that whichever is the case, you aren't going to change things.

Free Will Reconsidered

Melanie Chaparian

In the previous article, Earl Babbie presents the following rather simple defence of determinism. Every event in the world occurs because of cause and effect. Like every other event, human actions must be determined by cause and effect as well. If all of our actions are caused, we cannot possess free will because the same action cannot be both caused and free at the same time. Therefore, all human actions are determined, and no human actions are free.

An Argument for Determinism

Let's look at this argument in more detail. Babbie states that science assumes a deterministic model of the world. According to this model, there is an *inevitable* connection between a cause and its effect: if the cause occurs, the effect *must* also occur. For example, if heating water to a temperature of 100°C *determines* the water to turn into steam, then every time water is heated to that temperature it *must* turn into steam. Heating water to 100°C is the *cause* and the water turning into steam is the *effect*. We never entertain the possibility that boiling water or any other natural phenomena occur because of pure chance. It is the very nature of science to look for the causes of the phenomena it studies. Indeed, when scientists are unable to identify the cause of a particular phenomenon, such as the memory loss suffered by people afflicted with Alzheimer's Disease, they do not conclude that no cause exists but rather that it simply has not *yet* been discovered.

As Babbie notes, the deterministic view is not limited to the natural sciences such as physics, chemistry, biology and medicine. Determinism is also assumed by the social sciences, such as psychology and sociology, which usually attempt to study and *discover the causes of human behaviour.* Although we believe ourselves to be unique creatures, human beings are as much a part of this world as boiling water and Alzheimer's Disease. If everything else in this universe is the effect of some cause, the determinist argues, there is no reason to believe that human actions are not as well. The theory of determinism maintains that human nature, whether unique or not, does not exempt us from the forces of cause and effect.

The determinist argues that our distinctive nature only means that the causes which determine our actions are more complex, and therefore harder to discover, than those that cause other events. The *kinds* of causes determining human behaviour depend on the determinist's view of human nature. Some point to *heredity* as the primary cause of a person's actions. Those who adhere to the biological school of personality, for instance, argue that genetics determine such traits as intelligence, talents and temperament, which in turn cause an individual's actions. Other determinists argue that a person's behaviour is fundamentally determined by *environment*: the behaviourists point to rewards and punishments; Paul Chance, whose article appears later in this Issue of our textbook, points to early childhood rearing; and Doris Lessing, whose article also appears later in this Issue, points to membership in social groups such as family, profession, social class, religion or political party. Many, if not most, determinists, however, acknowledge that a *combination* of hereditary and environmental factors determines a person's actions. A Freudian psychologist, for example, believes that an individual's behaviour is caused by the way the *ego* moderates between drives of the *id*, which are determined by instinct or heredity, and the moral demands of the *superego*, which are determined by early childhood environment. Regardless as to the kind of causes they point to, all determinists agree that all human actions are determined or caused.

No matter how long and hard we may deliberate between different courses of action the "choice" we finally make has already been decided for us by hereditary and/or environmental causes over which we have no control. For example, Babbie applies the deterministic model to explain why a student is academically successful in college while her brother is a dismal failure. Babbie admits that the student earns her good grades in part because she studies hard, but he argues that her good study habits are determined by the parental expectations with which she was raised. Although she may be tempted to join the nightly college parties, she really cannot choose to do so; her upbringing does not allow her to make such a choice. Babbie also points to the relatively high intelligence that the student has inherited as another cause of her good grades.

Her brother, on the other hand, socializes at the expense of studying and consequently flunks out of college. Here again, Babbie does not see this as the result of a free, if foolish, choice. Rather, he argues that the parental expectations placed on the brother were *too strong*—so strong, indeed, that he is determined to rebel by going to all the parties instead of studying. Although he may feel guilty that he is not studying even while he is socializing, the brother cannot chose to study instead. In addition to parental pressure, Babbie cites the brother's relatively low intelligence as another cause of his poor grades. Thus, neither sibling really makes a genuine choice between studying and socializing. Instead, the course of action each takes is determined by causes over which neither has any control.

Nor do we have the freedom to make genuine choices concerning even the most important aspects of our lives. Our environment or heredity, or both, determine such things as which profession we enter, who we marry, and how many children we have. According to the theory of determinism, *all* human actions are the effect of causes over which we have no control; consequently, free will is merely an illusion.

Because we usually pride ourselves on our freedom, we may feel reluctant to accept the determinist's conclusion. But this in itself is not a good reason to reject determinism. It would be hard to deny that the deterministic model has helped to advance our knowledge of the natural world in general and the human world in particular. Discovering the cause of an event not only increases our understanding of that phenomenon but also allows us to *predict* and sometimes *control* its future occurrence. If, for example, we know that a virus causes an illness in the human body, we can predict that a person will become ill when infected by that virus, and, moreover, we can control that illness by finding ways to prevent the virus from infecting more people. Or, if we know that a moderate amount of parental pressure causes a student to succeed in school, we can predict that a student subjected to that amount of guidance will earn good grades, and we can control such successes by teaching parents how to provide the proper dose of encouragement. The deterministic model also helps us to make sense out of our personal lives. We are often remarkably successful, for instance, in predicting the actions of our close relatives and friends. If such predictions are not merely lucky guesses, the determinist argues, they must be based on our relatively extensive knowledge of the hereditary and environmental causes that determine the behaviour of those relatives and friends. The fact that we do not *like* the theory of determinism does not negate of the wealth of evidence for its accuracy.

A Critique of Determinism

In his famous lecture entitled "The Dilemma of Determinism," William James, an American philosopher and psychologist who lived from 1842 to 1910, defends *libertarianism*, the theory that human beings have free will. Before he actually begins his argument for this theory, however, James shows that determinism—its appeal to science notwithstanding—cannot be scientifically demonstrated.

Science cannot really tell us, for example, if the poor student's background caused him to rebel. The fact that he did attend too many parties does not in itself prove that the student was determined to take this course of action. Moreover, *before the fact*—that is, before the student entered college—no one, not even the most learned determinist, could ascertain whether the student's background would lead him to party or to study. For instance, it would not have seemed inconceivable to suppose that the extra parental pressure would prompt the student to study even harder than his sister. Nor would it have been unreasonable to surmise that his diligent studying would have compensated for his relatively low intelligence and ultimately earned him good grades. *Before the fact*, this series of events seems as likely to occur as the events that actually came to pass; thus, James argues, *after the fact*, there is no way to prove that the student was determined to socialize instead of study. The same argument applies to all human actions. James therefore concludes that the determinist cannot prove that all actions are the inevitable effects of prior causes. While this in itself does not disprove determinism, it certainly dispels the myth that determinism has the weight of science on its side, and, furthermore, suggests that libertarianism should at least be reconsidered.

An Argument for Free Will

Different libertarians disagree among themselves on how far human freedom extends. On one extreme, the existentialists claim that all human actions are free. On the other extreme, some libertarians only argue that actions performed in the face of moral demands are free. In this discussion, we will focus on the views of William James, who defends a relatively moderate version of libertarianism. According to James, we are free whenever we have a genuine choice between at least two possible and desirable courses of action. This does not mean, of course, that we are free to perform any conceivable action whatsoever. Nor does this even mean that we are free to do anything we may desire, for the action that we find most tempting may not be included within the choice before us. All that is required to render an action free is the existence of one other alternative action that it is possible for us to perform.

Essential to James's definition of free will is the existence of *possible actions*, that is, actions which a person is not inevitably determined to do but may perform nonetheless. If an action is the result of free will, then it is, before the fact, merely one of two or more genuinely *possible* alternative actions that the person can *freely choose* to perform; and, after the fact, it is correct to say that the individual *could have acted otherwise* by choosing another alternative. For instance, the poor student may have freely chosen to spend his time at parties instead of the library; and even though he made this choice, he could have chosen to study instead. It is the idea of possible actions that puts James in stark opposition to determinism, which states that every action is the *inevitable* effect of a cause.

We have already discussed James's argument that determinism cannot be scientifically demonstrated. He does not attempt, however, to disprove this theory nor to prove libertarianism true. This is because he believes determinism and libertarianism to be two alternative theories of reality, neither of which can be objectively proven true or false. Thus, he claims that the best we can do is to examine both theories to see which one offers us the most rational explanation of human behaviour. According to James, a "rational" theory should not only explain objective reality but must account for subjective human experience as well. James's defence of libertarianism consists in the argument that the free will position is more rational in this sense than determinism.

A significant fact of human life is the *feeling of freedom* that we often experience. James argues that any theory of human behaviour must adequately explain this feeling. Unlike determinism, libertarianism conforms to our ordinary experience: we often feel free to choose between alternative courses of action. Of course, the determinist argues that this feeling is merely an illusion because our course of action has already been decided for us by causes beyond our control. But the "illusion" persists in our inner, subjective experience nonetheless. For example, the good student probably *feels* that she could have chosen to go to more parties, and her brother likely *feels* that he could have decided to study harder. In his or her practical affairs, even the most staunch determinist probably *feels free* to choose between alternative courses of action. No matter how solidly convinced we may be that determinism offers us a rational account of all natural phenomena and perhaps most human behaviour, we still find it difficult—if not impossible—to *believe* subjectively that we are never free. Thus, determinism requires us to reject as illusory a universal human experience. Libertarianism, on the other hand, acknowledges the feeling of freedom as a natural part of the experience of exerting our free will. According to James, this is a good reason to adopt the free will thesis. While he concedes that determinism is a rational theory of reality from an objective standpoint, James argues that libertarianism is an even more rational position because it can account for our inner, subjective experience of freedom.

Another important fact of human experience that James believes a rational theory must explain are *feelings of regret*. Our dissatisfaction with the world, especially with human behaviour, leads us to regret; that is, to "wish that something might be otherwise." After flunking out of college, for instance, the poor student may *regret* that he chose to spend all his time socializing. And because we regret the actions of others as well as our own, his sister may also *regret* that he had not studied. The most significant regrets concern the moral sphere. We do not accept as inevitable the senseless murders, rapes, and cases of child abuse we read about in the newspaper; instead, we judge such acts to be bad or immoral to the highest degree and regret that they are part of our world.

A regret implies that something is bad, and "calling a thing bad means ... that the thing ought not to be, that something else ought to be in its stead." When we label someone's action immoral, we imply that it should not have been done and that the person should have acted otherwise. For instance, when we proclaim that a murderer is guilty of the highest moral offence, we mean that he should not have committed homicide and should have instead settled the grievance with his victim in a peaceful, humane manner. Regrets obviously assume the existence of free will. For this reason, libertar-

~ Review ~

Free Will Reconsidered

This article by Melanie Chaparian, like the previous one, explores one of the most basic philosophical dilemmas: does an individual possess free choice or is the path a person walks determined by circumstances beyond his or her control?

The author cites the work of the American philosopher/psychologist William James (1542–1910), who espoused the doctrine of "libertarianism." An advocate of free will, James argued that the theory that all human actions are the effects of prior causes cannot be scientifically proven.

James also observed that human beings have the capacity for feeling regret, and to regret an action implies an awareness of our ability to create consequences. Since we know we could have acted otherwise, we must assume the existence of free will.

rianism, offers us a better explanation of our regrets than does determinism.

The source of our deepest regrets is the recognition that the world is fraught with immorality. According to determinism, even the most heinous crimes are as much the result of cause and effect as the routine activities we do every day. Knowing the causes of immoral actions does not eliminate our regret that they occur, but it does make our regret merely futile hope. Libertarianism, on the other hand, recognizes immoral actions as the result of free will and, as such, acknowledges that other actions could have been performed instead. Since this applies to future as well as past actions, there exists the possibility that the world—although certainly imperfect—may be made a better and more moral place through free human action. Thus, from the libertarian viewpoint, regrets may virtually be taken at face value—as expressions of our belief that immoral actions *can* be avoided and *should not* take place. This, according to James, renders libertarianism a more rational theory of human existence.

James admits from the outset that his defence consists of the argument that libertarianism is more rational than determinism because it offers a better account of our feelings of freedom and regret. This is not a claim that can be proven objectively, but one that can only be "verified" by consulting our inner, subjective sense. Although James argues that determinism is also incapable of objective demonstration, he acknowledges that determinism appeals to a different kind of rationality, perhaps what we might call a scientific rationality. Even though James finds libertarianism to be more rational than determinism, it remains for each of us to study both theories to see which of the two *we* find to be the most rational.

Group Minds

Doris Lessing

People living in the West, in societies that we describe as Western, or as the free world, may be educated in many different ways, but they will all emerge with an idea about themselves that goes something like this: I am a citizen of a free society, and that means I am an individual, making individual choices. My mind is my own, my opinions are chosen by me, I am free to do as I will, and at the worst the pressures on me are economic, that is, I may be too poor to do as I want.

This set of ideas may sound something like a caricature, but it is not so far off how we see ourselves. It is a portrait that may not have been acquired consciously, but is part of a general atmosphere or set of assumptions that influence our ideas about ourselves.

People in the West therefore may go through their entire lives never thinking to analyze this very flattering picture, and as a result are helpless against all kinds of pressures on them to conform in many kinds of ways.

The fact is that we all live our lives in groups—the family, work groups, social, religious and political groups. Very few people indeed are happy as solitaries, and they tend to be seen by their neighbours as peculiar or selfish or worse. Most people cannot stand being alone for long. They are always seeking groups to belong to, and if one group dissolves, they look for another. We are group animals still, and there is nothing wrong with that. But what is dangerous is not the belonging to a group, or groups, but not understanding the social laws that govern groups and govern us.

When we're in a group, we tend to think as that group does: we may even have joined the group to find "like-minded" people. But we also find our thinking changing because we belong to a group. It is the hardest thing in the world to maintain an individual dissident opinion, as a member of a group.

Dissident—disagreeing

It seems to me that this is something we have all experienced—something we take for granted, may never have thought about it. But a great deal of experiment has gone on among psychologists and sociologists on this very theme. If I describe an experiment or two, then anyone listening who may be a sociologist or psychologist will groan, oh God not *again*—for they will have heard of these classic experiments far too often. My guess is that the rest of the people will never have heard of these experiments, never have had these ideas presented to them. If my guess is true, then it aptly illustrates my general thesis, and the general idea behind these talks, that we (the human race) are now in possession of a great deal of hard information about ourselves, but we do not use it to improve our institutions and therefore our lives.

A typical test, or experiment, on this theme goes like this. A group of people are taken into the researchers' confidence. A minority of one or two are left in the dark. Some situation demanding measurement or assessment is chosen. For instance, comparing lengths of wood that differ only a little from each other, but enough to be perceptible, or shapes that are almost the same size. The majority in the group—according to instruction—will assert stubbornly that these two shapes or lengths are the same length, or size, while the solitary individual, or the couple, who have not been so instructed will assert that the pieces of wood or whatever are different. But the majority will continue to insist—speaking metaphorically—that black is white, and after a period of exasperation, irritation, even anger, certainly incomprehension, the minority will fall into line. Not always, but nearly always. There are indeed glorious individualists who stubbornly insist on telling the truth as they see it, but most give in to the majority opinion, obey the atmosphere.

When put as baldly, as unflatteringly, as this, reactions tend to be incredulous: "I certainly wouldn't give in, I speak my mind ..." But would you?

People who have experienced a lot of groups, who perhaps have observed their own behaviour, may agree that the hardest thing in the world is to stand out against one's group, a group of one's peers. Many agree that among our most shameful memories is this, how often we said black was white because other people were saying it.

In other words, we know that this is true of human behaviour, but how do we know it? It is one thing to admit it, in a vague uncomfortable sort of way (which probably includes the hope that one will never again be in such a testing situation) but quite another to make that cool step into a kind of objectivity, where one may say, "Right, if that's what human beings are like, myself included, then let's admit it, examine and organize our attitudes accordingly."

This mechanism, of obedience to the group, does not only mean obedience or submission to a small group, or one that is sharply determined, like a religion or political party. It means, too, conforming to those large, vague, ill-defined collections of people who may never think of themselves as having a collective mind because they are aware of differences of opinion—but which, to people from outside, from another culture, seem very minor. The underlying assumptions and assertions that govern the group are never discussed, never challenged, probably never noticed, the main one being precisely this: that it is a group mind, intensely resistant to change, equipped with sacred assumptions about which there can be no discussion.

* * *

There are other experiments done by psychologists and sociologists that underline that body of experience to which we give the folk-name, "human nature." They are recent; that is to say, done in the last twenty or thirty years. There have been some pioneering and key experiments that have given birth to many others along the same lines—as I said before, over-familiar to the professionals, unfamiliar to most people.

One is known as the Milgram experiment. I have chosen it precisely because it was and is controversial, because it was so much debated, because all the professionals in the field probably groan at the very sound of it. Yet, most ordinary people have never heard of it. If they did know about it, were familiar with the ideas behind it, then indeed we'd be getting somewhere. The Milgram experiment was prompted by curiosity into how it is that ordinary, decent, kindly people, like you and me, will do abominable things when ordered to do them—like the innumerable officials under the Nazis who claimed as an excuse that they were "only obeying orders."

The researcher put into one room people chosen at random who were told that they were taking part in an experiment. A screen divided the room in such a way that they could hear but not see into the other part. In this second part volunteers sat apparently wired up to a machine that administered electric shocks of increasing severity up to the point of death, like the electric chair. This machine indicated to them how they had to respond to the shock—with grunts, then groans, then screams, then pleas that the experiment should terminate. The person in the first half of the room believed the person in the second half was in fact connected to the machine. He was told that his or her job was to administer increasingly severe shocks according to the instructions of the experimenter and to ignore the cries of pain and pleas from the other side of the screen. Sixty-two per cent of the people tested continued to administer shocks up to the 450 volts level. At the 285 volts level the guinea pig had given an agonized scream and become silent. The people administering what they believed were at the best extremely painful doses of electricity were under great stress, but went on doing it. Afterwards most couldn't believe they were capable of such behaviour. Some said, "Well I was only carrying out instructions."

This experiment, like the many others along the same lines, offers us the information that a majority of people, regardless of whether they are black or white, male or female, old or young, rich or poor, will carry out orders, no matter how savage and brutal the orders are. This obedience to authority, in short, is not a property of the Germans under the Nazis, but a part of general human behaviour. People who have been in a political movement at times of extreme tension, people who remember how they were at school, will know this anyway … but it is one thing carrying a burden of knowledge around, half conscious of it, perhaps ashamed of it, hoping it will go away if you don't look too hard, and another saying openly and calmly and sensibly "Right. This is what we must expect under this and that set of conditions."

Can we imagine this being taught in school, imagine it being taught to children. "If you are in this or that type of situation, you will find yourself, if you are not careful, behaving like a brute and a savage if you are ordered to do it. Watch out for these situations: You must be on your guard against your own most primitive reactions and instincts."

Another range of experiments is concerned with … a group of ordinary citizens, researchers, [who] cause themselves to be taken into prison, some as if they were ordinary prisoners, a few in the position of warders. Immediately both groups start behaving appropriately: those as warders begin behaving as if they were real warders, with authority, badly treating the prisoners, who for their part show typical prison behaviour, become paranoid, suspicious, and so forth. Those in the role of warders confessed afterwards they could not prevent themselves enjoying the position of power, enjoying the sensation of controlling the weak. The so-called prisoners could not believe, once they were out, that they had in fact behaved as they had done.

But suppose this kind of thing were taught in schools?

Let us just suppose it, for a moment … But at once the nub of the problem is laid bare.

Imagine us saying to children, "In the last fifty or so years, the human race has become aware of a great deal of information about its mechanisms; how it behaves, how it must behave under certain circumstances. If this is to be useful, you must learn to contemplate these rules calmly, dispassionately, disinterestedly, without emotion. It is information that will set people free from blind loyalties, obedience to slogans, rhetoric, leaders, group emotions." Well, there it is.

What government, anywhere in the world, will happily envisage its subjects learning to free themselves from governmental and state rhetoric and pressures? Passionate loyalty and subjection to group pressure is what every state relies on. Some, of course, more than others. Khomeini's Iran, and the extreme Islamic sects, the Communist countries, are at one end of the scale. Countries like Norway, whose national day is celebrated by groups of children in fancy dress carrying flowers, singing and dancing, with not a tank or a gun in sight, are at the other. It is interesting to speculate: what country, what nation, when, and where, would have undertaken a programme to teach its children to be people to resist rhetoric, to examine the mechanisms that govern them? I can think of only one—America at its birth, in that heady period of the Gettysburg Address. And that time could not have survived the Civil War, for when war starts, countries cannot afford disinterested examination of their behaviour. When a war starts, nations go mad—and have to go mad, in order to survive. When I look back at the Second World War, I see something I didn't more than dimly suspect at the time. It was that everyone was crazy. Even people not in the immediate arena of war. I am not talking of the aptitudes for killing, for destruction, which soldiers are taught as part of their training, but a kind of atmosphere, the invisible poison, which spreads everywhere. And then people everywhere begin behaving as they never could in peacetime. Afterwards we look back, amazed. Did I really do that? Believe that? Fall for that bit of propaganda? Think that all

~ Review ~
Group Minds

Even in societies that seem most free, there is still an overwhelming pressure to conform to group opinions and attitudes, Doris Lessing explains in this essay.

Lessing refers to several experiments that psychologists and sociologists have conducted in the last half-century that she says have added to our empirical knowledge about the human race. We must use this knowledge, she urges, in building our social institutions and in educating our children.

Lessing observes that the pressure to conform, to be one of the crowd, can inspire even a supposedly civilized person to commit a barbaric and inhumane act. She asserts that to prevent the rise of tyrants, we must make the masses aware of this unspoken and inherent "rule" of human nature; the lessons of psychology and sociology should be applied to make the world a better place to live and to oppose crowdlike, careless behaviour.

our enemies were evil? That all our own nation's acts were good? How could I have tolerated that state of mind, day after day, month after month—perpetually stimulated, perpetually whipped up into emotions that my mind was meanwhile quietly and desperately protesting against?

No, I cannot imagine any nation—or not for long—teaching its citizens to become individuals able to resist group pressures. And no political party, either. I know a lot of people who are socialists of various kinds, and I try this subject out on them, saying: all governments these days use social psychologists, experts on crowd behaviour, and mob behaviour, to advise them. Elections are stage-managed, public issues presented according to the rules of mass psychology. The military uses this information. Interrogators, secret services and the police use it. Yet these issues are never even discussed, as far as I am aware, by those parties and groups who claim to represent the people.

On one hand there are governments who manipulate, using expert knowledge and skills; on the other hand people who talk about democracy, freedom, liberty and all the rest of it, as if these values are created and maintained by simply talking about them, by repeating them often enough. How is it that so-called democratic movements don't make a point of instructing their members in the laws of crowd psychology, group psychology?

When I ask this, the response is always an uncomfortable, squeamish reluctance, as if the whole subject is really in very bad taste, unpleasant, irrelevant. As if it will all just go away if it is ignored.

Your Child's Self-Esteem

Paul Chance

Consider Alice, age five. Alice attends kindergarten, where she is making excellent progress. Her teacher thinks she is one of the brightest children in the class, though in fact she has no more natural ability than most. She is often the first to raise her hand when the teacher asks a question, waving it eagerly and sometimes calling out, "I know! I know!" If called on when she does not know an answer, she does not hesitate to make a guess. Sometimes these answers sound foolish to her classmates, but their laugh doesn't bother Alice—she just laughs right along with them. Alice tackles almost every assignment with enthusiasm. If one approach fails, she tries another. If her persistence does not pay off, she asks the teacher for help. Alice is as comfortable with other children as she is with her school work. She is a popular child, and in group activities, she often takes the lead. At home, Alice is eager to do things for herself. She is proud, for instance, that she can already dress herself completely, buttons, shoe laces, and all, without help.

Now consider Zelda, age six. Zelda is in the first grade. She did not do very well in kindergarten, and her progress continues to be slow. Her teacher believes that she is one of the least intelligent children in the class though in fact she has as much ability as most. She never volunteers, and if called on she usually refuses to say more than "I don't know." Zelda works on most assignments in a lackluster, mechanical manner and often abandons them at the first sign of difficulty. When her teacher asks if she needs help, she says merely, "I can't do it." Zelda is no more adept socially than she is academically. She has few friends, and in group activities she is usually the quiet one on the sidelines. At home, Zelda is more at ease and more loquacious, but not more self-reliant. She waits for others to do things

Loquacious—talkative

for her because she "can't" do things for herself. Her mother still checks her each morning to be sure that she has dressed herself properly.

Competence Has Little To Do with Natural Ability

Alice and Zelda are as far apart as the letters *a* and *z*. The differences that separate them are not, however, due to differences in native ability. The differences are emotional and motivational. Alice is obviously self-assured and self-reliant. She likes herself and her world. Although she could not put her philosophy into words, she is an optimist. She believes that she has some degree of control over her destiny, that success and happiness are goals an individual can achieve through effort. Zelda, on the other hand, is as filled with self-doubt as Alice is with self-confidence. Her self-esteem is low and she thinks the world a harsh, unfriendly place. A philosopher would describe her as a fatalist, a person who believes that what happens is largely a matter of fate or chance. Zelda believes that she can do little to shape her future, that success and happiness are things that "just happen" to people who get lucky. Although Alice and Zelda have about the same amount of intelligence, it is clear that Alice is making far better use of her abilities. The result is that Alice is a highly competent child, while Zelda is best described as helpless.

Why do some children become Alices, while others become Zeldas? This question has received intensive study over the past decade. Most researchers seem convinced that experiences in infancy and early childhood play an especially important role in the development of competence, so their research efforts have focused on experiences in the first three years of life. This is not to say, of course, that whether a person becomes highly competent or utterly helpless is unalterably fixed by age three. People can change at any age. Nevertheless, the evidence suggests that the kinds of experiences that are important to the development of competence typically *begin* in early childhood. What are those experiences? The research on this subject is complex and not easily reduced to a few simple, clear-cut statements. But over and over again, the studies reveal four elements common to the backgrounds of the most competent children but conspicuously missing from the backgrounds of the least competent.

The Importance of a Strong Parent-Child Bond

It may come as no surprise to most parents that one common element in the backgrounds of very competent children is a strong bond between the child and the primary care-giver—usually, but not necessarily, the mother. Dr Alan Sroufe, professor of child development, and his co-workers at the University of Minnesota, Twin Cities, have found, for instance, that infants judged "securely attached" at eighteen months of age were more successful at solving problems, such as getting an object out of a tube, at age two. They were also better able to elicit the help of their mothers to solve problems that were too difficult for them. They were, in other words, already more competent than children who lacked a strong bond with their mothers.

The Signs of a Secure Child

Dr Sroufe notes that it is possible to predict which children will be successful preschoolers by studying the relationship a child has with his caretaker at twelve to eighteen months of age. "Even by two years," he says, "secure children will be more enthusiastic, persistent, and cooperative in solving problems than insecure children will be." Children with a good, secure relationship with an adult can function well in a nursery school at a younger age than can children without such a relationship. "Apparently," Dr Sroufe concludes, "secure children have learned early how to explore and master their environment and function within clear, firm limits."

Perhaps the most extensive work on the relationship between a close attachment and child development is that of Dr Burton White, former director of the Preschool Project at Harvard University, and his colleagues. Their research followed the progress of 40 children, beginning at age one or two. The researchers went into the homes of these children every other week, 26 times a year, for one or two years, and then retested the children again at the ages of three and five. The researchers concentrated on the interactions of the infants with their mothers and others in the home. They concluded that a close social relationship "was a conspicuous feature in the lives of children who developed best."

Another way to study the benefits of a love bond, as it might be called, is by looking at the development of children for whom such a bond is notably lacking. One sometimes finds such children in poorly staffed institutions. Dr Sally Provence, professor of pediatrics at Yale University's Child Study Center, who has made a special study of such children, observes that they often become "subdued and apathetic." Given a little tender loving care, however, these children often liven up dramatically.

Providing a Stimulating Environment

Another common element in the backgrounds of competent children is a stimulating environment. Dr K. Alison Clarke-Stewart, associate professor of education and human development at the University of Chicago, studies the interactions of mothers with their firstborn infants, ages nine to thirteen months. She found, among other things, that mothers of competent children talked to or made other sounds when interacting with their babies more often than did the mothers of less competent infants. Dr White and his co-workers were so impressed by the role of verbal stimulation in the development of competence that they wrote that "live language directed to the child is the most consistently favourable kind of educational experience an infant can have during the eleven to sixteen month period." They go on to point out that language from a television or radio or speech directed elsewhere that the child overhears has little if any beneficial effect.

Freedom to explore can make even an ordinary environment more stimulating than it is from afar. An environment that is full of interesting objects a child cannot get to is less stimulating than one with fewer objects that are within reach. Dr White and his collaborators found, in fact, that freedom of movement was characteristic of the homes of competent children. The more freedom to explore about the house (within the limits prescribed by safety, of course), the more competent a child was likely to be.

The evidence for the benefits of a stimulating environment suggests that a dull, monotonous environment is a prescription for helplessness. This theory seems to be borne out by the classic research of renowned psychiatrist Rene Spitz, who studied the development of children living in the thoroughly monotonous world of a badly understaffed foundling home. These children had little to do all day but sleep or stare at the blank walls about them. Needless to say, such children do not develop normally, but the degree to which their development is retarded is striking. Dr Spitz offers this description of the typical child reared in such an impoverished environment: "These children would lie or sit with wide-open, expressionless eyes, frozen immobile face, and a faraway expression as if in a daze, apparently not perceiving what went on in their environment."

Fortunately for such children, a little bit of stimulation can have substantial benefits. For instance, psychologists Wayne Dennis and Yvonne Sayegh gave institutionalized infants in an otherwise impoverished environment items such as flowers, bits of coloured sponge, and a chain of coloured plastic discs to play with for as little as an hour each day. It is hard to believe that so little improvement in their thoroughly monotonous environment would make a great difference, yet their developmental ages jumped dramatically.

Interactions—with Parents...

It is, of course, possible to get too much of a good thing. Dr. White believes that too much stimulation, too many things going on around the child, may merely confuse him. This idea is supported by a study conducted by Dr. Jerome Kagan, professor of human development at Harvard University, who watched mothers as they interacted with their four-month-old infants. He noted when the mothers spoke to or cooed to their babies and what else they were doing at the time. He found that upper-middle-income mothers usually spoke to their children while facing them but did *not* simultaneously tickle them or provide other stimulation. Low-income mothers, on the other hand, were likely to talk to their infants while diapering, feeding, or burping them. It is probably not a coincidence, Dr. Kagan observes, that the children of upper-middle-income mothers typically show more precocious language development than do the children of low-income mothers.

Most researchers seem to agree that a varied environment is important to the development of competence, but the quality of the stimulation is more important than the amount.

A third characteristic of the backgrounds of competent children is frequent social interaction. Dr. White has found, for instance, that highly competent children have at least twice as many social experiences as their less competent peers. He says that "providing a rich social life for a twelve-to-fifteen-month-old child is the best thing you can do to guarantee a good mind." He also notes that first-born children have far more opportunities to interact with their parents than do later-born children. The rich social life of first-borns may have something to do with the fact that they are usually (though not always, of course) more competent than their siblings are. They are, for instance, more likely to obtain positions of leadership as adults than are later-born children.

... and with Others

Psychologist Michael Lewis, director of the Institute for the Study of Exceptional Children at the Educational Testing Service in Princeton, New Jersey, believes that the child's interactions with other people are more important than his interactions with any other part of the environment. "We learn about others through our interaction with them," he writes, "and at the same time we define ourselves." How does a child learn whether he is a boy or a girl, tall or short, strong or weak? Through his interactions with others who treat him as a boy rather than a girl, and who are taller or shorter, stronger or weaker, than he is. How does he learn whether he is competent or helpless? Partly, argues Dr. Lewis, through his interactions with the people around him.

Studies of social isolation have shown that even when other forms of stimulation are available, a dearth of social experiences can have devastating effects. Dr. Harry Harlow and his colleagues at the University of Wisconsin at Madison found that monkeys reared alone grew up to be timid, wholly inadequate individuals. Monkeys reared by their mothers but separated from other youngsters of their kind fared better, but still developed abnormally. Thus it appears likely that the more opportunities for social encounters a child has, the better. It is even possible to see social competence emerge as a result of such experience. When, for example, California psychologist Jacqueline Becker gave pairs of nine-month-old babies the opportunity to play with one another, she found that they interacted more and more with each succeeding session. When these youngsters were introduced to a new baby, they were much more likely to approach him than were infants who had less social experience.

A World that Responds

Probably the most important element in the environments of highly competent children is something that researchers call *responsivity*. A responsive environment is one that *responds to* the behaviour of the child. There is, in other words, some correspondence between what the child does and what happens to him. Under ordinary circumstances there is at least a minimal amount of responsivity in the life of every child. Take, for example, the baby nursing at his mother's breast. As Dr Martin Seligman, professor of psychology at the University of Pennsylvania, writes: "He sucks, the world responds with warm milk. He pats the breast, his mother tenderly squeezes him back. He takes a break and coos, his mother coos back…Each step he takes is synchronized with a response from the world." When a child's behaviour has clear, unequivocal consequences, he not only learns about those consequences but "over and above this," writes Dr Seligman, "he learns that responding works, that in general there is *synchrony* between responses and outcomes." This means, in turn, that the child exerts some control over his environment, and many researchers agree with Dr Seligman that "how readily a person believes in his own helplessness or mastery is shaped by his experience with controllable and uncontrollable events."

Synchrony—close relationship.

A responsive environment, then, inclines a child toward competence, while an unresponsive environment inclines a child toward helplessness. Dr Lewis illustrates the difference by describing the experiences of two infants, Sharon and Toby. One morning Sharon wakes up wet, hungry, or perhaps just lonely, and cries. Nothing happens. She cries again. Still no response. She continues crying for several minutes, but no one comes. Finally she falls asleep, exhausted. On the same morning another infant, Toby, awakes. She, too, is wet, hungry, or lonely, and cries. Within seconds she has the attention of a warm hand, a smiling face, and the food or dry diaper she needs. Sharon's world is unresponsive; her behaviour has no effect. Toby's world is highly responsive; her behaviour gets results almost immediately. Now, what is the lesson each child is taught by her respective experience? Sharon learns that making an effort to affect one's condition is useless. Things happen or they don't; what she does is unimportant. Toby learns that her efforts are worthwhile. What happens depends, in part, upon what she does.

Some readers may think at this point that responsivity is just another name for permissiveness. Give the child what he wants, pander to his every whim, deny him nothing. In other words, spoil him. Not so. A responsive environment is not one that gives a child everything and anything he wants. Responsivity means merely that an act produces clear, consistent consequences. Sometimes those consequences will be negative. For example, a four-year-old child who insists upon having cookies for breakfast may send his bowl of cereal flying. A parent might respond to this behaviour by saying, "Since you've thrown away your breakfast, you'll have to go without." Another parent might insist that the child clean up the mess he has made. In each case the child's behaviour has some effect, but the effect does not necessarily include getting a plate of cookies.

Handling a Baby's Cry

But what about Toby's crying? Sure, Toby learns that she can master her environment, but doesn't she inevitably become a cry-baby in the process? Doesn't she learn that the way to get what you want is by making a fuss? Interestingly enough, the answer is no. Psychologists Silvia Bell and Mary Ainsworth conducted a study of the effects of responsiveness on crying. They observed the interactions of mothers and their infants during the first year of the child's life. There were wide variations among the mothers in how often and how quickly they responded to their baby's cries. The most responsive mother, for instance, responded 96 percent of the time, while the least responsive mother answered only 3 percent of her baby's cries. Many parents would predict that the first infant would cry constantly. What actually happened, though, was that the children who could control their environment by crying soon learned to use more subtle tactics to exert control, and they also learned to do things for themselves. The researchers conclude that "an infant whose mother's responsiveness helped him to achieve his ends develops confidence in his own ability to control what happens to him." This means that he comes to do more things for himself, which means there are fewer occasions for calling upon Mom.

Other research supports the notion that a responsive environment leads to competence. In one study, for example, Dr Lewis and psychologist Susan Goldberg watched mothers interact with their three-month-old infants. They noticed that the behaviour of some mothers was likely to be a reaction to what the baby did, while the behaviour of other mothers tended to be independent of the baby's activity. The researchers found that the first infants, those whose mothers were responsive, were more interested in the world around them and were more attentive.

Toys That Foster Competence

Dr John S. Watson of the University of California at Berkeley demonstrated that the responsiveness of the physical world also is beneficial. Dr Watson designed a mobile that would rotate whenever a baby exerted pressure on a pillow. When an infant turned his head this way or that, the mobile would spin. Dr Watson found that with just ten minutes of practice a day, the infants learned to control the mobile within a few days. They also smiled and cooed as the mobile spun to and fro, apparently enjoying the control they exerted over the object. Other babies who saw the mobile spin but had no control over its movement did not show the same reaction.

Providing a child with responsive toys does not necessarily require anything so elaborate as Watson's motorized mobile. Psychologist Robert McCall notes that a mobile can be made responsive simply by tying a piece of soft cotton yarn loosely around a baby's wrist and tying the other end to the mobile. When the baby moves his hand, the mobile moves. Another inexpensive but highly responsive baby toy is the rattle, since it makes a noise only when and if the baby shakes it. Yet another example is a mirror, perhaps made of shiny metal so that there is no danger of broken glass. The child looks in the mirror and sees someone looking back. The person looking back does all sorts of things—smiling, laughing, frowning— but only if the child looking into the mirror does them first. As the child gets a bit older, a spoon and pie pan provide responsive, if noisy diversion. It may well be the case that the more responsive toys tend to be the least expensive. Toys that "do it all" rarely require much activity from the child. Thus, the *least* responsive toy available is probably the $500 colour television set, while one of the most responsive toys around is the $1 rubber ball.

There is evidence that if a child's environment is thoroughly *un*responsive, he is almost certain to become helpless rather than competent. Dr Seligman and his colleagues have conducted a number of studies that demonstrate just how devastating the lack of control over events can be. They have found that when a laboratory animal is unable to escape an unpleasant situation, it eventually quits trying. More important, when the animal is later put into another situation from which it could readily escape, it does not do so. In fact, it makes no effort to escape. Psychologist Donald Hiroto got similar results when he studied the effects of uncontrollable unpleasant events on college students. Some students heard an unpleasantly loud noise, which they could do nothing about. Other students heard the same noise but learned to control it by pushing a button. Afterward, the students were put into another situation in which they could turn off a noise simply by moving their hand from one part of a box to another. Those who had learned to control the noise in the first situation did so in the second, but most of those who could do nothing about the first noise made no attempt to escape the second.

~ Review ~

Your Child's Self-Esteem

Why does one child show great enthusiasm for learning, making friends, taking risks, while another, with about the same native ability, seems sluggish, shy, fearful? Why does one child have a positive attitude to life while another lacks self-confidence? One's feeling of self-competence tends to emerge at a very young age, and has little to do with natural abilities. Experiences in infancy and early childhood seem to play an important role. This section discusses *four factors* that affect childhood competency and self-esteem.

Obviously, the **quality of the bond** between an infant and his or her parent or caregiver has a fundamental influence. A baby with a strong bond to his or her mother, for example, often becomes more enthusiastic and cooperative, whereas the baby lacking a strong attachment to an adult often becomes subdued and apathetic.

Likewise, a drab, monotonous *environment*, filled with uncaring adults and objects beyond a child's reach, produces a dull-spirited child, while a richly stimulating environment, filled with safe objects to explore and people who converse freely with the infant or child, helps turn out a confident, sociable youngster. However, the **quality of the stimulation** is generally more important than the quantity.

Frequent social interaction also helps produce a happy, enthusiastic, confident child; it is through interacting that we learn about ourselves.

The fourth factor is **responsivity.** How well or readily does a child's environment respond to his or her behaviour? The infant who wakes up wet, hungry, and lonely, but whose cry brings forth no caring adult to attend to these needs, may learn through repetition of this experience that she has very little control over her world, further increasing her passivity and sense of helplessness as a school-age child. On the contrary, the infant whose parent is highly responsive to her cries learns that her behaviour can bring results.

In general, **the more responsive the environment the greater the competency** of the child. And conversely, **the less responsive the environment the greater the likelihood that the child feels helpless** and incapable of performing tasks that other children seem to accomplish effortlessly.

They simply sat there and did nothing. They had been made helpless, at least momentarily.

Helping a Child Master His World

Researchers have not, of course, deliberately set out to make children helpless by exposing them to unpleasant situations from which they cannot escape. They have, however, noted that children reared in unresponsive environments are not likely to become highly competent. Dr. Seligman points out that a lack of control was characteristic of the environment of Dr. Spitz's institutionalized children and may have been more important to their helplessness than the lack of stimulation they received.

All children are subjected to some unpleasant events that they cannot control. An infant's diaper rash is beyond his control, as is the misery of most childhood illnesses. And even the brightest child must eventually experience failure. But if the child is usually able to exert some control over the events in his life, this may give him some immunity against the adverse effects of unpleasant events he is powerless to control.

It appears, then, that the kind of experiences a child has in the first few years of life plays an important role in his development. The child who has a close, warm relationship with an adult; who lives in interesting surroundings; who has ample opportunity to interact with other people; and, most important, who lives in an environment that is responsive, has an excellent chance of becoming competent. The earlier these experiences begin, the better. "I believe," Dr. Seligman told me, "that motivation and emotion are more plastic than intelligence. I am no longer convinced that special kinds of experiences will raise a child's IQ by twenty points or induce him to write piano concertos at age five, as Mozart did. But I am convinced that certain kinds of experiences during childhood will produce a child who is helpless, while other experiences will produce a child who is competent."

There is in every child an Alice and a Zelda. The question is, which is to prevail?

QUESTIONS

1. State what the differences in the school performances of Alice and Zelda are due to.

2. Briefly explain the differences between an optimist and a fatalist.

3. State why, according to most researchers, some children become Alices (i.e., optimists) while others become Zeldas (i.e., fatalists).

4. List the two findings of Dr. Alan Stroufe's study and relate them to a common element in the backgrounds of very competent children.

5. State what Dr. K. Alison Clarke-Stewart found in her study of interaction of mothers with their first-born infants and relate it to a second common element in the backgrounds of competent children.

6. State what can make an "ordinary" environment more stimulating.

7. From Dr Jerome Kagan's study contrast both mother-infant interaction and the rate of infant language development in upper-middle income as opposed to low income households.

8. State the third common characteristic of the background of competent children.

9. Contrast how Dr White characterizes first-born and later-born children concerning parent-child interaction and obtaining positions of leadership.

10. State what Dr Harry Harlow and his colleagues found concerning monkeys studied at different levels of interaction and the conclusion that may be drawn from this.

11. Explain with an example what is the fourth element in the environment of highly competent children?

12. Contrast responsivity with permissiveness.

13. State the conclusion drawn from Bell and Ainsworth's study of the effect of responsiveness on crying.

14. Explain why, in terms of responsivity, a colour t.v. is not as good a toy as a rubber ball.

15. Explain how one group of college students in Hiroto's experiment learned to be "competent" while the other group learned how to be "helpless."

UNIT 2

CHANGE IN THE SOCIAL WORLD

Dynamics of Social Change

We make history ourselves, but, in the first place, under very definite antecedents and conditions. Among these the economic ones are ultimately decisive. But the political ones, etc., and indeed even the traditions which haunt human minds also play a part, although not the decisive one …

Frederick Engels

Introduction

John Steckley and Michael Badyk

What do we mean by the term "social change"? We mean that within a group of people at least one aspect of life has been altered significantly. For example, when we say that in Canada no households had televisions in 1951, while 90% did in 1963, we are talking about one form of social change taking place.

When speaking about social change, we often use the term "society." It can be used to refer to groups of people at a number of different levels: (*a*) a group within a country (e.g., French-Canadian society); (*b*) the country itself (e.g., Canadian society); or, (*c*) a unit beyond the level of a country but still recognizable as one group (e.g., North American society or Western society). So, society is just a particular group of people. Society itself is not uniquely human; many animals exist in social units. It aids them in their survival, and it was likely a necessary part of early human survival. We have retained this characteristic to this day.

Usually when we mention society we also use another term—**culture**. Culture is a totality of a way of life. It includes food, art, history and just about anything else that you can think of. Culture is passed from generation to generation. The process by which children acquire their culture through learning is called *enculturation*.

Culture is not passed down from generation to generation entirely intact. There are always changes caused by innovations and innovators within the culture or society. Change can also occur when one culture has contact with another. They trade ideas and materials. These two points (innovation and trade) are known as *acculturation*.

Social change is similar to change in the life of an individual. Alter one aspect of a person's life, and other elements are affected. We can see this when a person leaves high school and enters college. It is

CULTURE

Culture is a totality of a way of life. It includes food, art, history and just about anything else that you can think of. Culture is passed from generation to generation.

not just the education level that changes, but the person's entire life experience. There are *material* changes as well. The environment that the person encounters is different. The college student may have to travel further, by a different means of transportation, to an area he or she might not know. Locations of classrooms, offices, cafeterias and washrooms must be learned.

There are also changes in the student's *social* world. The population of the college is drawn from a broad area, and includes ethnically diverse groups. The student is drawn into new friendships with other people in the same program.

The student's world of ideas, or *intellectual* sphere, changes as well, and not just in what is taught in class. For example, the student learns to think of time in different ways. He or she may have more "free" time outside of the classroom, but must learn to budget that time to deal with a greater workload. The student also encounters new ideas, both inside the classroom and among friends, and develops a different perspective in this world.

Eventually these changes end up creating a set of social or cultural **values**. Values are those things that our society perceives as good, or wise, or right. In many ways these values are the items that allow us to recognize a particular society or culture.

Even though social change is inevitable, it is not always welcomed by everyone. People tend to be comfortable with the society they are familiar with. Sometimes this resistance to change can lead to serious problems of adjustment. These adjustment problems happen frequently when different cultures come into contact with one another for the first time.

There is a tendency to view things from the perspective of one's own culture. In other words, we tend to place our culture ahead of others that we come into contact with. This is known as **ethnocentricity**. Unfortunately ethnocentricity frequently involves stereotyping, discrimination, racism and prejudice. Probably the best example of this is the legacy of European/Native dealings over the past four or five hundred years. All too often we were taught that the Native Canadian cultures were primitive, made up of savages with nothing to offer the Europeans.

The Europeans also felt that they altered all aspects of the Natives' lives for the better. Technology, language, religion, and agriculture from Europe were all considered to be improvements. In truth, the aboriginal people were very sophisticated in all of these areas. Most

VALUES

Values are those things that our society perceives as good, or wise, or right. In many ways these values are the items that allow us to recognize a particular society or culture.

ETHNOCENTRICITY

Ethnocentricity is the tendency to view things from the perspective of one's own culture, placing one's own culture ahead of others that we come into contact with. Unfortunately, ethnocentricity frequently involves stereotyping, discrimination, racism and prejudice.

of the people living in Southern Ontario were growing crops—corn, beans, and squash—then unavailable to Europeans. They also had a more nutritious diet than that of most people living in Europe during the 16th and 17th centuries, and, as a consequence, were generally taller than most Europeans. Their axes, knives and arrowheads were manufactured from flint often obtained through complex Native-only trade networks. They spoke languages filled with terms and concepts for which European languages were silent. The fields, forests and waterways were alive with spirits, whereas Europeans just saw the physical world. But still the Europeans felt that they were superior.

But acculturation works both ways. What did the Native peoples give the Europeans? Many things; for example, their crops would eventually make up most of the food crops grown in the world, as they are today. One particularly important cultural trade item was the potato. It seems to be an insignificant item but it has changed the whole world. Over much of Europe the crop most frequently grown in the past few centuries was wheat. Wheat doesn't grow well in all places, either because of cold or wet summers, or a combination of both. Whenever the wheat crop failed starvation was widespread. The potato would thrive in the cold wet conditions because it had originated in the cold, wet mountains of Central and South America.

Potatoes are also much more nutritious than grains and they offer a big dose of Vitamin C, which was generally lacking in most Europeans' diets. Starvation was reduced, people were healthier and they lived longer.

In Russia, and what is now Poland, the potato was viewed as the "food of the devil" because of its almost magical health properties. The Empress, Catherine The Great, realized the importance of this crop and by royal decree forced the people to plant it. Now it is part-and-parcel of Russian culture, being used for food but also to make vodka, another Russian tradition.

Elsewhere it was adopted more readily. In Ireland, it caused a profound change. In 1754, Ireland had a population of 3.2 million; by 1845 the population soared to 8.2 million, plus another 1.75 million had emigrated out of Ireland. This population growth can be attributed directly to better nutrition from the potato. Irish dependence on the potato was so complete that when a potato blight (a fungal infestation) ruined the potato crop in the 1850s, thousands and maybe millions starved. They had no other crop to fall back on. Their lives were now tied to this foreign food.

We associate Ireland and potatoes to this day. Indeed, the package of potatoes we buy from Prince Edward Island shows a cartoon character consisting of a potato with an Irish hat in one hand and a shamrock (an Irish plant that is considered a good luck charm) in the other. This use of symbol is somewhat ironic since the potato originates here in the Western Hemisphere, not in Ireland.

In summary, trade in culture goes both ways. We end up with something new. In the U.S.A. you are almost forced to assimilate into what is known as the "American melting pot." You are an American first, and your ancestral background comes second. This decrease in cultural diversity is known as *assimilation*. Here in Canada we are more multicultural. You are encouraged to maintain your heritage.

Should we encourage people to assimilate into Canadian society? If so what exactly is Canadian society and culture when we have such a diverse grouping of citizens? These are difficult questions to answer. One way to get some clues about the influences on our society is to look at somewhat-less-complex or geographically-isolated societies.

In the article "Blood and Nerves" we will examine a fairly unique situation in an isolated part of Newfoundland. Before you read this article make sure that you are familiar with the terms *acculturation, enculturation, assimilation* and the three categories of change we discussed. They *all* occur in this article. And by all means avoid the trap of ethnocentricity. It is a different society, worthy of our study and provides a window on our past from which we can learn a great deal.

Language and Change—Bias in What We Read

Jill Le Clair

Social change often affects even the language we use. As a result of major social changes taking place in society—in particular the increasing involvement of women in the labour force and the changing ethnic composition of Canada—many people are now more critical about the written material they encounter. They are beginning to re-evaluate it for *bias* and *stereotyping*.

Biases in writing can take many forms. Possible biases you might find are described below.

Bias against women. Sexism (androcentricity) refers to seeing the world as male centred or through mens' eyes. Often authors write as if there is one perspective and that is male. Clearly, half the world is made up of women, so it is important to understand a woman's point of view. Examples of male sexism are: writing from a male viewpoint or framework; suggesting that males are the people who do things, whereas women are the people things are done to; omitting to discuss women, so they become invisible; and trivializing problems experienced by women. In preparing her book *Nonsexist Research Methods: A Practical Guide* (Boston: Unwin Hyman, 1988), Margrit Eichler was not able to find examples of reverse sexism in contemporary journals.

Bias against ethnic or racial groups. In ethnic or racial biases, assumptions are made about specific groups of people based on stereotypes. The focus may be on the ethnic group of the individual or it could be based on skin colour. *Stereotyping* is when a person assumes that one individual will behave in the way a specific group

~ Language and Change ~

Spot The Bias

Read the following statements and see if you can find anything in these quotes that leads you to think there may be something biased or overlooked.

SEXISM

1. *Sociologist Van den Berghe … interprets intergroup warfare as a rational means of gaining livestock, women and slaves, gaining or keeping territory, or gaining, controlling and exploiting new territory." (Shaw quoted in Eichler, 1988: 22)*

   This is a male point of view; intergroup assumes that the group is male, although the group does include women. Women are described as objects gained through warfare.

2. **INTERVIEW QUESTION:**
   Agree or disagree with this statement:

   It is generally better to have a man at the head of a department composed of both men and women employees. (Eichler, 1988: 43)

   Here the choice in answering the question is restricted. How can the person answering the question disagree or support the opposite view that women might make better heads of departments?

3. *The journalistic fraternity is very concerned about protecting its sources.*

   The language assumes that journalists are male—the "journalistic fraternity." The group is not referred to as a sorority or sisterhood.

4. *If a freshman student wants to register early he may apply at the registrar's office.*

   The term freshman excludes freshwomen. The assumption is that the new student is male.

5. *The nursing department is manned by twenty people.*

   Such a department obviously includes women. A more appropriate term would be staffed.

6. *God is viewed by Christians as all powerful. He can understand all that takes place in the world.*

   The assumption here is that God is male.

7. *Jacob Mincer … finds, for example, that quit rates in the union sector are about one-half as large as in the nonunion sector for young men and about one-third as large for men over 30.* (Frank quoted in Eichler, 1988: 28)

   Women are totally overlooked in this example. Sexism by omission is a very common form of discrimination.

ETHNIC/RACIAL/CULTURAL

1. *Christopher Columbus discovered America in 1492.*

   There were already communities in North America. A more accurate description would be: "Columbus was the first European to arrive in the Americas". Also his name is Anglicized—that is not how he spelled his own name.

2. *Canada was created in 1867.*
   By 1867, the First Nations had lived for many centuries in the territory we now know as Canada. The British government created the origins of the political unit we now call Canada in 1867 (excluding Newfoundland of course).

3. *The primitive Indian game of lacrosse was far from being the slaughter too often conceived in the history of sport classes. Rather it was a game of great skill, which demanded a high degree of stamina and endurance, and which was played with passion. It was a noble game, although a vigourous one.* (Jette quoted in J. Oxendine, *American Indian Sports Heritage.* Champaign, Illinois: Human Kinetics Books.1988: 47)

   It is unnecessary to describe the Indian game as primitive. Would the author describe English soccer games of the 19th century as primitive as well?

DISABLED

1. *In the past crippled persons were not permitted to participate in regular sport activities.*

   Today the term "crippled" is not used. The word "disabled" is preferable.

SEXUAL ORIENTATION

1. *Some homosexuals tend to seek out a single relationship, hoping to gratify all emotional needs within a one-to-one exclusive relationship. Such twosomes are usually based on unrealistic expectations, often accompanied by inordinate demands; in most instances, these pairs are caught up in a turbulent, abrasive attachment. These liaisons are characterized by initial excitement which may include exultation and confidence in the discovery of a great love which soon alternates with anxiety, rage and depression as magical expectations are inevitably frustrated.* (Bieber quoted in Isay, 1990: 146).

   The assumption is that somehow homosexuals have "weird" or unusual sexual relationships. The research does not support this view. Change the term homosexual to heterosexual and hopes for a great love are not any different.

BIAS IN WRITING

Biases in writing can take many forms. Possible biases you might find are:

- **Bias against women**
- **Bias against ethnic or racial groups**
- **Bias against the disabled**
- **Bias against homosexuals.**

has been expected to behave. An example of stereotyping is when a male student is on holiday in Europe and the hosts expect the Canadian student to be an excellent hockey player, when it is entirely possible that the student's preferred sport is basketball. Similarly, assuming that a person who has a black skin and comes from Kenya and lived in a small rural "undeveloped" village is jumping to conclusions. Many Kenyans, Nigerians, South Africans, etc., live in highly urbanized, modern cities.

Bias against the disabled. Often in the past those with disabilities were isolated from society or even physically hidden away. Even twenty years ago, people would talk about the "crippled," the "dumb" and the "retarded." Today it is expected, and it is the law under the Human Rights Code, that everyone is treated with respect. The most healthy and active person can become disabled in the few moments it takes for a car to go out of control on a road.

Bias against homosexuals. *Homophobia* is when people have a fear of people whose sexual orientation is to a person of the same sex. In many countries, homosexuals are labelled mentally deviant, put in jail or even put to death.

Blood and Nerves

Dona Lee Davis

This reading is about Grey Rock Harbour, a small outport or fishing village on the southwest coast of Newfoundland. Like many such communities, it traditionally was quite isolated. It could only be reached by boat.

During the 1960s, a number of major material changes took place that ended the isolation and strongly affected the community both socially and intellectually. A road was constructed, connecting Grey Rock Harbour with the outside world. Public electricity made television a part of daily life. A telephone system was installed. A fish-processing plant was constructed. Along with other changes related to the fishing industry, this drastically altered the social sphere of family relations (e.g., the relationships between husbands and wives, wives and mothers-in-law, young couples, single mothers and their parents). The technology of birth control helped create an intellectual "value gap" between young and old women.

At the same time, Grey Rock Harbour was designated a resettlement community, one to which people of other villages in the area were moved. This directly altered the social fabric of the community, bringing in people earlier considered to be "out-siders." This government ordered resettlement plan was instituted all over Newfoundland, and was a source of profound social change in that province.

The reading, taken from a book entitled *Blood and Nerves* and written by Dona Lee Davis, presents a look at what life was like for women "before" and "after the road."

BEFORE THE ROAD

Courting patterns were similar for all the "before the road" generations. Young men and women would stroll along (actually climb) village paths in like-sexed groups in the early evening and meet with the opposite sex, with some eventually pairing off. Besides these clandestine rendezvous, young women could meet men at church dances, lodge parties, weddings, and dances held on schooners. (In the 1950s and '60s, teens met in pairs at a local store.)

Most young people courted on the sly. Peer-group girlfriends and boyfriends knew who were "couples," since they were instrumental in getting them together. (Women reported learning about sex from peers, boyfriends or husbands, rarely from a mother.) When a young man finally came into a girlfriend's house, it was to ask permission to marry her. Mate selection was based on love; and if any objection were raised, it was usually by a mother. (There were cases of single women with children who waited for their own mother's permission on their—the mother's—deathbeds to marry the child's father.)

It is difficult to make definitive statements about courting customs. Different women had different morals, and some women report ideal rather than real behaviour. In general, premarital intercourse was considered common and natural. Nor was it common (or laudable) to have more than one partner at a time. Couples had a great deal of privacy, and often got together to go berry-picking and travel by boat to small islands for lunch. Absence of street lights made it easy to court near one's own house. Some parents allowed courting at home. "Courting" is held to be synonymous with intercourse, and then, as now, many couples "had" to get married. The common expression was, "Well, he flicked her" (made her pregnant).

The majority of young women married within the community. However, the large number of schooners in Grey Rock Harbour during the fishing season and the practice of serving resulted in a siphoning of females of marriageable age. It was common for women to be ten, fifteen or even twenty years younger than their husbands, since a man had to wait until he was "fishing full shares" to marry. It could take a long time to save up the capital to build a house, which was necessary if the family house was already full of married siblings.

Though many women did it, "dating" an outsider was frowned upon. A young girl was not supposed to become involved with an outsider or someone who was transient in the community. The rationalization was that if she got pregnant he could "just up and leave" without marrying her.

As noted a young woman was prepared, with all the necessary skills, for marriage by the time she was in her early teens:

> I got married at seventeen. Girls got married early in those days because married life was just as much hard work as being single so there was not much point in delaying it. Girls spent their lives doing washing, cleaning and cooking. Usually they would marry and go to live in their husband's house with his family. It was no different from life in your own home.

The alternative to marriage for a woman was to have a child and not get married. Most women with children eventually did marry; however, a couple could simply set up residence together. This was especially common for widows who took in boarders. There were very few spinsters, and women who were spinsters were considered to have something wrong with them, such as being mildly retarded. Extramarital affairs and divorce were almost nonexistent: marriage was "for keeps." The commitment meant more than the spouses' abilities to live up to the bargain. Marriage was viewed as a promise formally made, in God's house, to stay together for better or worse. Other than extreme drunkenness on the part of a man, or having children outside the marriage on the part of a woman, there was little justification for divorce. Couples who did not get along could separate, but that was rare.

One of the most salient characteristics of married life was the periodical absence of the husband. It is impossible to give a typical example of the pattern of male absence in "the old days." There was a great deal of variation from family to family in the fishing options a man chose to pursue, both from season to season and throughout his lifetime (although the general pattern from 1900 onward has been a change from an offshore to an inshore fishery). Most middle-aged and older women of today reared their families in a situation of long periods of absence of the husband. Consequently, the woman became the mainstay of her family, the operational head of household. The following is an example:

> Elsie's husband has been a longliner fisherman for 22 years. Reg fished longliners when they were first married. They were married on December 23, Reg left on January 15 and did not come home until June. In those days longliners went out from Cape Breton or Grey Rock Harbour depending on where the fish was. If the fish was off Cape Breton, Reg would leave for winter and not come back until the season

was over—January to June. The first winter they were married, Elsie went to Cape Breton with her husband. Just married and childless, she stayed in Glace Bay with a family of one of Reg's crew. After that she had to stay home and take care of the children when he left. When he fished from Grey Rock Harbour, from January to March, he would go out mornings and come back evenings. April to July he was gone on five-day trips, July to August he was home, and from September to December he was gone again on five-day trips.

Recently married women stayed with mother, mother-in-law, grandmother, or any other relative with space available. Women who had houses of their own and only small children asked a female relative, neighbour or serving girl to sleep with them. Having someone stay over was supposed to prevent loneliness, but it also provided a bit of security for people afraid of the dark; and, furthermore, two bodies make a bed much warmer.

When asked what it meant to be a fisherman's wife, women responded in terms of two recurrent themes: (1) worry about the absent husband and (2) the expectation, excitement and joy of homecoming.

"The life of a fisherman's wife is a life of worry." Middle-aged women felt they had good reason to worry in the past:

> I used to worry more when I was younger. In the old days there was more danger in fishing, more to worry about. There were no instruments for communication like there is now. For instance, a boat caught fire last week, and they were able to get help right away. In the old days you couldn't have done that ... In the old days there was a lot less choice. A captain who was an "old fish dog" would go out in hazardous weather while others stayed in. His crew didn't have much say in the matter, and the wives would be left at home to worry.

Homecomings were big occasions, particularly after long absences as the following three statements reveal:

> After the summer swordfishing, all the boats would come back at about the same time. When the first boats came back in, all the women would get right excited. Everyone baked pies and put them in the window to cool. Sometimes those pies got mouldy because the boats didn't all come at once. When the fall ships came in, you knew you'd have your husband home through the winter.

> Husbands would be a little anxious about coming home. They got all the news at once: births, deaths, pregnancies, etcetera. They were always glad to find wives and families healthy and faithful.

> My dear, a rest is as good as a change.

An important, widely joked-about element of homecoming was the resumption of sexual relations between husband and wife. Women had a healthy appreciation of sex, and the thrill of reunion was heightened by the long absence and suspenseful anticipation of return "any day now." Women view homecomings, even after short periods of absence, as times of intense, mutual appreciation between husband and wife. In addition, wives had gifts and small amounts of cash to look forward to.

Life Before the Road

The older the woman, the more likely her attitude that "the hard times were the best times. Even the food tasted better then." Although Grey Rock Harbour people were better off than people in other parts of Newfoundland, with their year-round exploitation of varied fishing resources, they were poor by contemporary North American standards. Even the merchant families lived like everyone else, and one bad season could ruin them.

Women pride themselves in their resourcefulness in coping with hard times:

> I used to make little nighties out of flour sacks for my girls. I bleached them and put lace on them. Each nightie was long, with a little piece of lace trim underneath. This was their Saturday night nighties they'd put on after their bath. They would go out on the bridge [porch] to play so that everyone could see their pretty nighties. They loved their nighties and pretended that they were little princesses.

Older women felt that the harshness of life in the past taught them to value the good times, and to appreciate the changes that modernization has brought about more than younger women. Middle-aged women, those who had reached adulthood before the road, felt that having the strength and endurance to live under the more demanding life situations of "the old days" has given them a deep quality that younger women lack. This status-enhancing quality, maintained by frequent reference to the past, is generally recognized and respected in the community.

Reciprocity was the community norm. People helped each other build houses, care for the sick, shear sheep, and raise children, and fed and fuelled those who had a bad season. People with disfiguring birthmarks, operable cripples and others, were helped by the pooling of community resources to provide medical treatment: "Before the road everyone was equal and willing to help."

In summary, life before the road was marked by seasonal patterns of male absence, hard work, poverty, and comparative isolation. Even children worked hard and became self-supporting before their teens. Marriage marked little change in status but brought new responsibilities in terms of childrearing and pleasing a mother-in-law. Childbirth was often difficult and hazardous, to be accepted and endured. A good wife was a woman who was easy to get along with, handled finances well, kept a good house, and raised her children well. Few women failed on any of these counts.

AFTER THE ROAD

As a result of the road, a fish plant was build in the early sixties by a former resident of Grey Rock Harbour. The plant processed frozen fish and fish by-products into fish meal for markets in the United States. At first, only young and old men worked at the fish plant, along with widows and young women saving for "bride's money." Today, however, most women working at the plant are middle-aged, and male workers represent all age groups. Working at the fish plant is considered to be an easier way to make a living than fishing.

The pattern of male absence from the household has also changed. Fishing trips are shorter ("He's just gone a dog's watch now"), allowing husbands and wives more time together. The majority of men "day fish," getting up between 2 and 4 a.m. to set gear, returning for dinner and a nap at noon, then leaving to bring in the fish and/or set more gear. Fishermen go home usually only to eat or sleep; otherwise they spend most of their time fishing or at the "stage" preparing gear or socializing.

Today there are five longliners that fish out of Grey Rock Harbour, employing local four- or five-man crews. All but one of these boats is owned by the fish plant. Their seasonal fishing schedule is as follows:

January—April.
Fisherman is usually home everyday but gets up about 1:00 a.m. to go fishing.

April—July.
Five-day trips. The ideal schedule is to fish from Monday to Friday and return home for the weekend; often this schedule is disrupted by bad weather.

August—September.
Refit, vacation, and fishing if there are any fish.

October—December.
Fishing when weather permits, may go by day, week or six- to seven-week stretches, depending on the weather, fish and skipper's judgment.

December.
Home for the twelve days of Christmas.

Whether they fish or not, men must report to the boat every day, although some skippers are more strict about this than others.

When at sea the skipper will call his wife and tell her how long the crew expects to be gone. It is her duty to relay this information to the wives of other crew members. Their fishing schedules are so erratic that wives report: "When he walks out that door, I don't know when he'll be back again."

Men who fish on draggers from much larger centres nearby are gone for ten days at a time, usually with a two-day rest at home between trips. Most men in the village who fish on draggers are from families who were resettled. Unfamiliar with the local fishing grounds, it was easier for them to find employment elsewhere.

Given that (1) the fish plant is an alternative to fishing, (2) the majority of men day-fish and (3) the shorter fishing trips, many changes in family relations that characterize the post-road era are related to the year-round presence of husbands and fathers in the community.

Childhood

The roles of children have changed dramatically. Compared to the child's former life of hard work and early responsibility of leaving or helping to support the family, children today grow up with few duties. Girls do not help with housework or cooking until they are in their teens. They do occasionally watch over toddler siblings and frequently run errands to stores or neighbours' houses, but they expect to be paid for these services. When a child is asked to do something the response is often: "What will you give me for it?" Instead of feeling that their children should be raised as strong, tough workers, mothers now feel that their children should be indulged: "I want to give them everything that I couldn't have," and "Life is cruel enough, they might as well enjoy it while they are young enough."

Adolescence, Courting and Marriage

Adolescence is the time of life for finishing school, finding work and courting. The period of adolescence is terminated by marriage for the male and by either marriage or birth of first child for the female. Men and women who do not marry and remain childless never really achieve full status in the community.

Young women who leave the community do so to attend the provincial universities, to find work as secretaries or clerks in larger centres or to marry men they have dated from nearby villages. Some still leave to go serving either because they come from poor or large families, or because they were adopted as youngsters. Young girls no longer serve in their own village. However, a teenager may be invited to live with a young married woman whose husband is away for long periods of time. Besides sleeping over, she is expected to do light housework and help tend young children. Young teenage women like this companion situation, as their young employer allows them more freedom that their mother would.

With the freedom from household chores that modern times have brought, young people have little to focus their attention on besides romantic liaisons. Each person knows all males and females in their age group well before courting ever begins. Teenagers meet in groups at hangouts such as the post office steps, restaurant and newly opened pool hall. No one dates more than one person at a time, and the norm is long-term steady relationships. Other activities include riding around together in cars (in couples), frequenting the local movie house and attending high school dances. A popular way for a couple to arrange for some private time together is through babysitting. One mother remarked, "Didn't seem as so many got pregnant before this babysitting racket started." As in the past, some parents allow courting in the house after the rest of the family have gone to bed.

Girls usually start to date early, at ages 11 to 13, choosing boys two to four years older. As a consequence, marriage occurs at an early age. Since young people can work at the fish plant and support themselves, it does not take long to save enough money to buy or start building a house of their own. Such a situation of independence undermines parental control, and contrasts sharply with days gone by.

As before, sexual intimacy is thought to be the natural consequence of romantic attraction. Young women may have a sequence of several boyfriends before they get married. According to one woman, youthful romances teach girls about men and get them ready to settle down. Young women are self-confident and aggressive in their relationships with young men: they call their boyfriends, arrange meetings and are practised in courting procedures. Teenage romances are popular topics of community gossip.

There is usually no formal proposal of marriage. The initiation of sexual intimacies is supposed to mean that the couple eventually plans to marry. The girlfriend simply informs her suitor that she is pregnant or suspects so. Parents are told, and the arrangements to marry are made. Marriage is no longer considered an unalterable commitment. Cases of couples who separate are becoming more frequent. Generally, divorce is too expensive and complicated to bother with, and so a couple will simply live separately or set up residence with a new mate.

However, today not all young women are pregnant when they marry, nor do all pregnant teens get married. Either partner may refuse to marry, or the parents may object to the marriage. Mothers still try to prevent marriages if they do not like their daughter's suitor. But most parents prefer not to force their children to marry, hoping that it will give them a better chance in life (better than their mothers who did have to marry early). Pregnant girls are no longer shamed into marriage. They often choose to work at the plant and leave the care of an infant with their mother or grandmother. Their children often become adopted into the family as an end-of-the-line brother or sister. Fathers do not legally have to support out-of-wedlock children, although it is considered a moral obligation. Mothers of illegitimate children receive $100 a month, plus a family allowance check from the government. Once a woman marries and becomes a faithful wife and good mother, she becomes as respectable as any other married woman.

Motherhood/Young Mother

It is necessary to distinguish between young mother and middle-aged mother, as they are characterized by a different reproductive pattern. The major role differences between young and middle-aged women today stem from the fact that today young women complete childbearing early in their marriage—by age thirty—whereas many middle-aged women in their late thirties and forties continue to have children.

Today, couples who did not have to get married may postpone childbearing to a more convenient time. Nevertheless, the general pattern is marriage followed soon after by the birth of children. Today, newlyweds prefer to live with married brothers or sisters rather than with parents. Of those who do live with their parents, the majority live with the wife's mother rather than with the husband's. Thus many of the mother-in-law problems previously experienced by the young wife are avoided. If a wife does live with her mother-in-law, her husband is at home more often than in the old days to be a buffer in any difficulties that arise. A husband and his mother-in-law do not have much difficulty in getting along, as he is seldom in her company. Newlyweds are not as financially dependent as they used to be, and mothers-in-law are more indulgent than they were in the past.

The newly married woman is usually busy fixing up her home and starting a new family. She has learned housekeeping in her late teens, at which time her responsibility of caring for younger siblings and babysitting has provided her with a basic experience in childcare also. Brides often consult their mother for advice and may even temporarily reside with her after the birth of the first child in order to learn the fundamentals of early infant care.

Conditions surrounding pregnancy and birth have changed considerably since the road. A young woman who suspects she is pregnant will go to a doctor for confirmation of pregnancy; some may wait six weeks and others four or five months before they "make sure." But once pregnancy is confirmed, they will visit the doctor only if they feel something is wrong. A woman will participate in her regular activities until she gets "quite big"—about the seventh month of pregnancy. Despite the fact that they themselves, and even their younger brothers and sisters were born at home, young women feel that it is necessary to be hospitalized for parturition. The fact that the nearest hospital is thirty miles away can present major problems.

Even though most people do not have cars, a woman who goes into labour ("takes sick") can easily find a ride to the hospital. However, in winter, the severity of storms can block off roads for days. For this reason, a woman who is expecting in the winter will stay with a relative who lives near a hospital during the last month of her pregnancy. The husband stays behind and works or continues to fish while the wife is away having the child. When the baby is born, the father will pick up the mother and baby or accompany them on the busride home.

It is felt that pregnancy and birth weaken the health of a teenage mother, and much help and attention is given her when she returns home. Women today do not choose to breastfeed. It is viewed to be old-fashioned, unnutritional, immodest and an unnecessary drain on the mother's health.

Women today are more knowledgeable about pregnancy and birth and have more trust in hospitals than their mothers had in deliveries by midwives. Very few women die in childbirth today. Young women regard many of their mothers' and grandmothers' beliefs about pregnancy and birth as old-fashioned and ungrounded in fact (except for the causes of birthmarks, which are still widely believed).

Young women have different attitudes toward birth control than women whose reproductive careers began twenty years ago. They feel that limiting family size is a key to an improved lifestyle, mainly in terms of less work and better material conditions. They are not as resigned to their fate as childbearers as their mothers were. In fact, many women justify the early termination of their reproductive careers by pointing to their mother's misery. Two children are now considered the ideal family size.

Most young mothers who are in their late twenties and early thirties today continue to live according to their mothers' lifestyle and values. Any future changes will be initiated by those young teenagers who are presently marrying. It is their values that are particularly hard for the middle-aged women to cope with.

Motherhood/Middle-aged Mother

[These women]…have passed through childhood, courting, marriage, and young motherhood in the traditional ways. As such their present middle-aged roles have roots in the past but are influenced by the present. These middle-aged women are most likely to feel the mixed blessing of the loss of such cherished values as hard work and endurance and the benefits of a technologically improved lifestyle. They do not cling to the old ways as their own mothers do, but at the same time they do not adjust to change as readily as their young married daughters do.

The issue of contraception, with its combination of negative and positive viewpoints, is just one example of the many ways in which middle-aged women straddle the value gap between young and old women in the village. Although they feel that young unmarried women should "prepare themselves" so that they do not have to get married, they also feel that courting without the risk of pregnancy is irresponsible and promiscuous. Sex for sex sake is seen as enviable but selfish and morally wrong. Sex is viewed as a part of family life, and, as such, should entail mutual male and female obligations. Young married women's use of contraception is regarded with a twinge of regret and envy; for example, "You can't blame them. If I had the pill when I was young, I'd have used it too." Yet, for middle-aged women, part of the great pride of being a Newfound-lander stems from the acceptance of duties and burdens which make one hard and strong. The use of birth control by younger women (especially sterilization) is seen as a weakening or deterioration of the "Newfoundland Race." "They got it too easy these days, just run off and get fixed, just like it was nothing at all." Birth control is frequently a topic of conversation among middle-aged women. They concede that it is nice to have reliable means of birth control, but at the same time, they are proud of their ability to do without it. Their large families and unquestioning acceptance of fate are viewed as status-enhancing. They view themselves as models of strength and endurance that younger married women should look up to.

At middle age, lifestyles vary from woman to woman more than at any other stage of life. Among the factors contributing to this variation are patterns of husband's absence, family size, comparative ages of husband and wife, and widowhood. A middle-aged woman's husband may fish in one or a combination of fishing technologies, or he may work at the fish plant, or be retired (the consequences of which are discussed below). Those women who have a large number of children or children spaced widely apart are more likely to have young children still at home to care for than others who were finished with childrearing years ago. The woman who is married to an elderly man who is too feeble to accompany her to social occasions and who requires nursing care or constant supervision finds herself in a much different situation than the middle-aged woman who is married to a man her own age. Marital history also affects a woman's perception of her present life. By the time a woman reaches 40 or 50 she may have been widowed and remarried at least once. Some remarried widows have "mixed crowds," children of their own and their new husbands to care for. Other widows, who remain single, may lead a "singles" lifestyle more or less patterned after that of younger married women. Of all these factors, those most commonly held to affect women's adjustment to middle age are childbearing/childrearing and husband's absence.

The childrearing duties of the middle-aged woman are decreased by the presence of older children who care for younger brothers and sisters. However, women have babies or toddlers who are too young to be entrusted to the care of siblings. Some women even find themselves with two families: "Once one crew of them was growed up, she gone and had three more little ones, one right after another." "Change-of-life babies" are a common occurrence and are regarded with mixed feelings, particularly if the mother is in her late 40s or early 50s; it is feared that something could be wrong with the child or that the older mother will not have the health and energy to raise it properly. Both parents are teased, and the woman usually blames it on her husband: "The old creamer gave me a change-of-life baby." However, as well as being viewed as a curse, in that they tie a woman to her house at a time when her peers are free from childcare, change-of-life babies are viewed as gifts from God, to be spoiled and become the pride and joy of their parents.

Just as an individual woman's roles at middle age may vary with childrearing duties, so they vary with the pattern of her husband's absence. A woman whose husband continues to trip-fish, or changes from inshore fishing to plant work, finds little change in her married life; however, a woman whose middle aged husband changes from trip-fishing to either day-fishing or plant work finds her daily schedule altered:

> Ken quit working on the boat last year. We were talking about it the other night. This is the first time in our marriage we've slept in the same bed every night for a whole year. It's nice not to have to worry about him being gone, but he takes more for granted now. He doesn't appreciate how I cook and clean for him like he used to after he'd come back. I don't have the freedom I used to either. When he was gone I'd have the whole day to myself. I could get up when I pleased

and come and go to suit me. Now I have to be there for dinner and supper. I'm tied to the house just like there was still small children there.

Regardless of the situation of middle-aged women, the majority share (1) worry over their teenaged children or grandchildren, and (2) participation in a wide range of community activities. The role of mother of teenage children is fraught with difficulty. "Little children hold you to the home, but teenagers are worse because they can get into more trouble." Mothers of teens constantly worry about pregnancy, dating in cars, and fighting (teenaged boys frequently get into fights when they visit nearby villages). In order to keep from worrying women are urged to "get out of the house and do something." This means participation in community-wide organizations and activities open to women, which often become the focus of a middle-aged woman's life.

"Old Woman"

It is easier to divide a woman's life into stages for the old days than it is for the present. In the past, childhood, puberty and courting, marriage and childbearing, a mother-in-law stage, and old age were clearly demarcated segments of the life cycle. In modern times the middle stages of the life cycle have begun to blend into each other. There is no longer an age-grade or status demarcation equivalent to the "Granny" of the past. And older women are no longer the heads of household during extended periods of male absence. Nowadays, a reference to an "old woman" would mean a woman who was at least 70 years old.

It is harder for this group than any other to adjust to change—changes that had taken place when they were finished with childrearing and were advanced in age. Their attitudes toward their place in life, the young people in the community, and other changes discussed in this chapter vary from woman to woman. Some feel that "the world has gone to the dogs," others that "this must be a little like heaven." They have a strong sentimental sense of good time gone or lost, but they also have a practical recognition that certain hardships are no longer necessary. Apart from the very young, most villagers accord old women respect for being survivors of the hard days.

Old women pass their time visiting, talking on the telephone, watching television, and knitting or making handicraft items for their

~ Review ~

Blood and Nerves

This is a sociological study of the men and women of Grey Rock Harbour, an isolated fishing village in Newfoundland. It describes the changes in the way of life that occurred after a road was built which linked the town to the outside world. In addition, the author highlights the tension that developed between these changes and the old habits that persisted.

First, the author discusses life before the road: courting rituals and premarital sexual customs, the marriages that frequently happened between pregnant girls in their mid-teens and fishermen who were often several years older, the post-marital absence of the husband away on fishing trips lasting several months, the simultaneous independence and loneliness of the fisherman's wife as she anxiously awaited her husband, the joy of homecoming. Life before the road was characterized by hard work, poverty and isolation. Women managed household affairs; children were raised to help.

Along with the road came a fish processing plant, a telephone system, electricity, television and, all at once, it seemed, Grey Rock Harbour entered the modern world. Inevitably, this had a marked effect on the social order. The fishing boats changed their patterns, trips became shorter and more frequent, and the fishermen were home more. Life became easier, so children did not have to help out as much as before. Modern innovations like "the pill" reached the town for the first time because of the road, causing traditional courting and marriage patterns to shift. A "value-gap" emerged between the younger and older women of the town.

Like an anthropologist studying some unknown culture, the author, Dona Lee Davis, describes these and other changes in Grey Rock Harbour. In this excerpt from her book *Blood and Nerves*, she skilfully documents how a simple connection to the outside world (a material change) can have profound effects on the social and intellectual fabric of a once-isolated community.

relatives and church sales. If an old woman can no longer care for herself, she may move in with a daughter or some other relative. If she has a house to herself, a young related couple may move in and care for her, eventually inheriting the house. Some old people who are severely disturbed or senile are sent to old-age homes.

Many old women in their late seventies and eighties are widows. If they are capable of caring for themselves, they live alone, and may even take over full-time care of a great grandchild. A close relative will check in on them daily, and they will be given help with spring cleaning, washing and cooking by their daughters. Children may be sent over to sleep at night so they will not feel lonely.

Since 1949 (when Newfoundland joined Canada), old people have been receiving Social Security cheques and are financially independent from their families.

QUESTIONS

1. State what the age difference was between husband and wife "before the road," and explain why that was so.

2. State why "dating" an outsider was frowned upon "before the road."

3. Explain why it could be said that a woman became "the mainstay of her family, the operational head of the household."

4. State the two recurrent themes regarding being a fisherman's wife.

5. List the four main characteristics of life "before the road."

6. List three reasons why husbands and fathers were more often present with the family "after the road."

7. Explain how the roles of children have changed.

8. State how marriage has changed with respect to separation and pregnancy (two ways), and comment on why you think this is so.

9. List four reasons why many of a newlywed wife's problems with her mother-in-law have either been avoided or lessened.

10. State what is different "after the road" concerning women's attitudes towards home births, breastfeeding, traditional attitudes towards pregnancy and birth control.

11. Illustrate with the issue of contraception how "after the road" middle-aged women "straddle the value gap between young and old women in the village." Include reference to the values of responsibility, freedom and pride in endurance.

12. State one reason why older women have less influence "after the road."

Change and the Family Meal

John Steckley

We tend to look at change in two ways. If the change is technological, we usually think it is good, taking us closer to "Star Trek: The 21st Century Generation." If the change is in the social world, we seem to feel it is bad, taking us away from an earlier, better time. Yet both types of change are quite similar and are often closely linked. Neither technological technique nor social form are carved in stone, not etched in our DNA (genetic programming). It is just as natural for humans to have different types of families as it is for us to have varied means of sending messages— through words spoken, written by hand, typed, printed, faxed or flashed over video screens.

Both types of change enable us to gain something new and compel us to lose something old. We are well aware that technological innovation brings with it new skills, but we often overlook the fact that it can sound the death knell of old skills as well. One reason we hold feats of ancient large-scale construction in awe (and sometimes foolishly assume the ancients could not have done them without the help of aliens) is because we have lost their technological expertise. Take, for example, that 4,000-year-old marvel, the enormous stone rings of Stonehenge in England. Without our modern moving equipment we could not move the smaller 8,000-pound stones of the inner circle of Stonehenge the torturous 300-mile journey they took from the Presely Mountains in Wales (where the stone was quarried) because we have lost the knowledge of how to do it.

Change in the social world can bring gains that we applaud as well as the losses we more typically mourn. Child labour laws in 19th-century Britain (such as the Act of 1833 that reduced the maximum work week of a child under 11 to 69 hours, and of a young adult under 18 to 84 hours) substantially reduced the presence of children in textile mills and other factories. Only the more short-sighted factory owners and shareholders wore black at the funeral of that social form.

The connections between technological and social change are strong. Change in one area affects the other (with the former often driving the latter). The industrial revolution of the late 18th and 19th centuries brought new and much more powerful sources of energy (initially coal-fired steam) and the monster machines driven by this energy to the world of manufacturing. This had a powerful affect on the family, as thousands left the countryside and went to work in the factories, mines and other newly-developing businesses in the cities. As countries industrialized, people waited longer to get married—they could not depend on getting a piece of the family farm, so they had to save enough money to establish a household. In Canada, during the great industrialization period of 1851 to 1891, the average age of first marriage went up from 23.8 to 26.1 for females and 26.8 to 29.2 for males. It is not higher than that today. The number of children in a family began to drop because children were no longer as much in demand; there were cheap, home-grown farm labourers, and more women entered the work force prior to marriage. (It has been estimated that in 1891 in Canada, one out of every eight paid workers was a woman, suggesting that perhaps at least one-quarter to one-third of all Canadian women worked before getting married.)

Let's look at the family meal to illustrate the linking of technological and social change. The changes in the family meal also show how change in the family is a natural adaptation to changing conditions rather than a lamented deterioration in life.

First, we need some kind of definition of what the family meal is. For our purposes here, the family meal is an event in which all of the family members get together at one time and place to eat the largest meal of the day. As a daily event it is very much the product or innovation of a society in which farming is the main food-producing activity. Such daily feasts were relatively unusual in the earlier established lifestyle of hunting and gathering societies where eating occurred more casually whenever food was available, a person was hungry or someone was visiting. Large-scale family meals in such societies typically involved more than one family, perhaps the whole community, and it was usually a ceremony celebrating the success of the hunt. (Think of the scenes in the movie *Dances with Wolves* after the Lakota Sioux and Kevin Costner had returned from hunting the *tatanka* [buffalo].)

Industrialization altered this act of family life as much as any other. The time shifted for one thing. Instead of being a massive midday meal it became a night-time affair. Lunch was born. Many of us have learned about the differences between city and country meals after going to the country to visit grandparents. The midday meal is often called "dinner" and it is huge; the night-time meal is called "supper" and it is usually merely big.

The role of the father also changed. The father on the farm was not usually far away from the other members of the family. He often saw, worked and talked with his wife and children during the day. When dad went to work alone in the industrialized city he became isolated from the rest of the family. The family meal was one time in which he could become reacquainted with his wife and children. But it was also the long-awaited and dreaded time for "Wait until your father gets home"—new tension entered the family meal.

Tension also came from other sources as the family meal moved into the twentieth century. "Scientific" child-raising of the first few decades dictated that children should not be pampered by getting their own way, but needed firm discipline. "Let them cry; don't give in to them or you will fail as a parent," the books said. The family meal became an experimental test area for that theory and "making them eat the right things" also became important.

The majority of Canadians didn't live in cities until the second decade of the twentieth century. This move changed children's eating habits in a number of ways. The economies of food alter when food is purchased in the city rather than grown on one's own farm in the country. Meals will have less volume and less variety at any one sitting. This made life tougher for children with fussier appetites. Opportunities for alternatives more suited to a child's particular tastes—junk food—also became available. Corner stores were close by. Part-time work and allowances as payment for work done at home meant that children had money to spend on "treats." "Spoiling your appetite" became a new sin.

The test for the new meal-time experiment began with the words, "You're going to sit there until you're finished your brussels sprouts. There are starving children who would love to eat them." Children who did not finish their food were sometimes forced to remain at the table in a battle of wills with their parents.

Anthropologists say that behaviour becomes ritualized when its performance takes on a significance that is more symbolic than a reflection of something practical. For example, in Western society wearing ties is a ritualized activity, symbolizing that a man is formally dressed, no matter what else he is wearing. During the twentieth century, the family meal became ritualized and parents became custodians of the rituals, the ones responsible for the rituals being performed correctly. An important part of this job was to see that the family meal was a certain length of time, like in "more cultured times when we (the parents) were young."

Radio became the first great iconoclast (ritual or symbol breaker). The children had their favourite radio shows that they did not want to miss. Parents had them too, but they didn't want the "meal heathens" to know that. In many homes across Canada, the "great radio compromise" must have taken place. The sacred words of this important contract were "We will turn the radio on for your program while we are eating if you promise to be quiet and to eat at least some of your brussels sprouts." It was the beginning of the end for the traditional family meal.

And then came television. The wandering eyes of the viewer would follow the restless ears of the listener. Family members began a migration towards the TV, a move that cut a path across the time territory of the family meal. Eventually, television even came with its own meal and it own table—the frozen TV dinner and the TV tray!

All this is somewhat ironic. Television tries hard to push the so-called traditional family. Commercials preserve the housewife whose world revolves around the three c's—cooking, cleaning and curing. You see more such women on the screen than in your neighbourhood.

Studies show that the more television children watch, the more traditional views they have towards female roles. And yet the networks try hard to keep the airwaves "clean" during "family viewing hours." You'll not see significant nudity nor hear words from the street (or the schoolyard) during prime time.

Still, television promotes the move, or should one call it the trek, from the family table at dinner time by offering some of its most enticing programs for the entire range of family members. Here's the schedule for six o'clock, Wednesday, May 1, 1991: for the little ones,

"Polka Dot Door;" the next age group has YTV's "Rock'n Talk;" one group older has Much Music's "Spotlight;" then for all ages, "Star Trek: The Next Generation" and the "Cosby Show;" and finally, for the more elderly, fantasy traveller (for they are the true "cruisers"), "Love Boat." Did the networks miss anyone?

Our cooking technology has joined the family meal revolution. Consider the following scene from an episode of "Star Trek: The Next Generation." Commander Riker has just prepared a "real" omelette rather than making one the usual way with a food replicator. Data, the android, questions why Riker would go to such trouble rather than have a computer instantly produce the same omelette from whatever raw material the replicator uses. Doctor Polaski replies that cooking your own meal was an important part of an ancient twentieth-century ritual, linking long preparation with the eating of a meal together as a significant social occasion. The implication was that with individuals being able to produce instant meals to their own tastes whenever they wanted, the family meal became obsolete.

In a sense she was right, even for today. We have a kind of instant food replicator now: the microwave oven. No longer is a family forced to have dinner together because the cooking apparatus is taken for long periods of time—even half an hour can be long if you are hungry—just to prepare one basic dinner. We now have more choice. With rapid-fire microwave ovens, separate meals can be prepared quickly whenever a person wants, whatever that person wants (as a variety of "microwaveable" dishes become available). Children soon learn its operation, often faster than adults do. New technology such as this benefits best the new-of-mind, with no traditions to get in the way.

Should we mourn the decline of the family meal? Think of it this way. One of the indignities of being in a hospital, one of the most depersonalizing aspects of hospital life, is that you are forced to eat at hospital dinner time and to take whatever is being served (because "it is good for you"). Do we miss that when we return home? Isn't that a lot like the traditional family meal?

Perhaps the present author is prejudiced. I grew up dreading the family meal. I remember the shame of my bad marks being announced at dinner for the whole family to hear, sisters not too sympathetic (parents neither) to the excuses I gave. I recall my father constantly watching and judging my sloppy eating habits and wondering out loud why I couldn't eat like a "normal human being." I firmly believe that my family meal experiences are why I eat so quickly now and why it took me a long time to learn how to eat at a "leisurely" and "civilized" pace in a restaurant, rather than bolting down my food and bolting out the door to "freedom."

What does that leave us with? Let's look first to the hunters and gatherers discussed earlier. In traditional hunting and gathering cultures people shared food when circumstances permitted. It was something special, a willing decision of the participants. Perhaps that is where we are going today, with family meals being infrequent, but desired on special occasions.

And maybe technology is offering us solutions, if we choose to see them. With video rentals being a rising phenomenon, more and more families are watching films together. Along with that comes a technologically produced "family snack," popcorn made in a micro-wave. The shared experience of movie and popcorn is usually an enjoyable one. Perhaps our childrens' grandchildren will look back to that as the family meal that makes them feel sentimental; by then there might be food replicators, and new social forms.

The author admits that so far he has been overstating his case. The important thing is this: it should not be forgotten that in virtually all change there are both positive and negative aspects. In stressing one, you should not ignore the other.

At the beginning of this article we looked at great historic techno-logical enterprises such as Stonehenge in terms of skills lost through change. That does not mean that we should see that change in purely negative terms. We are fortunate that we have the new heavy moving machinery and don't have to resort to the "tricks" of the past (which probably involved strenuous labour on the part of a lot of people).

Likewise, the decline of the family meal as we have come to know it is also two-sided, both good and bad. Perhaps the negative aspect lies foremost in the area of values, a kind of intellectual change. The family meal taught, among other things, that the family had a signif-icance beyond that of the individual, that a family need could be more important than an individual need sometimes and that some compromise is necessary in life. Those are important lessons. You don't have to go to the extreme of a Thomas Hobbes to believe that too much individualism can be destructive to society. Acting like good cooperative family members would certainly look good on us all—from powerful politicians and corporate leaders, to high-sala-ried athletes, and the rest of us.

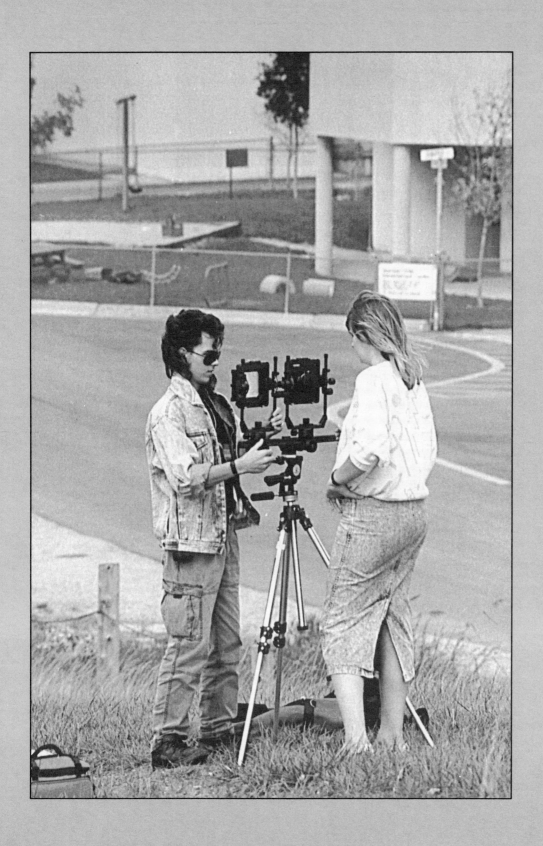

ISSUE 2

Public and Private Roles

It is understood that in a developed society *needs* are not only quantitative: the need for consumer goods; but also qualitative: the need for a free and many-sided development of human facilities, the need for information, for communication, the need to be free not only from exploitation but from oppression and alienation in work and leisure.

A. Gorz

Introduction

John Steckley

A society provides for its needs and wants by mobilizing its work force in a certain pattern. This pattern involves such elements as how long and when people work, where they work, who they work with and their relationships to the ones in charge, the goals of work and people's attitude towards work. The pattern varies enormously from time to time and from society to society, depending on material factors such as the importance of kinship or bureaucracy in organization, and intellectual factors such as whether or not it is considered morally "right" to own slaves or have children working in factories.

Today the pattern of work is changing rapidly. In part, this is because of changes such as the development of micro-processors and the application of computer technology to countless tasks. It is also due in part to social development, such as women becoming a permanent part of the paid labour force, taking on a widening range of jobs.

In addition to our public roles, we also have a private side to our lives. The roles we play here are focused on our relationships with others—friendship, marriage, etc. A major part of our private lives is directed toward "romance." Romance is another aspect of our lives, like work, that can be studied as something that goes through change.

Romance can be studied in at least two different ways. One is the way typically followed by social scientists, in which "romance" as an idea is related to other changes in the world, especially the social world. Writers using this approach discuss such issues as the effects on romance of the kind of participation each sex has in the work force, and how romance relates to the interpersonal dynamics of marriage.

Forming connections between the different aspects of life is only one way of discussing change in romance and other elements in the intellectual world. Another is to look at the ideas themselves, as is done in literature and other arts. Artists often explore images in terms of universal life experiences—such as love—and how such images either continue or are replaced over time.

In our public and our private lives we are constantly exposed to change—change that we either embrace or resist. Either way, it has an influence on us. This unit looks at some of the ways that change may affect us.

Change, Law and the Workplace

Kathy Casey

Compared to twenty years ago, today many more women, visible minorities and disabled employees can be found in offices, schools, industries and medical centres. These workers are qualified for their positions and work productively at their jobs. However, some feel disadvantaged, that they are not receiving equal treatment in the workplace. Others are discriminated against and harassed, even though it is public policy that every person is free and equal in dignity and rights and can expect to live and work in an environment that is exempt from discrimination and harassment.

In order to understand why people are treated differently and, in some cases, unfairly, let's examine what discrimination and harassment are and review how the legislation in Ontario attempts to prevent unfair treatment and remedy the effects.

Now, *discrimination* is a tricky word. Sometimes, definitions of the term are devised to accelerate the interests of those people who claim they are being discriminated against. However, at its simplest level, discrimination merely means making a choice, and making choices is an essential part of everyday life for individuals and organizations. These choices are governed by many factors including attitudes, traditions and rules. When these factors have the effect of limiting the opportunities of certain groups of people because of their sex and colour, for example, then the problem of discrimination arises.

DISCRIMINATION

At its simplest level, discrimination merely means making a choice, and making choices is an essential part of everyday life for individuals and organizations.

When these factors have the effect of limiting the opportunities of certain groups of people because of their sex and colour, for example, then the problem of discrimination arises.

When our different treatment of people is based on stereotypical perceptions rather than real characteristics, then we are illegally discriminating. For instance, some women are not hired or promoted to senior management positions because of the attitude that women have family obligations and therefore won't make good senior managers. As well, some blacks are not hired or promoted because of the attitude that blacks are lazy and won't make good employees. Ultimately, illegal discrimination is based on prejudiced attitudes about people that result in unfair treatment of people.

Discrimination may also be defined as an action or behaviour that attaches exaggerated importance to physical differences between people. When we assume that people have certain characteristics because of their skin colour, disability or sex and then treat them unfavourably, we have created a situation of illegal discrimination.

Harassment may be defined as repeated vexatious or distressing conduct or behaviour that is known or ought to be known as unacceptable and unwanted. Harassment takes many forms: for example, sexual, racial, gender, age and ethno-cultural. However, what is important to note is that all forms of harassment are uninvited and unwelcome. Furthermore, harassment is a form of discrimination. It occurs because people have internalized the stereotypes and prejudices that exist in our society.

Harassment is based in the abuse of power—real or perceived. It is generally carried out by members of a dominant group against members of a minority group. Incidents of harassment tend to be repeated and to grow in intensity. Victims often say nothing because of fear or embarrassment. The person doing the harassing then feels a distorted sense of power and continues his or her demeaning treatment of others. It is important to note that, because people often accept the stereotypes and prejudices of the dominant culture, a person can harass another person or group of people of the same gender, race or ethno-cultural background as himself or herself.

Despite public policy, there are many indications that racial and sexual harassment are on the increase today. Signs and buttons presenting "Keep Canada White" have been displayed in public. Also, anti-female slogans have been heard on some post-secondary campuses in opposition to women studying in non-traditional programs.

Acts of discrimination and harassment are illegal in Ontario. All persons in the province are protected under the *Ontario Human*

HARASSMENT

Harassment may be defined as repeated vexatious or distressing conduct or behaviour that is known or ought to be known as unacceptable and unwanted. Harassment is based in the abuse of power: real or perceived. It is generally carried out by members of a dominant group against members of a minority group.

Vexatious—annoying.

Rights Code. First enacted in 1962 as a consolidation of various anti-discrimination provisions, the *Code* provides, among other matters, that every person has a right to freedom from discrimination and harassment in a number of areas and various different grounds. The areas are services, goods, facilities, accommodation, contracts, employment and membership in associations and trade unions. The grounds are race, ancestry, colour, ethnic origin, citizenship, creed, sex, handicap, age (18–65), marital and family status, receipt of public assistance, record of offences and sexual orientation. For example, you cannot be denied accommodation because of your colour, denied education because of your handicap, or denied employment because of your religion (creed). As well, according to the legislation, you cannot be the object of harassment which could consist of slurs, jokes, stares, isolated treatment and/or suggestive touching or remarks.

If you think that you have been discriminated against or harassed by someone in your workplace, then there are a number procedures to follow. If you work in a unionized environment, you can speak to your union representative. Alternatively, or as well, you can file a complaint internally through the Human Resource Department in your company or externally with the Ontario Human Rights Commission.

Another type of legislation in Ontario has come about because of the historical undervaluation of the work that women workers do. It is the *Pay Equity Act.* Historically, men and women have tended to do different work, and the work that is performed by women has not been paid as well. This undervaluation has resulted in a wage gap: the difference between the average earnings of men and women. Currently, the wage gap in Ontario means that women earn 36 percent less than men.

A lot of the mistaken ideas about the role of women in the workplace and the worth of their work are based on the assumption that women are secondary workers. Some believe that women's contribution to the economy is less important than that made by men and that women don't really need employment income. Moreover, a lot of the jobs available to women are secondary jobs—part-time, temporary, dead-end and poorly paid.

This idea of secondary workers and secondary jobs—secondary, meaning less important—has caused some people to undervalue the work that women do. This is one of the main factors contributing to the wage gap. Though the wage gap stems from a number of reasons (such as difference in education, differences in experience, prejudice, job ghettoes and hours worked), a third of the wage gap exists because of the myth that the work women do is of less value.

To bridge the wage gap, *Pay Equity* was enacted as of January 1, 1988. The Act requires an employer to pay men and women the same wage for work that is different but of equal value. Pay equity is not to be confused with "equal pay for equal work" which means that if a woman is doing the same job as a man she will be paid the same wage.

Pay equity compares different jobs to see if the jobs are of equal value to the employer. Although the jobs may be different, their contents may be similar and therefore comparable.

To compare jobs, the criteria used are skill, effort, responsibility and working conditions. The *Pay Equity Act* requires employers to compare female job classes to male job classes using the four criteria. When it is found that the female and male job classes are of the same value, yet the female jobs are paid less, compensation in the female job class must be improved. Both men and women within the underpaid female-dominated jobs will receive adjustment.

If you currently work in a female-dominated job class (one in which 60 percent or more of the members are women), and if you are interested in seeing how your position has been compared, your employer is required upon request to show you the evaluation method used. If you are concerned that you are not being paid fairly, you can ask the Pay Equity Commission for assistance.

The *Ontario Human Rights Code* is an example of legislation that has been enacted to prevent unfair treatment of all workers in the province. The *Pay Equity Act* is an example of legislation to remedy past discriminatory treatment of all workers in female-dominated job classes. Nevertheless, some pro-active employers have not waited for legislation. Instead, these employers, as well as adhering to provincial legal requirements, have voluntarily created employment equity programs within their company. Employment equity is a planning process adopted by an employer to examine how women, the disabled, visible minorities and native persons are recruited, hired, trained, promoted and represented within an organization. It seeks to identify and eliminate illegal discrimination in a company's processes and policies and tries to remedy the effects of past illegal discrimination. These remedies may include programs aimed at changing representation within and across occupational groups so that target group members are appropriately represented throughout the workplace. Canadian and Ontario laws specifically require that programs designed to change the effects of past discriminatory behaviour are not in themselves discriminatory.

Employment equity is a voluntary program undertaken by an organization to ensure that non-discriminatory employment practices are carried out within the workplace. By having such a program, an employer is broadcasting that discrimination based on sex, race and disability is no longer acceptable. Recognizing that certain groups within our society have a tradition of being unfairly discriminated against, employment equity programs counter the long-term effects of such discrimination to give these groups real equity of opportunity in the workplace.

Change is difficult for every generation. We hear that we are losing what has been important, that other areas will also change, that we must adjust and learn new ways when we are already comfortable with what we know. However, change is the norm of the human condition. We must confront the paradox. While we are always seeking new knowledge and new ways of being, we resist change. However stubborn our resistance may be, one thing is evident. The workplace has changed from what it was just a short time ago, and not only the government but also individual employers have responded to that change in a variety of ways. New legislation and new programs have been created in response to the multicultural, multinational, dual gender workplace that we now have. Examining our own behaviour in an attempt to understand and change, rather than to defend, allows us a new perspective on a changing environment, a perspective that will allow us to accept how others differ, to respect those differences, and to value ourselves and others as unique individuals who have a worthwhile contribution. As a result, we all grow in our understanding of ourselves and each other, an understanding that will increase our ability to live and work together in harmony.

On the Meaning of Work

Mitchell Lerner

There's a story told about a young man who brings the ruler of a peaceful kingdom a secret method of making bread without labour. At first everyone, ruler included, is delighted because it seems that hunger will be gone and the need to work will vanish. Then, painfully, reality sets in. What will people do with time on their hands? The king orders the young man killed. "The devil," as the saying goes, "makes work for idle hands." As the king belatedly understands, work is a necessity, an inescapable part of the human condition.

No civilization can survive without work. But what is the nature of this activity that by necessity is part of your life and mine? This essay presents several interpretations of work from ancient to modern times.[1]

One of the earliest interpretations goes back to the Judaeo-Christian roots of western civilization to the first story in Genesis. Eve having eaten from the fruit persuades Adam to do the same and together they are banished from paradise to "a life of toil and sweat of the brow." This kind of work means drudgery, repetition, punishment and suffering.

> Accursed be the soil because of you.
> With suffering shall you get your food from it.
> Everyday of your life
> It shall yield you thorns and thistles and you shall eat wild plants.
> With sweat on your face shall you eat your bread

---

[1] In these considerations I have been generally influenced by Hannah Arendt's discussion of work. I am also indebted to some theological interpretations and to some concepts of Peter Berger.

Until you return to the soil
As you were taken from it.
For dust you are
And to dust you shall return.

In this fundamental Judaeo-Christian understanding of work, humankind did not deserve the gift of paradise, the gift of a complete world. We got instead an incomplete world—filled with necessity and condition. To survive, we must work. It is not a very pleasant role we have to play since according to this view work is a punishment.

At face value this interpretation of work as punishment is intolerable. Every religion has a work ethic because few can imagine work without some reward. We view work as a mixed blessing—something people love to hate, but can't see doing without. Therefore, we redefine work in both religious and secular philosophies so that work offers something positive. So, this early view gets modified.

Rational moral thought does just that. It holds that our expulsion from paradise and the subsequent necessity of work has a reason: to develop moral character. We attach certain values to work. Work keeps us out of trouble. It reduces the wastefulness of idleness. Work challenges us to use our talents and abilities, and helps develop personality. It is said to reduce self-centredness and arrogance, moderating the excessive lifestyle in favour of the modest one.

Work separates the authentic from the image. Think of two bike riders on the street: same racing gear, same bikes, same clothes. You cannot tell one from the other. Only in the race is the true racer distinguished from the hopeful novice. Without exception, the real thing, not the appearance, shows through work.

So, in rational moral thought, the Fall from paradise becomes advantageous since work fosters positive qualities in us: generosity, because by working we give; faith and good will because we *hope* without knowing that the fruit of our labours will be good. In fact, work mirrors our human condition. We strive in the face of the unknowable, we seek means to great ends, we are forever impatient with the pace of our progress. Ultimately, work is a supreme test for all of us. Through work we succeed or fail; become great or small; are judged to be worthy or petty, good or bad, high or low.

The trouble is, though, that this profound and ennobling view of work doesn't fit easily into our modern experience, so we must look further. This brings us to our next interpretation.

Labour or Work?

Hannah Arendt, the influential modern philosopher, wrote much about the meaning of work in her book *The Human Condition*. She suggested that our understanding of work goes back as far as the ancient Greeks. Greek culture distinguished between craftsmen, those who made things, and labourers, those who worked with their bodies. In ancient Greek society, slaves and women laboured, performing menial tasks. Labouring was in Aristotle's description "the meanest, because the body is most deteriorated."

Arendt points out that this distinction between work and labour exists in many languages. In French it is *travailler* and *ouvrer*, and in German it is *arbeiten* and *werken*. The German word *arbeit* originally referred to farm labourers. In English, the word *labour* connotes a sense of drudgery and suffering as found in the biblical story of Man's Fall, while the word *work* connotes effort that is directed toward the accomplishment of making something. So we get phrases like "the works of Shakespeare, Beethoven, and the Beatles" and by contrast the "labours of Hercules" that involved back-breaking physical tasks.

This distinction between "work" and "labour" helps us to think about what we will be doing the rest of our lives. Will we be labouring, which suggests a kind of slavery? Or working, which suggests a more meaningful connection to the activity and the possibility of producing something? For the most part, we share with the ancient Greeks the feeling that physical labour is a menial occupation holding little status in society because labour leaves little trace behind.

So, working is making something that stays. For us and our friends in ancient Greece, where modern civilization was born, work holds status because it means leaving a trace of your existence, a "body of work." On the other hand, labourers, who make neither a complete thing nor leave any notable contribution to humankind, are relegated to the periphery of society. In the last century, labourers sought to correct this flaw in the scheme of things by organizing into collective political units. As a result of the labour movement, the status of labourers was raised, both intellectually and socially. This was something the ancient Greeks never accomplished.

For the ancient Greeks the highest form of work allowed for as much leisure time as possible for the pursuit of philosophy and virtue. In our day, the labourer is equally entitled to leisure, protec-

WORK VS. LABOUR

Hannah Arendt, the influential modern philosopher, notes that the distinction between *work* and *labour* exists in many languages.

This distinction between "work" and "labour" helps us to think about what we will be doing the rest of our lives. Will we be labouring, which suggests a kind of slavery? Or working, which suggests a more meaningful connection to the activity and the possibility of producing something?

WAGE LABOUR

Karl Marx, the 19th-century socialist philosopher, believed that industrialization turned labour into a product to be bought and sold on the marketplace. When people sell their labour, they are exchanging an essential part of themselves for money.

tion, dignity and an OHIP number, while the philosophers, and some craftsmen, are often relegated to the unemployment lines.

Wisdom is best pursued when food, shelter and other basic human needs are met, even though, according to some, we gain much wisdom from scrambling to meet our basic needs of survival. In ancient Greece, where the pursuit of wisdom became an ideal, only twenty percent of the eligible population could participate in politics, philosophy and pure thought, while eighty percent had to work.

Our next interpretation of work demonstrates that wisdom derives not from the luxury of philosophy but from the experience of the common labourer.

Karl Marx on Work

Karl Marx, the 19th-century socialist philosopher, had much to say about this question. Marx believed that industrialization turned labour into a product to be bought and sold in the marketplace. He called it labour power. And every individual had about the same share. As the factories of the industrial revolution churned out more and more product, more and more labour was required. People abandoned the land because increased agricultural efficiency freed them to move to cities where a better life was possible. People moved from being generalists, capable of many things, to being specialists, capable of one or a few things only.

When people sell their labour, they are exchanging an essential part of themselves for money. And this process of trading labour for a wage leads to measuring self by the wage, not by ability. Even people who defined themselves as workers rather than labourers are not immune. On the industrial assembly line, in the steel or textile mills, in many human spheres, work became increasingly subdivided into limited operations performed by separate workers. While this maximized productivity, it minimized craftsmanship. Workers became increasingly adept at repetitive tasks as the various aspects of the work became disconnected.

When work is divided into component parts—we call this the *division of labour*—the individual worker finds it increasingly difficult to improve through work. He or she therefore seeks self improvement elsewhere. Aware of a growing split between public and private roles, the worker may attempt to integrate the two, with some success. However, the division of labour ultimately requires a division of self. And the modern struggle becomes one of composing one's identity.

For example, a doctor's social identity is distinct from his or her private self which is found at home. The patients know nothing of that doctor's private life. The sphere of work is geographically and socially separate from the private sphere where the "real person" is known.

So, fragmenting the production of a thing into isolated tasks has consequences beyond the workplace. The worker in a sweater factory who only sews labels day in and day out, may feel detached from the product, from the manufacturing process, and from himself as an individual capable of more than repetitive tasks. This detachment is called *alienation*. And it is not restricted to the assembly line but is a social fact found in middle-class occupations as well. We have assembly-line education, medicine and law where teachers, doctors and lawyers are so specialized that they are attached to small parts of the overall process.

Alienated work leaves no trace of our presence as individuals. The industrial division of labour redefined workers as labourers because they no longer make a whole thing but a part of it. This notion of "alienated work," of being fragmented into parts in the process of production, and in ourselves, has been the negative side of work since the industrial revolution.

Marx wrote his ideas in the 1800s when working conditions were absolutely intolerable, when owners of mines would hire children because they were small enough to dig coal in the smallest seams and workers died early in life from breathing metal dust in cutlery factories. His ideas have never gone away. The long sweaty hours in unhealthy conditions that characterized the working environment of the past can still be found in the developing countries.

"Modern" Work

Work remains a constant but the kinds of work change with the times. Today, we need to be seduced to work by an illusory guarantee of security, fulfilment and advancement. The promise of "making it" is deceptive because it doesn't remove the necessity for having to work, but only sweetens it. Winning the lottery doesn't mean you no longer have to work. "Making it " refers to having it all now; and even though it is a culturally esteemed value, it is not the same goal as "making something." It is ironic but people who focus on making something often end up having really made it.

Today many occupations seem to offer more freedom from having to labour to meet our basic daily needs. Machines take the place of manual labour. Motors replace the strain of lifting and pulling. Workers operate and monitor machines that do everything from cutting metal to stitching leather. In an explosion of technological change, photography, telephones, radio, television, nuclear power, rubber and plastics, medicine, and computers redefine lifestyles at a pace never before experienced, leaving little time to reflect and plan.

Alienation is still a reality in the modern world. And along with it comes the challenge of finding meaning in work.

The Meaning of Work

Finally, whether work implies suffering and drudgery, or leaving a trace of your existence, or if work means alienation, the work you choose is probably the most important decision you will make. There is something irrevocable about that choice. Your lifestyle gradually envelopes and defines you and you become whatever occupation you have chosen: technician, accountant, housewife, teacher, nurse, farmer, truck driver, writer. The work we do folds us into various known and unknown quantities: measurable players in the game of life. It is inevitable; even if we remain idle, we are defined.

To many of us, ultimately, work means maturity. It helps us to identify and accept ourselves: to teach us our limits and possibilities on the testing ground. It is not enough to be a "good person," or a "promising individual." Work, in the final analysis, defines a person, clearly and mercilessly, for all the world to see. As the humanists say, we have some control over the circumstances of our lives—we have some choice of occupation, of deed. In the end, our lives are measured by what we accomplish and leave to memory. We all strive, secretly and openly, to make a difference, to make our existence worthwhile for others to benefit from. So the challenge laid down to Adam and Eve, to the ancient Greeks, and to us is the same—to make something of value when nothing of value is possible without engaging the human condition, without modifying the world; that work is the ultimate pain and pleasure of life, both necessary and desirable.

Men, Women, Equality, and Love

Cheryl Merser

Not long ago I made plans to meet a married friend at her apartment after work, an hour or so before she expected her husband home for dinner from the racquetball game he played every Tuesday night. That way, we decided, we'd be able to talk by ourselves before her husband and the man I was living with, who had a late meeting, joined us for dinner.

I arrived at the apartment only a moment after Diane did, when she was still taking off her coat and dumping the day's accumulation—briefcase, pocketbook, umbrella, an over-full bag of groceries, a lemon tart in a bakery box, and a lone shoe with a new heel on it—onto the floor. Diane was her customary cheerful and frantic self, and I suddenly felt the adrenaline charge I always get in her company; she's a real-life version of one of those superwomen you read about in magazines, always with energy to spare. A partner in a large public-relations firm, she has handled her career as deftly as I've seen other women steer baby strollers over a curb, and she has always seemed to know exactly what she wanted: a happy marriage, a high-powered career, no children, good friends. She also tutors reading one night a week, sews, exercises during her lunch hour … and after I've seen her, I usually go home and clean out a drawer.

"Pour us a glass of wine while I go change," she ordered, and before I'd even finished with the corkscrew, Diane had disappeared and reemerged, not an executive in her mid-thirties now, but dressed in corduroys and oversized red sweater, her brown hair in a ponytail. As we talked, she bustled around, tidying up, and I followed her from room to room. First she made the bed, then laid out fresh towels, rinsed the breakfast coffee from the coffee-maker, threw away the morning paper, and arranged a bouquet of flowers that had been sticking out of her briefcase when she got home. Absently, I found myself helping; I put the umbrella in its stand, straightened a cushion, wiped off a sticky countertop. The ritual was familiar: I'd seen women smoothing out the edges of domestic life for as long as I can remember, and I've done it myself, willingly or sometimes resentfully, for a man due home.

While she chopped shallots, I set the table. I told her about a mutual acquaintance who had lost his job, and about another, whose good news was that she was pregnant—she'd wanted a baby for ages. Diane was worried about someone else we both knew, with boyfriend troubles, who needed to get out more; couldn't I take her to lunch? She told me about a new account she had at work, and that she wasn't getting along with one of her colleagues. Then I tested a theory I was trying to work through for this book, something about the changing roles of parents, and she gave me the name of a book she thought would help. At one point, she paused in her chopping to say, "I wonder what they talk about at racquetball," and we speculated on that for a minute. Soon the halibut, surrounded by herbs, tomatoes, and the shallots, was ready for baking. Broccoli for steaming was set out on the chopping block next to a loaf of French bread; the rice was measured, the salad ready, and two new candles were lit on the table in the dining area. The apartment, which had looked abandoned only a few minutes before, now looked lived-in and magically cozy. We moved into the living room, decorated in shades of mustard and dusty blue; the lighting was just right. And when Diane's husband, Joel, walked in and announced, the way Ricky Ricardo might have done in an old *I Love Lucy* episode, "Boy am I tired," Diane and I both started to laugh.

However, to compare my friends' marriage to Lucy and Ricky's, with Lucy's wide-eyed conniving and Ricky's blustery machismo, would be absurd. In fact, even the labels "husband" and "wife," as I've always thought of them, with the masculine and feminine roles and responsibilities they evoke, don't sound right. While my parents were married, my father was surely a husband, my mother a wife; their marriage, like most others I remember from childhood, seemed heavy with unexamined and mechanical dependencies. Joel and Diane instead are like two great pals but closer. Their dependence upon each other is not of the "where are my gloves, honey?" kind, but private—you can't see it at first glance. What they seem to be held together by are not the mechanics of marriage, as I've thought of them, but simply by love.

While Joel went to change out of his business clothes, I asked Diane why, on top of her job, she did the rest—the cooking, the shopping, the candles, the tidying up. "I do it," she said, "because I don't know how not to. Nobody's making me be a woman or a wife." But then she went on, and later I wondered whether she had confessed more than she meant to, or less: "My marriage is fine," she said. "I mean, it's not perfect, but I'm happy, even if I'm not doing it right, or equally. But the strange thing is that, close as we are, I thought marriage would be different—that it would be one 'thing' with two people inside. With us, it's more like two separate marriages, his and mine. Joel probably thinks he does half the work, but he doesn't. I don't think he knows what my side of the marriage is like. Half the time, talking to him is like talking to a can of soup— about my feelings, for one thing, or things I worry about at the office. He doesn't get it. He doesn't know. I guess," she concluded vaguely, "men are just different."

Though I'm not married myself, I knew right away and all too well what she meant. A few years ago, I would have been disheartened or angered by her comments, to say nothing of that scene at dinner— the stereotypical bustling women and the tired-and-hungry husband-arriving-for-dinner, oblivious to the care and trouble that went into it. I would have argued that men don't have to be "different." After all, our generation, Diane's and mine, was out to prove that there need be no built-in distinctions between the sexes. We would share everything, fifty-fifty, from boardrooms and floor-waxing to the emotional "chores" of love, marriage, and family. For the first time in history, the motto of marriage was to be: Don't treat me like a "wife" and I won't treat you like a "husband." But now, since more of my friends have paired off and since I've been living with a man myself, I've had a better chance to know liberated men and women not on paper but in action, which is to say negotiating new and untried rules of equality—and making their inevitable private compromises in the name of love.

Off and on that evening, I thought about Diane's compromises, and, as Joel cleared the table, I tried to imagine how the marriage looked from his "side," the compromises or sacrifices he himself must have made, and whether he too would argue that women and men are "different." I tried to bring the subject up over coffee, but Diane glanced at me uneasily, and Joel and my boyfriend looked politely puzzled, as if I'd asked them a question in Chinese. Quickly, we switched to more general conversation and never returned to the question of why men and women are "different."

As I write this, relations between the sexes—on the surface at least—seem more troubled to me than ever before. Divorce Court reveals a terrible and different drama on TV every day. In the past year, there have been no fewer than three best-sellers about misogyny, variations on the theme of men hating women. Newspaper life-style pages report continually on the strains of two-career marriages and second marriages; the dilemma of whether to have children or not; the failure of old-fashioned marriages in new-fashioned times; of tensions that arise when the woman makes more money than the man (as 20 percent of working wives now do); and of the many adult relationships that fall apart before they even reach the prenuptial agreement stage. When I hear friends despair over the 50-percent divorce rate and think about all that could possibly go wrong, I marvel instead at the marriages I've seen that do manage to succeed. And I marvel at the power of love, or if not love, at least what Dr. Johnson called the "triumph of hope over experience."

The experts have little in the way of good news to tell us. "Contrary to the common wisdom," says Letty Pogrebin in *Family Politics*, "married men are generally happier and healthier than bachelors, but single women are happier and healthier than married women." And yet married men are sexually unfaithful as much as 20 percent more than married women—who themselves are not exactly laggards in the infidelity department these days: One pessimistic estimate suggests that two out of three of all contemporary baby-boom marriages will be accompanied, from one side or the other, by an extramarital affair. If this prediction holds true, not only will we divorce more than our parents did, we'll also beat them at infidelity—we, the generation for whom equal partnerships, uncomplicated sexuality, and honest communication were supposed to be not a romantic ideal but the norm.

What's gone wrong? Can it really be that—despite all the much-deplored sexual inequality of the past—love, marriage, and family were nonetheless stable and trustworthy aspects of life all through history and are only now, for the first time, in terrible shape? Of course not. In the first place, the definitions of marriage, family, and

Misogyny—hatred of women.

even the role we expect love to play in our lives are not fixed but fluid; these definitions need revising with every generation. In the second place, liberation, as many men and women like Joel and Diane have seen at first hand, has its price—and the costs to love, marriage, and family can be painfully high. Is feminism to blame for the tensions today between men and women? Is the problem, as fundamentalist preachers insist, a widespread moral breakdown? Or are we facing something at once more mundane and more serious: Is the historic equilibrium between the sexes burdened now by an economy that forces men and women to compete for scarce resources in order to survive? There's no simple answer. But one explanation that makes sense to me comes from an odd source, for I wouldn't have thought that new research about the life cycle could tell us so much about men, women, and love.

Conventional postindustrial life-cycle wisdom has it that, for the most part, men and women go through life on parallel and complementary tracks, which intersect at mid-life and then run parallel again. As Erik Erikson, and others—from Carl Jung to Gail Sheehy—have outlined the adult life cycle, the healthy male would reach maturity, begin to define himself professionally, take on a wife, and start his family. At mid-life, having fought to earn a living for his family, he would see death around the corner and, for the first time, stop to take a look at the world. His so-called "feminine" qualities would emerge. Suddenly, his nurturing side would come out and possibly a newly discovered gentleness. He would no longer have to prove himself in the "masculine" realm; he could begin to express himself in a fuller, sensuous, more visibly open-hearted way, without threatening his manhood. The phrase "life begins at forty," for example, comes from a best-selling book by that title published during the Depression, which proposed that a man's happiest years would come after the struggles of early manhood. It's no coincidence that until now, men had tended to become more sentimental and loving as they aged—think of the man who is a more indulgent and demonstrative grandfather than he was a father, and not just because the child is someone else's direct responsibility.

A woman's life cycle took place on the other track. She would reach maturity, secure both her professional and personal identities vicariously through loving a man, and, once married, would assume the posture of wife and usually mother. In general, she had no separate identity but acquired her stature from those to whom she was connected, the way small children are braver when they're

Vicariously—done through another.

hanging onto their mothers' skirts. As she cared for her husband and family, however, she would deplete her nurturing instincts. At mid-life, her primary work completed, and her husband now more "feminine" in sensibility, she too would envision death and become more assertive, joining the outside world she had not been a part of until now. (Think of the age at which Betty Friedan became an active feminist—mid-life.) Having provided love and nurturing all these years, the woman was restless to find out about herself. Thus, at mid-life, men and women became more alike, as their rigorous gender differences mellowed, grew less important, and began to fade. The point to remember here is that this emotional merger could not have happened—or happened so dramatically—without the earlier enforced separation of the sexes by the roles each was expected to play.

There were always variations on these broad patterns, of course, and no one knows for certain whether they were culturally or physiologically determined, though it is known that men and women seem to "exchange" hormones sometime in mid-life, when oestrogen and testosterone, the feminine and masculine hormones that determine sexual differences, diminish in women and men, respectively, a decline which appears at least in part to effect these mid-life personality transformations. Hormones aside, though, what is more important is that the world has changed significantly since Jung, Erikson, and their followers recorded these conventional life-cycle assumptions. The men and women of the postwar generation no longer make their ways through life on these traditional parallel and complementary tracks: We're thrust instead, men and women together, onto the same track, travelling in a single train.

> *I say the "young men and boys" rather than the "young people" because the problems ... belong primarily, in our society, to the boys: how to be useful and make something of oneself. A girl does not have to, she is not expected to, "make something" of herself. Her career does not have to be self-justifying, for she will have children, which is absolutely self-justifying, like any other natural or creative act. With this background, it is less important, for instance, what job an average young woman works at till she is married. ...*
> PAUL GOODMAN, *Growing Up Absurd*
>
> *American girls did, and no doubt do, play down their intelligence, skills, and determinitiveness when in the presence of datable boys, thereby manifesting a profound psychic*

discipline in spite of their reputation for flightiness.
ERVING GOFFMAN, *The Presentation of Self in Everyday Life*

The comments above, from immensely successful books of their time, show how deeply influential Erikson's views of the life cycle were until our postwar generation came of age—with its new ideas about the roles of women and men, its uniquely high percentage of ambitious and educated women, and in a flailing economy where "woman's work" now includes coming up with half the rent. From the structure of the workplace to the rituals of dating, the premise, as every feminist will tell you, was the same: Women, at least in the first half of life, were to be responsible for making men's lives in the "real" world possible. What Goodman and Goffman are saying is that not only were women responsible for washing the socks and raising the kids—more important still was their role as psychological help-mates: Under the terms of the traditional life cycle, women's work was to give the men in their lives unqualified emotional space and support, to do everything possible to ensure that these men could live out their potential and their dreams. For women, there was only one legitimate dream. In exchange for money to buy laundry soap, women were expected to give up their names, their own dreams, and their souls to a man, his job, his house, and his children. And for all its drawbacks on both sides, this formula, in its way, worked for a long time: The life cycle was lived out much as it was laid out, as if Erikson's formulas were as much a biological imperative as the arrival of baby teeth or puberty.

Now consider the new life-cycle "formula" for men and women in the first half of life today: Upon reaching maturity—and we are the first generation for which this is so widely true—we do not complement each other so much as compete with each other, as we all, men and women alike, try to succeed, achieve autonomy, and find out who we are. Despite any superficial deference to the old formulae like Diane's and Joel's and whether we think about it or not, we're all competing in the marketplace for jobs and status and, just as important, we're also competing for the emotional space and support that used to be a woman's most self-sacrificing gift to her man. We can no longer afford the accommodations to gender that men and women have made in the past: I don't know many women who would "play dumb" on a date or who dabble tentatively at a job, trusting that a husband will be along shortly, and I don't know many men who'd dare to present themselves any more as sole kings of the castle. Most of us—literally—no longer make "gender deals" of the you-peel-the-carrots-and-I'll-pay-the-rent sort, or if we do, we negotiate them carefully; such deals are no longer almost automatic. Today, there are two people to contribute to the rent, two people who need the unqualified emotional support that pursuing a vocation or personal dream requires, and maybe no one to peel the damn carrots. Or to put it another way, in most relationships today, there are two adults with the same needs—Diane and Joel, for example—and no longer a man and woman whose separate needs justify a working, give-and-take balance.

"Gender characteristics," writes Alice Rossi, a former president of the American Sociological Association who has recently written on gender and the life cycle, "are clearly modifiable under changed social circumstances, as men and women take on either greater or lesser similarity of roles and experience. ... Political and economic pressures are now blurring traditional gender roles in the first half of life." In other words, the post-war women Rossi refers to have had to subdue their loving, nurturing instincts for the sake of self-assertion—a stage which, in Erikson's day, wouldn't have emerged till mid-life. Similarly, to make sense of this new world, men have had to tap their feminine sensibilities, if only rhetorically—or if only by learning the pragmatics of ordering Chinese takeout for themselves—much earlier than they would have tapped them in the past.

It follows that once gender distinctions have begun to blur in the outside world, so too will they be transformed in the intimate worlds of love and marriage—unarguably crucial benchmarks of adulthood. Where once men and women "borrowed" inner resources from each other (stoic man would put his arms around his crying wife, as if she were crying for both of them), now we strive ideally to cultivate inner resources of our own against any eventuality: Men are encouraged to learn to cry for themselves in much the same way that women have been encouraged to face the world apronless and head-on. Our expectations from love and marriage are high, even so, for to believe that men and women are not "different" is to expect complete understanding from a mate, to fail to allow for the unknowable mysteries between people and the sexes that in all likelihood make complete understanding too much to expect. We all have, as Virginia Woolf once said of women, our "own contrary instincts."

If to be an adult now means to internalize all the strengths and virtues of both sexes, it also means that we've abandoned those you-peel-the-carrots-and-I'll-pay-the-rent rules and roles of gender. Why then the new strain on relationships? Shouldn't it have worked out instead that, with some of the pressure off both sides, love and marriage would be all the easier? Why is my friend Diane unable to find the point, the center, of her marriage? The answer is disquieting: In loving relationships that require neither "husbands" nor "wives", where the traditional rules and roles have been cast out, there's love and only love at the center. If we don't need to borrow so freely any more from each other's strengths and resources, or to depend on each other for rent and peeled carrots, our only need for each other is our human, compelling, and unrelenting need for love. And love, of course, is a problem.

UNIT 3

CONFLICT AND COOPERATION

■ **ISSUE 1:**
The Individual and the Collective

■ **ISSUE 2:**
Relations between Collectives

The Individual and the Collective

One always bakes the most delicate cakes
Two is the really superb masseur
Three sets your hair with exceptional flair
Four's brandy goes to the Emperor
Five knows each trick of advanced rhetoric
Six bred a beautiful brand-new rose
Seven can cook every dish in the book
And eight cuts you flawlessly elegant clothes
Do you think those eight would be happy
if each of them could climb so high
and no higher
before banging their heads on equality
if each could be only a small link
in a long and heavy chain
Do you still think it's possible
to unite mankind …

Marquis de Sade in the play Marat-Sade,
by Peter Weiss, adapted
by Adrian Mitchell.

Introduction

John Maxwell

Our experience tells us that human beings are social animals. We work together, play together, make war together—in fact, very few human activities are truly solitary. Human beings live in a cultural environment; that is, an environment of beliefs, values, rules, objects, and tools which they have created. Even individuals who are physically isolated from others maintain their social ties through culture.

The first reading, "The Individual and Society," presents several models of human nature and of human society. Each model can be used as a basis for deciding what view to take on issues of social importance. For example, viewing human nature as essentially selfish and always looking out for "number one" leads one to see social problems differently than if one viewed human nature as essentially social and cooperative. For instance, consider the different views one might take on the need for and value of punishment for crime.

To view society as more than the sum of its members invites the question whether the individual in a society, especially a complex one, is somewhat less than his or her constituent portion of society. Auden's poem "The Unknown Citizen" provides an unsettling view of a person's place in society.

Of course, often collective action is more effective than individual action. If my driving interest is to obtain food, I may be able to do this more effectively by hunting or farming with others. Ultimately a group may discover that a degree of specialization is required. They may also find after a period that the interests of some members become dominant or that some are getting greater benefits from group activities. At this point the group must be seen as a collection of groups rather than as a single group and we are confronted with the problem of our second issue—collectives.

The Individual and Society

John Maxwell

Human beings are social animals. This means that most of our behaviour occurs in the context of interaction with other people; very few human activities are truly solitary. In fact most of our behaviours, our attitudes, our values, and even some aspects of our personalities are learned as we interact with others. Even those characteristics which are determined by our heredity are modified to meet the demands of our social experience.

We know from our experience that society is a structure of rules (broadly defined to include traditions, customs, laws, conventions, etc.) which define the relationships between individuals and their society. Much of our behaviour is determined by the specific social institutions in which we participate. These institutions define our roles in much the same way as a script and stage directions define the roles of actors on the stage. There is certainly room for individual interpretation and expression but by and large our behaviour must fit within socially structured guidelines.

One of the tasks of social philosophers and social scientists is to explain how individuals are integrated into the social world, how they become and remain part of a society and why the society persists over generations. The answers to these types of questions are not easily derived from our immediate experience and often require that we generate speculative theories to help us make sense out of our experience. There are many theories which attempt to explain the phenomenon of society. We may prefer one theory over another simply because it provides the answers we *want* to believe. However, no single theory has answered all of our questions satisfactorily and we are constantly challenged to develop new understandings which more closely reflect social reality.

In this chapter we will briefly review four theories which purport to account for the relationship between us and our society. We will concentrate on how each of these theories deals with:

1. *Assumptions about human nature:* Are human beings basically good or basically bad? Are we governed by reason or by passion? Are we basically self-interested or altruistic?

2. *The relationship between the individual and society:* Are all people seen as being equal? What, if anything, should people have to say about the way they are governed? Why should people obey the rules? What is more important, the individual or the society?

3. *The role of "authority" within the society:* Who has the authority to make decisions? How do they get and maintain this authority? What responsibilities do the "rulers" have to the people they "rule"?

4. *The question of altruism and self-interest:* Are self-interest and altruism mutually exclusive behaviours? How do self-interest and altruism relate to such things as "good" and "evil"? Which attitude (self-interest or altruism) is better for the society at large?

First of all, we must understand what it is that we take for granted about our own society. These unquestioned beliefs about the relationship between ourselves and society colour the way we view any theory which purports to explain the relationship. Our society is built upon the principles of liberal democracy, socio-political and economic freedom, and individualism. These principles derive from the great social, political, and scientific revolutions of the 17th, 18th, and 19th centuries in Europe. For example, most North Americans are taught (and probably believe) that the best way to resolve a dispute is to vote and that the best decision is the one that gets the most votes. Most of us also are generally willing to act in accordance with a group decision and believe that the "principle of fairness" insures that we will not always be on the "losing end" of the decision.

That there is a structure of basic rules does not mean that they are always operative nor does it mean that they apply universally. One of the constant complaints in our society is that the rules which are theoretically based on the principles of democracy are not applied to everyone, at all times, or in the same way. Our system permits and even encourages us to raise questions of fairness and justice. An important question is why it is that even those people who suffer the worst injustices and benefit least from the "principle of fairness" continue to support the basic principle of the system.

THOMAS HOBBES

Until the fourteenth century in Europe the dominant theory of society was tied to the religious doctrines of the Catholic Church. In short, people were taught that the social order existed because God had created it and that to question the social order was to question the will and wisdom of God. Thomas Hobbes (1588–1679) was concerned with developing a theory which would explain social order without attributing this order to a super-natural power. In his book *Leviathan*, Hobbes speculates on "The Natural Conditions of Mankind." In attempting to explain social order Hobbes makes certain assumptions about human nature and the behaviour of pre-social human beings.

Hobbes assumed that human beings in their natural state are essentially non-social and that they are driven, as are all other "wild" animals, by basic passions (lust, greed, etc.); in nature there is no morality and no system of rules to govern behaviour. These basic passions cause human beings to be suspicious and aggressive in their relations with each other. The unregulated desire for self-gratification naturally puts people into conflict with each other and leads to the situation which Hobbes described as the "warre of every man against every man," a situation in which "might is right."

Fortunately, human beings are, according to Hobbes, rational creatures and ultimately their "reason" leads them to see that ordered relationships with others are beneficial. In other words, the rational human being understands that self-interest may be advanced through cooperation with others. This cooperation can only develop if there are rules which govern the relations of people with each other. Since there is no "natural" commitment to the rules, people will only abide by them if they see the immediate satisfaction of self-interest or if there is some power strong enough to enforce the rules. Consequently, people willingly submit to the power of one person, the sovereign, who is able to impose order and, through the use of force, maintain a stable society.

Thus, social stability is a human product, a matter of a "social contract" to which all people at least tacitly submit. What we call "morality" is nothing more than a system of conventions (i.e., agreed

Thomas Hobbes assumed that human beings in their natural state are essentially non-social and that they are driven, as are all other "wild" animals, by basic passions (lust, greed, etc.); in nature there is no morality and no system of rules to govern behaviour.

John Locke believed that people will naturally act altruistically (i.e., in the interest of the group) and it is an element of God's plan that self-interest is best achieved through cooperation.

upon rules) designed to regulate our basically self-interested behaviour. It is only through the exercise of force (or the potential use of force) that the sovereign has the authority to create and enforce a structure of rules. The sovereign invents these rules to satisfy his own needs and the needs of those whose support he seeks in order to maintain power; his only commitment to rule well relates to the fact that his self-interests are furthered if he does so. The only check on the sovereign's behaviour is the threat of organized rebellion.

Hobbes's view of people and society is often described as "pessimistic" in that it is based on the assumption that the "natural" human being is at best un-social and at worst anti-social. Some two hundred years after Hobbes's death Sigmund Freud developed a theory of the personality which shares this "pessimistic" view of human nature and describes the "person" as the product of an ongoing conflict between natural self-interest and the demands of the society. This theoretical conflict is often expressed as the struggle between "good and evil" and has a long tradition in our religious thought and in our literature and clearly colours the way we see ourselves and our society and other societies.

JOHN LOCKE

In his *Second Treatise on Civil Government*, John Locke (1632–1704), like Hobbes, attempted to build a theory of social behaviour based on certain assumptions about human beings in the "state of nature." Locke assumed that God created human beings to live harmoniously in the state of nature (compare this to the Garden of Eden). With few exceptions people recognized each other's "natural rights" and sought to meet their needs through cooperative action. Locke believed that people will naturally act altruistically (i.e., in the interest of the group) and it is an element of God's plan that self-interest is best achieved through cooperation.

Locke's theory is based on an "optimistic" view of human nature. "Optimistic" theorists typically believe that if people behave badly it is not because they are "naturally bad", rather it is because the social structure is imperfect or because they are not aware of the rules of good conduct or the consequences of their actions. Locke argued that there are laws of nature which govern human behaviour. As rational creatures human beings should use their intelligence to discover what these laws are and live by them.

Government and other social organizations are created by human beings to facilitate cooperation and to exercise control over those few people who choose not to follow the laws of nature. Government (the sovereign) is obliged by the laws of nature to rule in the best interests of the society at large. If the sovereign abuses the privileges of authority then the people are authorized (by the laws of nature) to overthrow him.

KARL MARX

John Locke suggested that the negative aspects of human behaviour (greed, lust, etc.) are not natural but are the products of either ignorance and error (regarding appropriate behaviour) or some minor and correctable fault in the social structure. Karl Marx (1818–1883) very definitely saw "evil" as a social product, specifically as a result of the relationships (and therefore the attitudes and values) imposed upon people by the structure of the productive system dominant in the society. In other words Marx is saying that people are victims of the social structure.

Marx argued that the system of material production in the society historically has created social structures which divide people into two types—those who own and control the basic means of production and those who actually do the labour. In the pre-industrial days the two groups were the landowners and the peasants; in industrial Europe the two groups (classes) are the capitalists and the workers. According to Marx the peasants/workers are the "slaves" and the landowners/capitalists are the masters. The two groups are in a constant state of conflict because the self-interests of each group are diametrically opposed—in other words what is "good" for the boss is "bad" for the employee and vice versa. Because it controls societal resources, the "master class" controls all the important institutions in society and it uses these institutions to further its own interests. So it is that Marx argued that the landowners/capitalists controlled organized religion and used religious institutions and beliefs to control the peasants/workers. The "authority" of the ruling class is based upon the control over the institutionalized means of force (i.e., the police and military).

Marx believed that primitive societies operated communally—that is, the people cooperated in the attainment of common goals. In such communities self-interested behaviour is moderated because people are committed to the group and its goals. He argued that the only

Karl Marx saw "evil" as a social product, specifically as a result of the relationships (and therefore the attitudes and values) imposed upon people by the structure of the productive system dominant in the society.

John Stuart Mill agreed with Locke that reason will over-rule the "baser" aspects of human behaviour (self-interest, greed, etc.) provided that people have sufficient information about the issue and the consequences of its various possible resolutions.

truly stable society must be a communal society and that the conflict of interests in other forms of society must eventually lead to open violence and revolution. Marx believed that the ultimate revolution would be a product of the conflict between the capitalists and labour in the industrial/capitalist society and that this revolution would produce a communal/industrial state in which the principle of "from each according to his ability, to each according to his needs" would apply. Of course this revolution would not occur until the oppressed masses use their natural reasoning abilities to recognize that they were being systematically exploited and to develop a systematic plan for revolutionary activity.

JOHN STUART MILL

Democratic theory is based on an "optimistic" view of human nature. Democracy assumes that the decisions made through the democratic process are, at least in the long run, the best decisions and that individual self-interests are best served through willing compliance with these decisions. The authority of the leaders in a democratic system is simply based on their position as agents whose task it is to act in accordance with "the will of the people."

As a democratic theorist John Stuart Mill (1806–1873) had great faith in the ability of the "common man" to participate in the democratic process and to make sound decisions based on a rational consideration of the issues and possible consequences. In other words Mill agrees with Locke that reason will over-rule the "baser" aspects of human behaviour (self-interest, greed, etc.) provided that people have sufficient information about the issue and the consequences of its various possible resolutions. Mill recognized, of course, that many issues do not have an inherently right or wrong side, that there will often be issues where all sides can be supported by sound reasoning.

Mill cautioned that the democratic system could lead to "majoritarianism," a situation where a majority shared a broad set of interests which were at odds with the interests of a minority—in such a situation the members of the minority would always be complying with the rules established by the majority.

Majoritarianism is not a threat if a society is truly "pluralistic." In a pluralistic society the social, political, and economic interest groups are continually shifting and there is no large scale control by a single

~ Review ~

The Individual and Society

In this unit, the ideas of four philosophers concerning human nature and society are summarized, beginning with the 17th-century English writer Thomas Hobbes.

Hobbes believed that human beings are motivated chiefly by self-interest. He believed that they want to preserve their own liberty but also wish to acquire dominion over others. This perpetuates a constant state of war. However, because of the natural impulse toward self-preservation, people are also capable of living harmoniously in groups by submitting to a central authority or sovereign who is able to insure stability and peace. Self-preservation outweighs self-interest, according to Hobbes, as citizens behave as though they had a "social contract" towards their ruler and towards each other. Hobbes saw morality as a socially agreed upon convention and man as a base creature of passion, which fostered Hobbes' pessimistic view of humanity.

In contrast, John Locke, a young contemporary of Hobbes, saw human beings as peace loving and eager to cooperate with others. Within his optimistic view of mankind, wars and other evils occur not because human beings are essentially bad but rather because of flaws in the social structure.

The notion that class structure victimized whole groups of people was a key feature of the writings of Karl Marx. Marx was a 19th-century German socialist-philosopher whose ideas affected global politics in a profound way and did not diminish in influence until the late 1980s.

According to Marx, an industrial society produces inequalities among citizens. A class structure emerges with two basic categories of people, the capitalist-owners and the peasant-labourers, whose most basic interests are diametrically opposed. The result is a perpetual state of conflict that inevitably leads to violent social upheaval. Convinced that communism is the only stable form of social organization, Marx thought that the capitalists would hold power only until

the oppressed masses recognized their exploitation when they would rise up and revolt.

But unlike Marx, a British contemporary by the name of John Stuart Mill saw a great deal of good in the common man. Mill was a proponent of democracy and a believer in the inherent tendency of human beings to reason. He felt that people are well disposed towards the idea of submitting themselves to the "will of the people." However, he cautioned against "majoritarianism," a situation where the intolerance found in a majority dominates and denies the rights of a minority. The risk is lessened in a "pluralistic" society containing many interest groups.

Whole shelves of books have been written about each of these major theories. They are but four of the many social theories that attempt to define the complex relationship between an individual and his or her society in a given age.

interest group. For example, I might be a member of a minority group with reference to a particular economic issue (let us say the issue of free trade with Mexico), but my views on another issue (perhaps multi-culturalism) are those shared by a majority of Canadians. In a pluralistic society (or at least one which is believed to be pluralistic) people are willing to "go along with the majority," because they believe that in the long run they will frequently be part of the majority.

SUMMARY

Each of us relates to society within the framework of a set of traditions, customs, laws, conventions, and beliefs. The four theorists briefly presented in this article have attempted to understand the nature of the relationship between the individual and the society.

Hobbes begins with a "pessimistic" view of human nature which says that "the baser passions" are the dominant factors in determining our behaviour. On the basis of this assumption Hobbes theorizes that society can only be maintained through the agency of a self-interested ruler whose position is ultimately dependent on the use of force. People obey the ruler because they fear his power but also because they recognize that an ordered society is in their best interests. *look at bright side turn out to be best in life.* *life holds more evil than good*

Marx has an "optimistic" view of human nature but a "pessimistic" view of society—it is the structure of social institutions which interfere with our natural desire to live in communal societies. Until the final revolution occurs we must live under the stress of a society in which a ruling class controls societal resources and oppresses and exploits those who are ruled.

Locke holds an "optimistic" view of human nature and sees society as the means through which human endeavour is "enabled." Society provides the coordinating structures which permit us to cooperate to achieve our collective and individual goals. There are some flaws in the social structure and these may combine with human ignorance and error to create conflict and injustice but these problems can be remedied through the use of reason.

Mill's commitment to democratic theory presumes an "optimistic" view of human nature; democracy can't work unless people respond intelligently, fairly, and humanely to the challenges of living in society. Majority decisions may not always be the best but in general they reflect the collective wisdom of the people—as the people become better educated on the issues they will make better decisions. Majoritarianism is a danger in our type of democracy (based on the principle of majority rule) but this danger is minimized if the society is pluralistic and the composition of interest groups varies depending upon the issue.

QUESTIONS

1. Outline the main points of each of the models of society presented in this article.

2. Using the principles of comparison and contrast discussed in the beginning of this book, fill out the grid on the following page that contrasts Hobbes, Locke, Mill, and Marx on their theories of human nature.

3. Should individuals riding in cars be required by law to wear seat belts? The harm that may come to them from being in an accident while not wearing a seat belt is primarily to themselves, though the general effect of many injuries is the raising of insurance rates to everyone. Aside from the rightness or wrongness of seat belt legislation, are seat belt laws enforceable? Analyze these questions from the point of view of each of the models in the preceding article.

4. Should all tobacco use be banned? Does the analysis of this question raise the same considerations as the seat belt issue? If so, do the conclusions implied by each of the models for the tobacco issue correspond to those for the seat belt issue, or are there different considerations? If the latter, what are they?

5. Suppose you read in the newspaper that a certain politician said that unemployment insurance benefits should never be paid to anyone who has resigned from a job voluntarily. What models of society could that politician believe in?

Theories of Human Nature

THINKERS

ELEMENTS	HOBBES	LOCKE	MILL	MARX
The nature of the individual				
Relationship of the individual to society				
The role of authority				
Importance of a fair contract				
Self-interest *vs.* altruism				

Dené Strategy to Counteract the "Tyranny of the Majority"

John Steckley

T he Dené are a group of Native peoples who live in the Northwest Territories, the Yukon and in the northern areas of the western provinces. They speak languages (such as Chipewyan, Carrier, Hare, Loucheux, Dogrib and Slavey) that belong to the Athabaskan family of languages. Like all First Nations of Canada, they have experienced the "tyranny of the majority" in having a culture that is quite different from that of the non-Native majority.

In the western part of the Northwest Territories, where they make up most of the population, the Dené have proposed the establishment of Denéndeh ("Land of the Dené") as a new province. As proposed in the early 1980s, Denéndeh was to have the following features:

1. *Employment and labour legislation* that respects the fact that hunting, trapping and fishing are still key elements in their local economy (i.e., bringing money in and saving them hundreds of thousands of dollars on the high cost of food brought in from the south), self-sufficiency (i.e., making them not completely dependent on the notoriously short-term employment opportunities in the North that come from construction and oil and gas extraction projects) and cultural identity.

2. *Making Native languages official* so as to guarantee (where numbers warrant) that government material, legal proceedings and some education is provided in the first language of the Dené people. (This does not mean that every document would be printed in every language.)

3. *Establishing a minimum guarantee that 30% of the seats in the provincial assembly* are filled by Dené, even if and when their percentage of the population drops below that figure.

4. *Establishing a Dené senate,* a political body composed entirely of Dené elders (those wise in the ways of the traditional culture). The members of the Dené senate would have the power to veto any legislation adopted by the provincial assembly or community councils if they thought such legislation would seriously harm aboriginal rights. They would outline their objections and send them back to the lower political bodies for re-examination and change.

QUESTIONS

1. Would each or any of these measures help guarantee that "the tyranny of the majority" that the Dené experience would lessen?

2. Is there any other measure that the Dené could propose that could lessen the effects on them of having a culture that is quite different from the non-Native majority?

3. Would these measures create a localized "tyranny of the majority" of Dené over non-Dené? If so, would this be the same thing?

The Unknown Citizen

W.H. Auden

(To JS/07/M/378
This Marble Monument
Is Erected by the State)

He was found by the Bureau of Statistics to be
One against whom there was no official complaint,
And all the reports on his conduct agree
That, in the modern sense of an old-fashioned word, he was a saint,
For in everything he did he served the Greater Community.
Except for the War till the day he retired
He worked in a factory and never got fired,
But satisfied his employers, Fudge Motors Inc.
Yet he wasn't a scab or odd in his views,
For his Union reports that he paid his dues,
(Our report on his Union shows it was sound)
And our Social Psychology workers found
That he was popular with his mates and liked a drink.
The Press are convinced that he bought a paper every day
And that his reactions to advertisements were normal in every way.

Policies taken out in his name prove that he was fully insured,
And his Health-card shows he was once in hospital but left it cured.
Both Producers Research and High-Grade Living declare
He was fully sensible to the advantages of the Instalment Plan
And had everything necessary to the Modern Man,
A phonograph, a radio, a car and a frigidaire.
Our researchers into Public Opinion are content
That he held the proper opinions for the time of year;
When there was peace, he was for peace; when there was war, he went.
He was married and added five children to the population,
Which our Eugenist says was the right number for a parent of his generation,
And our teachers report that he never interfered with their education.
Was he free? Was he happy? The question is absurd:
Had anything been wrong, we should certainly have heard.

~ Review ~

The Unknown Citizen by W.H. Auden

The "Unknown Citizen" in Auden's poem of the same name does not seem like a particularly noble hero, does he? In fact, his primary quality is that he has managed to keep himself entirely out of trouble.

A competent worker and a good consumer, he led a statistically "normal" life—neither complaining nor arousing complaints from others. He had few positive attributes to speak of. He was just a small voiceless cog in a big machine. What kind of state might erect a marble monument to honour a person like that?

In many respects, this state has much in common with contemporary Western society, especially the America of several decades ago, when the poem was written. It is a nation of automobiles, phonographs, radios, refrigerators, unions, factories—and a highly compartmentalized government bureaucracy that pervasively keeps a close (and not entirely innocent) watch on its citizens.

This poem is an ironic view of a society that sees itself as an ideal place to live, a Utopia, but one that is actually highly intolerant of individuality and free expression. The Unknown Citizen complacently accepts the status quo (and the irony) without protest. Now a monument has been erected to remember his name—even as that name is forgotten for all time.

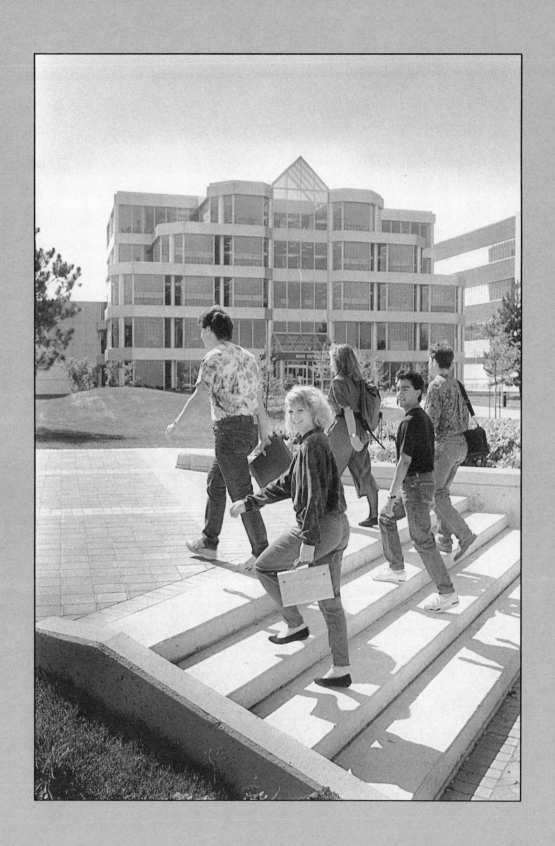

Relations Between Collectives

Man is not a solitary animal, and so long as social life survives, self-realization cannot be the supreme principle of ethics.

Bertrand Russell

Niccolo Machiavelli

Antanas Sileika

Countries do not have friends. They have interests.
CHARLES DE GAULLE

Niccolo Machiavelli was a statesman and diplomat who lived in Florence from 1469–1527, and it is important to understand the world that he came from before going over a few of his ideas. At the time Machiavelli lived, Italy was a collection of city states that were perpetually jockeying with one another for advantage. They formed complicated, shifting alliances and in addition foreign countries often looked upon the Italian peninsula as ripe for occupation.

Machiavelli became a victim of this complicated, cut-throat world, when new rulers, the Medicis, took control of Florence. They first tortured him and then banished him to a small family estate. Machiavelli was desperate for new employment, so he wrote a kind of political handbook called *The Prince* and dedicated it to the Medicis in attempt to gain their favour.

Both Machiavelli and his book have been attacked ever since because Machiavelli was so unsentimental that he sounded perfectly wicked. His premise was that the world was a very dangerous place for a prince, and the book was supposed to be a guide to survival. Machiavelli called his ruler a "prince," but today we would call a person who has just come to power by force of arms or scheming, a dictator. Machiavelli's book told a dictator how to take power and how to hold on to it.

To this day, a ruthless political schemer is called "Machiavellian."

Do 400 year-old ideas have any relevance today? Let's take a look at some of the principles Machiavelli advocated, and then see if we can find any examples of modern Machiavellian behaviour in politics.

Some of Machiavelli's Ideas from *The Prince*

How to Keep a Principality One Has Conquered

A prince who has just taken power by force of arms or scheming is in a dangerous position. He may still have many hidden enemies and he must make himself safe from them. Machiavelli suggested that most of the population in a newly taken country should be left in peace. They should be allowed to keep their taxes, languages, and customs because they are familiar with them. After all, a new prince can not afford to antagonize everyone. However, the members of the former ruling family must be eliminated entirely—elimination, of course, means murder. Machiavelli said that as long as any members of the ruling family remained, there was a danger they might surround themselves with followers and overthrow the new prince. To protect against this, they must all be murdered.

With pointers such as this, one can see how Machiavelli gained his reputation for wickedness. And yet, this barbaric principle was followed in the recent past. Let us consider the fate of the Romanovs, the ruling Czars of Russia who lost power to the Communists in 1917. To consolidate their power, the Communists had the Czar, his wife, and all their children murdered. The Communists feared that if any Romanovs lived, they might yet return to power. Almost four hundred years after his death, Machiavelli's principle was being applied.

The Nature of Human Beings

The wish to acquire, says Machiavelli, is a normal part of human nature. We all want things, and when we have them, we want more. The same is true of countries. Furthermore, we tend to admire countries and rulers that are rich and powerful, and tend to despise those that are poor. Machiavelli suggests that it is worth trying to become as powerful as possible by virtually any means because people admire the rich. People may not actually despise the poor, but no one looks up to them.

It cannot be denied that people admire "winners." Even though Canada and many other countries could be placed on almost the

Niccolo Machiavelli's book, *The Prince*, told a dictator how to take power and how to hold on to it.

To this day, a ruthless political schemer is described as being "Machiavellian."

same pedestal, let us restrict our attention for a moment to the USA, perhaps the richest of Western countries. The United States is certainly admired by many, and the admiration is not always for the democracy and freedom enjoyed by Americans. More precisely, poorer foreigners admire the United States because it is a rich country. At the very moment when many Eastern European countries are becoming politically free, thousands of emigrants want to leave those nations for the USA. Why should this be so when the citizens of East European countries either enjoy the same freedoms as Americans or will do so very soon? It is because they admire success, and in this case success means money.

How to Keep Vices from Affecting One's Hold on Power

Machiavelli believed that most people could not be free of all vices. By vices, we mean character flaws that lead to extravagance, violence, sexual perversity, etc. He believed it was natural for people to have weaknesses. A prince had to be very careful about vices, though, because certain of them could cost him his principality. A prince who had a weakness for spending money might no longer be able to pay an army, for example, and therefore leave his country open to attack. Machiavelli suggested that a prince might allow himself certain vices, as long as they did not weaken his hold on the state. In other words, it may be good to be virtuous, but virtue is not possible for most people to attain.

In modern times, we like our politicians to be squeaky clean, but Machiavelli would say that this is impossible. John F. Kennedy is remembered as a remarkably appealing president of the United States. Many think of his time as one of great hope. Thirty years after John F. Kennedy's death, we have learned that the man had a weakness for women that led him into numerous affairs, among them an affair with Marilyn Monroe. For some people, this knowledge lowered Kennedy's appeal. It was disappointing to learn that such a seemingly upright man repeatedly betrayed his wife. Machiavelli would not have been surprised, though, because he would have said that the vice was not important. After all, it did not affect Kennedy's ability to rule.

How to Hold a Newly Acquired Country

The problem with holding a country that is far away is that armies of occupation cost a great deal, and one can beggar oneself by maintaining large numbers of soldiers. Machiavelli suggested that a cheaper method is to confiscate the land of a small number of local people and to send colonists to occupy that land. The colonists will be grateful to the prince for their new land, and help him hold it against the hostile locals.

We don't think of colonies very much in modern times, but we should remember that North and South America were colonies of various European powers. It would have been very expensive to force the native peoples into submission using only paid soldiers. It was far cheaper to give land to people, colonists, and to have them dominate the local inhabitants. The native people of North America were forced into submission by a distant power not merely because the power was more technologically advanced, but because emigrants were sent to this continent to establish the rule of the distant powers.

Is It Better to be Loved or Feared?

Most individuals would of course prefer to be loved, but Machiavelli says that this is not easy for a prince because it is difficult to make the majority of people love you. People will only obey you if they love you or fear you, and since the former is impossible to achieve, it is better to have people fear you.

Again, an attempt to strike fear into the hearts of one's subjects may sound horrible, but let us consider just one of this century's dictators. Joseph Stalin ruled the Soviet Union for almost thirty years, and in his time he was responsible for the deaths of millions and the imprisonment of many more. His secret police were feared, and several million Ukrainians were starved into submission to his policies. Machiavelli would say that Stalin understood how to stay in power.

On the Nature of War

Machiavelli believed that wars were an expression of humanity and were therefore impossible to avoid. Admittedly, Machiavelli lived in a time when the most powerful weapons were cannons, and so the danger of fighting a nuclear war could never have occurred to him. If we restrict our argument to conventional wars, of which there have been over 150 since 1945, we might agree that there is no use in saying there *should not* be wars if they continue to happen. Machiavelli said wars would always happen, and therefore one should never try to avoid war. Instead, the prince should always choose to fight a war when it is to his advantage.

Should a country only fight when it is attacked? This sounds like a very noble sentiment, but countries that live in dangerous circumstances can not afford to be sentimental. In the late 1970s, it became clear that Iraq was preparing to build nuclear arms. The laboratories for research and the plants for construction were already largely in place. The state of Israel could not afford to allow Iraq to become a nuclear-equipped country because Israel and many of its neighbours were in a perpetual state of tension. Therefore, the Israeli government decided to launch a pre-emptive strike. Using its air force, and without an explicit declaration of war, Israel destroyed the labs and plants that would have given Iraq the ability to build nuclear weapons. Machiavelli would have nodded approvingly at Israel's application of his principles.

Realpolitik—A Modern Extension of Machiavelli's Ideas

We have looked at a few paraphrased examples from Machiavelli's book of thirty-six chapters. Now let us get a little closer to modern times.

The German term "realpolitik" was coined to describe the policies of Otto von Bismarck, the nineteenth-century German chancellor who said that he recognized the right of no other nation when it came to foreign policy. "Realpolitik" refers to an unsentimental attempt to further the policies of one's country, specifically, to gain material or political advantage.

A believer in realpolitik would say that there is no use talking about high moral standards. People *should* not steal, but many do. People *should* be more easily satisfied with what they have, but they are not. Countries *should* respect other countries and co-operate with them, but they do not. In other words, in a world dominated by national self-interest, only the self-interested can survive.

A Comparison of Two Articles

While we are on the subject of *should,* this might be a good moment to discuss the ideas of both Toby Fletcher and Niccolo Machiavelli.

Toby Fletcher's article, *The Future of Sovereignty*, calls for a new world order, a loose federation of states that could deal better with problems such as war, pollution, and hunger. This type of call for a new world order has become increasingly popular since World

Life in Hell
© 1991 by Matt Groening

War II. Decolonized states and developing countries have called for changes in the economic system we live in, as they see this economic system favouring the Western countries, mainly Europe and North America. Also, Fletcher points out, pollution, hunger, and war are international problems, and we need international bodies to control them.

A critic of Toby Fletcher might say, however, that he describes the world as it should be, and not the world as it really is. A critic might therefore say that Fletcher's ideas are idealistic and have little chance of being implemented, for no nation will ever give up sovereignty unless it is forced to do so or sees some overwhelming advantage. Certainly, economic and political union is moving forward in Europe, but the opposite is happening in the Soviet Union and Yugoslavia, and the very idea of centralization, at least in economic terms, has fallen out of favour as Eastern European economies begin the route to reforms. In short, there is no clear and definite move towards

~ Review ~

Niccolo Machiavelli

This article is a summary of some of the pragmatic and often shocking ideas about how to run a state as advocated by Niccolo Machiavelli, a Renaissance-era Florentine states-man and political analyst. His handbook on the subject, written in 1513, is entitled *The Prince*.

Italy in the 15th-century was a patch-work quilt of frequently battling principalities with constantly shifting loyalties. A close observer of this frenzied political scene, Machiavelli, a ruthless political schemer, believed that "might makes right." A ruler must do whatever must be done to cement their hold on power. Ethics do not enter the picture. Political foes must be murdered; no amount of lying, cheating and treachery was beneath the political leader whose object was to subjugate another people or state. "Such intellectual honesty about politi-cal dishonesty would have been hardly possible at any other time or in any other country ... " Bertrand Russell writes in his *History of West-ern Civilization*.

One of Machiavelli's dictums for rulers is that "it is better to be feared than loved," and many 20th-century tyrants from Joseph Stalin to Saddam Hussein, seem to have modeled themselves on this advice. Many modern leaders also seem to share Machiavelli's belief that treachery was inevitable, even advantageous under certain circumstances. The 19th-century German notion of "real-politik" which rationalizes unethical conduct if it advances the national interest, seems based on Machiavel-li's bleak perception of politics.

Despite, or perhaps because of, his pessimistic vision of humanity, Machiavelli's name has entered the English language. Underhanded and manipulative political leaders are still commonly referred to as "Machiavellian."

world political union, but a kind of tension exits between centrifugal (away from the centre) and centripetal (towards the centre) forces.

Fletcher's assumption that people like orderliness in line-ups is certainly not true for most of the world. Anyone who has waited for a bus in France, Italy, or Egypt knows the type of jockeying that happens when the bus arrives.

Can one therefore say that Fletcher is wrong and Machiavelli is right? The problem that most people have with Machiavelli's ideas is that they paint a picture of a world that functions purely out of motives of self-interest. Many of us would like to believe that the world is not really so amoral.

This leaves us with a fundamental dilemma. In international political terms, we can imagine a far better world, but what is the use of imagining a better world if it cannot be achieved? Machiavelli might have said that we can imagine a "kinder, gentler" world all we want, as long as we do not delude ourselves into believing it is really possible to achieve.

The Future of Sovereignty

Toby Fletcher

Much of our every day life is guided by widely-accepted, but unwritten rules of conduct called manners. For instance, many of us try to get a cup of coffee in the cafeteria before that first class in the morning. Although we may be late, we will line up and wait patiently, as long as it's clear that we are served in the order we arrived. But that quiet patience can quickly turn to anger as we see a late arrival butt into the line ahead of us. Why? What rule or tradition or custom has been broken? There is no sign which states "Line up or else." Who said a bunch of strangers are supposed to line up? Why do we feel this deep sense of injustice, even outrage, when someone is rude or impolite?

Our favourite teachers are often the ones who clearly describe a reasonable set of rules governing how classes will be managed and especially how course work will be evaluated. If the rules are clear, fair, and consistently applied, we usually accept the results of those rules. If it is clear how a paper is to be marked, we usually accept the grade we get because it is clear how the grade was determined. We keenly feel a sense of injustice if we get an unjustified low grade and we often feel a sense of being devalued if we get an unjustified high grade. Teachers and students are happier with clear and fair rules in the classroom.

The principles of proper manners and academic regulations can be generalized from the relationships among individuals to the interactions among nation states. The peoples and nations of the world have been merging more and more into an interdependent global society. Advances in technology have improved communications around the world to the point where "spaceship earth" is a concept most people can readily accept. Supersonic jet travel, live rock concerts played and televised simultaneously on two continents, instantaneous transfers of huge sums of money from Hong Kong to London to New York to Los Angeles to Tokyo, timely news and information reports from anywhere to anywhere—all of these technological applications have clarified that we live on a small, finite planet. Countries rely on each other for trade and economic stability, for security and peace, and for help and friendship when disasters strike. Unfortunately, world politics have not kept pace with world problems. Only forty years ago, the world and its resources seemed limitless, inexhaustible, yet we had just developed the means to annihilate it. Commenting on the nuclear bomb, Albert Einstein said: "It has changed everything except our way of thinking, and so we drift toward unparalleled catastrophe." We are technically quick and politically slow, with the result that our technology has far exceeded our social and spiritual development.

Our biggest problem is that while the world has become a finite, integrated whole, we continue to think that all political power should be kept at the level of the nation. Global politics are still dominated by a view of the world that prevailed before growth and technology made us so interdependent. In this view, the world is an aggregate of sovereign nations having neither rights nor obligations toward each other. Sovereign-nation thinking relies on "might makes right" and divides the world into East and West, North and South, "us" and "them." People are citizens of the country to which they owe their highest loyalty. We support two standards for humanity—we look after the welfare of our own citizens, but disclaim any political or ethical responsibility for the plight of people in other countries. Just as sovereign-nation thinking sets up boundaries to compassion and responsibility, so it sets up barriers to cooperation around the vital interests which all people, all nations have in common. An intolerable irony: each nation trying to put its immediate interests ahead of the overall interests of the world worsens the global crisis and no one's interests are truly served. Everyone who has a television has seen the images of starving children in Ethiopia. We know there is a problem of properly distributing the food we produce to ensure that everyone is fed. Last year, the world's military expenditures totalled $1,000 billion spent to buy weapons to hurt others and protect ourselves. Imagine potential changes, if even half of those dollars went to help feed the hungry or to improve agricultural methods and technology.

Millions of young people have been killed or maimed in over 150 wars fought since 1945. We are poisoning our air, our water and destroying our habitats. Our situation begs us to change, begs us to rethink our assumptions, to go beyond the sovereign-nation system to conceive a new world order.

Humans are social and cooperative. We are born into groups, nurtured by groups, socialized by groups, and very early on in our lives we begin to influence, create, and develop groups. We form groups for many reasons: to protect ourselves, to gather food, to teach the young, to have fun, to solve problems, to do things. We form families, clans, tribes, churches, nations, provinces, states, countries, empires, dynasties, teams, associations, leagues, companies, corporations, and conglomerates.

If we want the nations and peoples of the world to live together as a peaceful, interactive community, then we need some form of government. Most people, even those who don't like government, accept that to be able to live together socially, we must have a way to make decisions and take action on matters affecting the community as a whole. Many people resent government for being restrictive, cumbersome, and expensive, yet ignore the freedoms and benefits provided.

Metropolitan Toronto is a very complex operation. We have developed a structure where elected officials draft by-laws which greatly influence our urban behaviour—how fast we drive, where we can park our cars, how many dogs and cats we can own, how high fences can be between neighbours, and now even where we can smoke.

Most of us comply with these by-laws most of the time and we know the consequences of breaking them. Disagreements are settled at City Hall.

We rely on our cities to provide us with water, electricity, sewers, police and fire protection, and garbage removal. For bigger issues such as education, health care, highway safety, and liquor control, we turn to our provincial government.

In order to balance the potentially conflicting regional interests among provinces, we have a national government which attempts to address issues such as monetary policy, taxation, postal service, defence and trade.

We create organizations to accomplish things, but very often our organizations are not as efficient nor as effective as we would like them to be. Describing problems, then explaining possible solutions can be very frustrating, and there is always the terrible temptation for those in power to dictate to the powerless. But the best solutions invariably result when everyone who has an interest or will be affected has some influence on the outcome. Giving people a voice, consulting, and consensus-building, take time. Sharing power and giving up authority are extremely difficult to do.

More and more now we are confronted by problems that threaten all humans, problems which transcend city and state boundaries, problems which require national governments to cooperate and collaborate—two activities which many governments are reluctant to do.

Canadian values of regionalism, interdependence, multiculturalism, and national problem-solving could provide the foundation for a global political framework. Newfoundland, Quebec, Ontario, and British Columbia are very different and distinct components of Canada. Disputes among them are settled at conferences, in the courts, or in their legislatures. It is extremely unlikely that citizens of one province would actually go to war against citizens of another province. It is not that there is no conflict; it is that the conflict is appropriately managed.

Federalism is a system of government in which a number of states form a union but remain independent (or sovereign) in their internal affairs. A federal government can be weak or strong, depending on how responsibilities are divided between central authority and the component states.

The United States of America is an example of a strong central government with fifty relatively weak states. The European Community is an excellent example of twelve sovereign, diverse states joining together to form a remarkably effective and powerful federal union. Canada's federal system lies somewhere in between.

Countries have associated with each other for a variety of reasons:

1. *geographic*, such as the Organization of American States (OAS), the Organization for African Unity, the Pacific Rim, the Arctic Nations;

2. *colonial*, e.g., the Commonwealth, the Francophonie;

3. *military*, e.g., the North Atlantic Treaty Organization (NATO);

4. *political*, e.g., the Western democracies, the Communist Bloc, the nonaligned countries;

5. *religious*, e.g., Arab League;

6. *economic*, e.g., the Organization of Petroleum Exporting Countries (OPEC), the Group of Seven, the European Community (EC).

Economic partnerships seem to be the most enduring, egalitarian, and effective. Countries seem to be much more willing to surrender certain sovereignty rights for economic gain. The best example of this is the European Community. By 1992, the EC will become a single market of 325 million consumers—far greater than the U.S.-Canada free trade zone of 265 million. The EC comprises twelve remarkable nations: Belgium, Britain, Denmark, France, Greece, Ireland, Italy, Luxembourg, Netherlands, Portugal, Spain and West Germany. Remarkable because of their ethnic, cultural, political, and historical diversity. Many of these countries have been at war with each other and are still intensely nationalistic, yet they will share a common currency and passport; they will recognize common patents and professional designations; citizens can live, work and move freely anywhere within the community. These countries have established a democratically-elected parliament to pass legislation to deal with common problems—for example, their environmental challenges. But each country retains a distinct identity and internal control over social policies, language, culture, and internal security. Together, they are the strongest economic union in the world. The EC exemplifies a working model of "harmonious diversity" achieving effective unity.

With the remarkable changes that have taken place in Eastern and Central Europe since the collapse of the Berlin Wall, the EC may well expand to include the East Bloc economies and provide "associate" status to the newly-emerging Baltic nations. Economic realities have overwhelmed ineffective political organizations and democratic ideals and institutions are replacing totalitarian repression and elites.

The supremacy of the huge US economy is declining but will remain very powerful throughout the 90s. The contest between the old "superpowers" is over but that does not mean that we do not face many multi-lateral, global concerns for which we need global cooperation:

- reducing armed conflict
- managing population growth
- reducing defence budgets
- distributing food
- reducing debt
- disposing of hazardous waste
- protecting the environment
- establishing human rights
- accommodating refugees.

To have world federation, we need world institutions. Although we are a long way from a federated world community of nations, we do have a number of global organizations, e.g., The United Nations, The World Court, The World Bank, The International Monetary Fund (IMF). The U.N. is constantly criticized for being weak and ineffective, yet its strength is in being a forum for even the weakest nation to voice its concerns. The U.N. has survived since 1945 precisely because it relies on consensus, the lowest common denominator, and the single veto. From tribe to feudal kingdom to nation-state, from town to city to metropolitan area, there has been an historical trend to ever larger social groupings. When we transcend sovereign-nation thinking, we become citizens of the world, loyal members of humanity. Global interdependence requires new definitions. Our personal and national interests can only be served through a more sophisticated, cooperative and collaborative relationship among nations.

World federation will not be cheaper nor necessarily more efficient as a bureaucracy, but if we create a principled world order in which every individual and every nation assumes certain global responsibilities in exchange for certain guaranteed rights, then world federation will be more effective in dealing with our global challenges. Strong economically based associations of nations would reduce the need for elaborate defense systems and free up huge amounts of money which could be used to eliminate hunger, promote health and education. Open, unrestricted communications and news services would reduce totalitarian oppression and provide the opportunity for global human rights.

Minimal world governance means establishing at the global level the principles and institutions we already recognize as fundamental

~ Review ~

The Future of Sovereignty

The principles that govern good behaviour among individuals should also be applied to govern the conduct among modern states, Toby Fletcher writes in this essay.

Technological changes have advanced communications and travel so rapidly that it is possible to perceive the world not just as a conglomeration of nations but as a unified "spaceship earth." In this modern world, Fletcher writes, the concept of "nationhood" is old and divisive; people need to put the global agenda ahead of nationalistic goals.

The author proposes that nations should invest in agricultural technology, not weapons, and co-operate to find fair solutions to a host of global problems such as food shortages and starvation, pollution, exploitation of resources and war. As there is government on the municipal, provincial, and federal levels, so too the nations of the earth ought jointly to establish a world government.

According to Fletcher, the global government would be composed of a democratic legislature and a justice system, and impose sanctions against transgressors of international law. A global police force would also be necessary to enforce compliance.

to our social order at the civic, provincial, and national levels. These include:

1. A democratic legislature to develop a body of world law setting out basic rights and obligations;

2. A system of world courts for interpreting those laws in cases of dispute;

3. A set of sanctions to motivate compliance with the laws; and

4. A recognized, fully-resourced and effective global police force.

These principles are familiar to everyone and are as relevant on a global scale as on a local one. International trading partnerships, associations, and communities seem to be the best way of establishing collaborative, productive relationships among nations. Clear, just rules of international behaviour are simply our best hope for a peaceful, prosperous future.

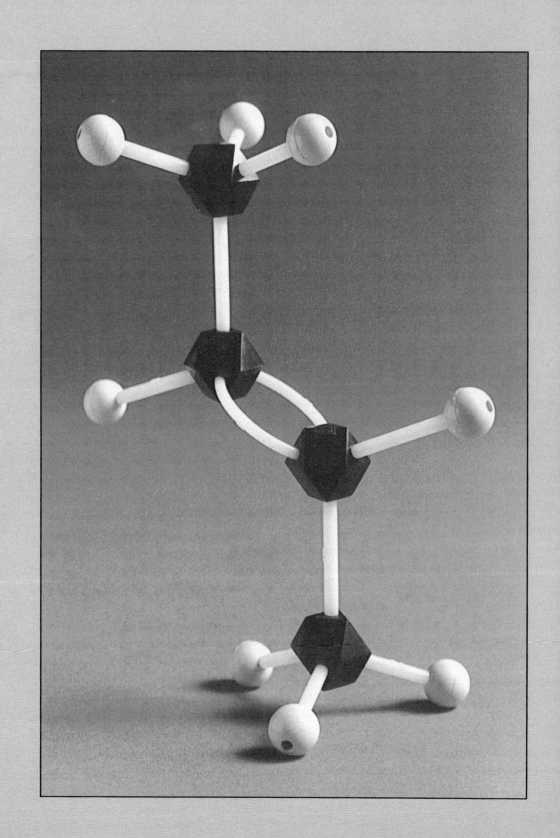

UNIT 4

PERCEPTIONS OF THE NATURAL WORLD

Science and the Natural World

I cannot believe that God plays dice with the cosmos.

Albert Einstein

The release of atom power has changed everything except our way of thinking, and thus we are being driven unarmed towards a catastrophe... The solution of this problem lies in the heart of humankind.

Albert Einstein

Curiosity and Discovery

Michael Badyk

I don't think that it really matters where or how we got it, but we have it—curiosity. All you have to do is look at children. Every day and moment is full of curiosity and discovery. Watch toddlers entering a room. Their heads will go from side to side as they look around and take it all in. The next thing they do is find things that they can reach. They'll explore and touch and look at everything they can. Anything that produces a reaction when touched will be a special delight for children.

If necessary, children will put something that they find curious into their mouths. I remember being with a friend of mine and her son when her son was about 16 months old. The little guy came into my living room, wandered over and grabbed a large rock that was on top of a stereo speaker. He then shoved half of it into his mouth. He wanted to see what it tasted like. That is probably a legitimate use for the sense of taste. As adults we suppress that sense, except for food. But people like geologists often taste rocks to test for salts and other minerals, so we can use it for more than food.

I've always liked to watch kids around Christmas time or on birthdays. Just put a present down in front of them, but tell them that they can't open it yet. They go crazy. They'll whine or plead and when they finally realize that you won't give in, they will know that they can't take the easy way out by coercing you and then their senses will start to kick in.

They'll look at it first. This might supply a clue. That's one sense. Then they'll touch it. That will give them a better sense of size and shape, building on what their eyes told them first. That's two senses that have kicked in. They'll also probably pick it up. More information. Weight. Density. They will probably also shake the box, and see what sound it will make. Hearing: sense number three. While they're this close they'll also check the box for any odours. Sense number four. Not much luck there under most circumstances. The same with taste. Kids tell me that wrapping paper tastes awful. Sense number five. All engaged. Most children may now try to guess what's in there, and they'll probably question you as to the success of their guess. Adults usually give in at this point and let the gift be opened.

If your senses allow your curiosity to be satisfied then you have made something that in general you can call a *discovery*. That's the best part about being young. Almost everything is a discovery. This curiosity/discovery cycle is precious and it must be fed and nurtured throughout a person's life. There are trails to walk, mountains to climb, books to read and many moments to savour.

Curiosity and Science

Many people have misconceptions about what science is and what it does. A dictionary will say that "science is a branch of knowledge." Perhaps a better way to put it is that science is a tool or an aid to help us explore our universe, under the influence of our curiosity. It's not as concise as the dictionary definition, but explains things a little bit more clearly. If we had that gift-wrapped present in our hands and we couldn't open it, then maybe we'd invent the X-Ray to check inside. That to me is science—exploring the small and the large.

We have done a reasonable job at explaining many facets of life on earth, but there is still a great deal to learn. The question remains "How did we as humans and our universe come to be?" This ancient question is not going to be solved soon. It might never be. There is plenty to explore and discover and to stimulate our human curiosity.

What carries us forward to acquire new knowledge is the **scientific method**—a series of logical steps that we have developed to get to the truth or the solution in the most economical way. This series of steps works quite well, but there are some underlying points that must be kept in mind.

Tentativeness. The first is that scientists must be *tentative* about conclusions. They are rarely 100% positive that what they have established is the truth. They might have made a mistake somewhere that has given them a false impression that they have uncovered the truth or solved the problem. "Good" science will never state a result

THE SCIENTIFIC METHOD

The scientific method is a series of logical steps that we have developed to get to the truth or the solution in the most economical way possible.

The Scientific Method

The steps leading to a solution in science can be broken down as follows:

STEP 1: State the nature of the problem.

STEP 2: What is a possible solution or the truth in this case? *(Developing an hypothesis.)*

STEP 3: Come up with a way to test your solution. *(Designing an experiment.)*

STEP 4: What results does your test provide? *(Collecting the data or observations.)*

STEP 5: What is your conclusion? *(Producing an interpretation of the data or observations that you collected.)*

to be an absolute. Words such as "maybe" or "perhaps" are the correct terms that should be used.

Verifiability. Another underlying point is something called *verifiability.* This means that the way in which scientists get their results can be repeated by others, and they will get exactly the same results. If they don't, then either their experiment was done incorrectly, or the experiment is wrong in the first place. If a number of people can obtain the same results independently then the results must be reasonable. It's simply a way of checking.

Empirical Observations. The final point is that you must have results that include *empirical observation.* These are observations that you can detect with your senses. If it is a problem that you can only think about, but not really test or produce results that you can sense, then the results will largely remain unproven or inconclusive.

Laws and Theories. The whole process that we just went through points to solving a problem and establishing the truth. If you can conclusively say that what you have discovered is the truth and it will stay that way wherever you go in the universe, and under any possible condition, then you can call your result *a law.* These are exceedingly rare commodities.

Usually, we only manage to come up with a possible explanation and these are called *theories*. They will remain only an explanation until we gather more information or come up with another explanation to establish the truth.

Theories and laws extend far beyond just the realm of science. So far in the *Humanities* text we have examined many theories. In psychology, the "four schools of thought" discussed earlier are really theories. More work needs to be conducted before any of these could be accepted as a law. If a law is developed it most likely will combine aspects of some or all the existing theories as well as new, yet-to-be-discovered information. For aspects of society it may be ludicrous even to try to establish sociological laws. Will it ever be possible to devise a law that explains how we select a mate? There are some well-known and understood factors, but the elements of chance always make it difficult to come up with a universal rule (a law).

Later in the text when we deal with the role of art we will see the attempt that has been made to develop explanations as to why people like certain works of art, or why some works can be termed "good." The complexity of variables here is such that the rational side (objectivity) may never be able to eliminate the need for the emotional (subjectivity). It would be a shame if artistic laws became "carved in stone" or captured in some formula. One of the pleasures of the arts is the surprise of something really new.

Unlike the subjects just described, we do have laws in the natural sciences. They are great and important discoveries, and nowadays we take them for granted. This can lead to the false conclusion that we know everything about the natural world, but there is an immense quantity of work still to be done. Even our understanding of something basic like light is still theoretical (either it's a particle or wave depending upon the situation).

There is enough in our existence (and even the origin of our existence) to keep our curiosity fuelled for a long time. Science and curiosity will continue to work together and we will continue to experience the joy of discovery. Thomas Huxley stated it very poignantly at the turn of the century: "It's not that the universe will live up to our imagination, it's whether our imagination will live up to the universe." These are words that have been pondered for many years, and ones that will continue to be discussed for ages to come.

"It's not that the universe will live up to our imagination, it's whether our imagination will live up to the universe."
Thomas Huxley

The Path of Scientific Development

Tom Olien

The three primary activities involved in scientific development are: **(1)** observing; **(2)** structuring the information; and **(3)** discovering or creating an underlying mechanism. Inherent in each activity is a relentless (or an on-going) process of reflection, checking equipment, correcting observations, updating technique, confirming speculation and questioning theory. The result is the process shown in the chart on the next page. This process parallels the steps of the scientific method, the discipline of curiosity used by individual scientists as described in the previous article.

Observing

Scientific activity starts with observation. Initially, observations were limited to the five human senses. We now live in a world with powerful extensions to our primary senses. A simple set of binoculars drastically changes our ability to identify a bird in the woods or to see the stars and planets with a clarity that the most astute astronomer of four hundred years ago could not imagine.

Many instruments measure features of the universe that go beyond our senses. A voltameter measures electrical potential, a feature of an electric circuit unseen by human eyes except in the high values that produce a dangerous shock. A compass can detect the direction of the earth's "invisible" magnetic field, while other instruments measure its strength. The Herculean forces between the rock faces of sliding continental plates can now be measured, as can the temperatures of outer space or the heat in the core of a nuclear

The Path of Scientific Development
The Process

OBSERVING
- instrumentation
- skill in specific techniques
- patience and "objectivity"

STRUCTURING AND USING THE INFORMATION
- patterns and laws
- applied mathematical tools of analysis
- empirical rules for design and extension

DISCOVERING/CREATING AN UNDERLYING MECHANISM
- a creative leap beyond reasoning
- a simple, elegant unifying principle
- constantly creating new possibilities and being tested against new observations

reactor. Today, in most industrialized countries there is a significant industry associated with the development, manufacture, sales and operation of scientific instrumentation.

Scientific observation requires skill. It requires the persistence of a keen nature observer waiting for hours to see the mating habits of an obscure species, the diligence in washing and sterilizing every piece of equipment over again to maintain the germ-free environment necessary for medical research, or the technical skill of the operator of a multimillion dollar electron microscope.

Behind the specific skills, every area of scientific observation requires a unique "objectivity." Scientific "objectivity" should allow one to "see" what is really there and not what one hopes to "see." The ability to achieve this ultimate abstract objectivity is at best tainted by human frailty and at worst perverted by the massive personal, social, economic or ideological consequences of the impact of a given observation. In spite of these complications, the process of scientific observation usually converges to the point where all competent observers agree that they "see" the same thing in the same set of circumstances.

THE DEVELOPMENT OF SCIENCE

The three primary activities involved in scientific development are: (1) observing; (2) structuring the information; and (3) discovering or creating an underlying mechanism.

Structuring the Information

Once a body of data has been accumulated from reliable observation, the next task is to attempt to make some sense and order out of the data.

Science assumes that every action follows some pattern, usually some cause and effect connection. Sometimes the connections are fairly simple and obvious. Two of you may just manage to push a stalled car out of an intersection, but six of you could move it much more easily and quickly. The connection between force and motion is fairly obvious.

At other times the connections are complex and obscure. The connections between cigarette smoking, lung cancer and heart disease are not so obvious. Statistically, there is a relation because large samples of smokers consistently show higher incidence of these problems than non-smokers, but we are unable to link one person's smoking of one pack a day to an onset of lung cancer in a specified number of years. There are too many other factors involved to be able to make specific cause-and-effect connections.

The search for patterns or laws is a long-term goal of science. The methods include cataloguing samples, making diagrams, lists and graphs. Statistical analysis and other powerful mathematical tools are also used. The details of a discovery may be tucked away in seemingly random data or "noise." Finding patterns in such circumstances is not unlike the capacity of the human ear to pick out a faint cry for help in the midst of the roar of a hurricane.

Laws and empirical regularities can be developed from these patterns and reapplied by science and society. Taller cathedrals and longer bridges can be built from what was learned in earlier research. An element in the same column, but next row of the periodic table can be expected to have similar properties to the one in the previous row. This may be enough guide or warning to allow one to make a useful compound or avoid a potentially explosive one.

At this stage of observation we may have some very useful rules for how things work, but we do not know why they work as they do. There is no obvious fundamental mechanism, only rules, often very complex and arbitrary ones connecting certain facts and events. There is still a need for a unifying principle to simplify and make sense of the regulations.

Discovering or Creating an Underlying Mechanism

The discovery of grand themes and fundamental theories is the crowning achievement of the creative human mind in the arena of science. The theories of universal gravitation, relativity, evolution, continental drift and the role of DNA in genetics are examples of underlying mechanisms.

These themes did not emerge from reason alone. Like an artist, scientists must step beyond the structured data and rules. Typically a person or a group makes an educated guess, an intuitive leap, that opens a new possibility and a new way of thinking. The genius of the process of science is that it doesn't stop with a good guess, but sets to testing it thoroughly. The creative guesses that were wrong have long since disappeared leaving us only the heroic tales and legacies of the ones that worked.

A fundamental theory (such as gravity) is often simple. It is seen as an elegant and aesthetically pleasing unifying principle. Looking back, most people would say it is obvious; it looks so right and natural.

The discovery of an underlying mechanism creates new possibilities. It begs to be used and tested in new areas. Great advances in scientific development and technological application take place following the breakthrough of a major scientific theory. Each extension is also a test of the new theory. Applications that work confirm the theory. When the extensions of the theory begin to break down and adjustments are needed to get consistent results, a new understanding of the fundamental mechanism is brought forward. In this way, the process moves on—never complete, no matter how convincing, powerful and elegant a particular theory may be at one time.

From examples in celestial mechanics, genetics and neurology we can see how these three stages develop.

The Path to an Underlying Mechanism in Celestial Mechanics

Global navigation in the fifteenth century revived interest in the stars and planets. Little change had been made to the Ptolemaic system of the universe from second-century Rome. The Ptolemaic theory held that the earth was the center of the universe and that the earth was at rest with no rotation or motion. The sun, the stars and the planets rotated around the earth. The system was adequate for

The Path of Scientific Development

Celestial Mechanics

OBSERVING

- **Copernicus** (1473-1543): an idea—earth not the centre .
- **Tycho Brahe** (1546-1601): an observatory —new precision of information about planets.
- **Galileo** (1564-1642): used telescope to observe rotation of sun and the revolution of the moons of Jupiter.

STRUCTURING AND USING THE INFORMATION

- **Kepler** (1571-1630): develops three laws of planetary motion.
  1. the orbits of the planets around the sun are elliptical, with the sun at one focus;
  2. the line drawn from the sun to a planet sweeps out equal areas in equal times;
  3. the square of the period of the planet is proportional to the cube of the radius.

DISCOVERING/CREATING AN UNDERLYING MECHANISM

- **Newton** (1642-1727): the law of universal gravitation.
  All objects in the universe attract each other. The force increases with the product of their masses and decreases with their distance apart.

$$F = \frac{Gm_1m_2}{r^2}$$

the needs of the time (it worked as a system of navigation) but was very complex.

Copernicus suggested that the system would be simpler if we treated the sun as the centre of the system of planets and rotated the earth daily to allow for the rising and setting of the sun and moon and stars. It seems obvious now, but was not in the context of his time. Religious dogma and our own ego demanded that we see ourselves and our earth as the pinnacle of God's Creation, and thus the centre of it all. But the simplicity and elegance of the Copernican suggestion was convincing and encouraged a new wave of thinking.

Galileo made use of the newly developed optical lenses to make a telescope. His observations of the rotation of the sun and of moons revolving around the planet Jupiter did much to challenge the dogma that had kept a static world view dominant for so many centuries. He was also instrumental in developing the experimental method and theories of terrestrial mechanics that would be vital for the next leap.

In the meantime, Tycho Brahe, a Danish astronomer, had made meticulous observations of the heavens. His observations were extensive and some one hundred times more accurate than previous observations, pushing the very limits of accuracy of the unaided eye. Johann Kepler, a German mathematician and astronomer, applied his skills to this new accurate data to develop the three laws of planetary motion. These laws correctly described and predicted the motion of the earth, moon and planets about the sun, but lacked any explanation of why they should be so.

The explanation came from the leap made by Isaac Newton. Galileo had described the action of gravity for earthbound objects such as stones and cannon balls. The leap that Newton made was to ask if gravity actually extended to the moon. Again, it may seem obvious, but it represented radical new thinking at the time, and only a few decades earlier would have been ruled out as heresy by both church and science. Newton calculated and found it worked for the moon. In fact, it worked for all the planets, with the sun as the gravitational centre of the solar system. Kepler's laws could then be deduced as a consequence of universal gravitation rather than as a separate set of rules for our planetary system.

The mechanism of universal gravitation could be applied to all objects on the surface of the earth and beyond. It explained the pattern of the tides and allowed for accurate predictions, such as the date of return of Halley's comet and the existence of the planet Neptune, finally observed in 1846.

The Path to an Underlying Mechanism in Genetics

Genetics presents a current example of the path of scientific development. Mendel is credited as the father of genetics based on his systematic observation and explanation of the patterns of genetic inheritance. The physical location of the "inheritance material" was

---

The Path of Scientific Development

Genetics

IDEA — organisms "inherit" characteristics
of the parent

OBSERVING	**Mendel** (1822-1884)—observed the inheritance pattern in peas
STRUCTURING AND USING THE INFORMATION	• introduced the basic form of the laws of genetics • many people use the laws of genetics to improve grains and livestock and to understand and control some genetic diseases
DISCOVERING/CREATING AN UNDERLYING MECHANISM	**Watson and Crick** —the DNA molecule reveals the code that governs all genetics

---

Black box—a term scientists use to describe a situation in which we know essentially what something does, but we don't yet comprehend how it operates (like machinery covered up by a black box).

found in the chromosomes. These appear under a microscope as small sausage-like objects within the nucleus of the cells of an organism. But there are a small number of chromosomes and a very large number of genetic features for even the simplest organism. The gene is the package of information coded for a particular characteristic. The sense of what form this "gene" could take was unknown.

For over half a century increasingly complex rules of genetics were developed and applied to improvements of grains and livestock and to an understanding of hereditary diseases. But the gene itself remained a mystery. The fundamental mechanism driving genetics was an illusory black box with many patterns of input and output understood, many more not understood and the action within the black box unknown. It was the study of nucleic acids, culminating in the illumination of the structure of the DNA molecule by Watson and Crick in 1953, that opened the black box and caused the revolution in genetics. Just as mechanical engineers, armed with the foundations of mechanics, generated the industrial revolution in a previous era, now genetic engineers equipped with an understanding of the fundamental genetic structure are developing tools

---

The Path of Scientific Development

Neurology

IDEA—the basis of perception and consciousness is associated with the electrical activity of the brain

OBSERVING	**Eccles**— physiology of individual neurons - the action potential **Sherrington**—physiology of nerve sequences involved in reflexes
STRUCTURING AND USING THE INFORMATION	**Penfield**—memory triggered at specific sites within the brain **Edelman**—groups of neurons form the basis of perception
DISCOVERING/CREATING AN UNDERLYING MECHANISM	no single simple process is able to present itself as the fundamental structure and operating mechanism of the brain

---

and techniques that can systematically control the features of plants, animals and human beings. The implications are exciting and frightening but with the basic mechanism understood there is no turning back the exploration.

The Path to an Underlying Mechanism in Neurology

Neurology is the study of the nervous system and encompasses many domains of study: anatomy, physiology of the neuron, psychology, psychiatry, neural pathology. Each area has many rules and laws that can be used to predict actions in response to specific causes or stimuli. The drug *curare* was used by South American Natives on poisoned arrows. We now know that this drug blocks the transmission of nerve impulses to muscles and thus leads to paralysis. Our clear understanding of its action allows us to use curare in controlled ways during major surgery to avoid muscle reflex. Psychiatry has used electro-shock and drugs to control certain extreme psychiatric illnesses and has models of the actions of the brain that suggest why these methods are effective.

But the field of neurology is full of seeming contradictions. Wilder Penfield in working with epileptic patients was able to stimulate specific points in the brain and have memories brought to consciousness. Thus, specific memories seem to be located in a specific place in the brain. But it is also known that brain injuries to these areas do not necessarily remove the memory, but rather it seems to be stored like a hologram within a large domain of the brain. However, in spite of all we know about the brain, all the rules and patterns we have sorted out so far, we do not have a clue about the fundamental mechanism of the brain. From the neck up we are a virtual black box. Each promising hypothesis soon runs into contradictions that will not let it stand as a candidate for the explanation of the operation of the black box. And so we stumble along, making the best we can with the rules we have obtained so far, and looking enthusiastically to the time we will break-through to a clear view of this most intriguing of all fundamental mechanisms.

The Illusion of Fundamental Mechanisms

The illusion that the power of a few fundamental mechanisms holds out to us is that we will be able to explain the universe fully. But again we are forced to let in newer and grander theories that reject previous notions or treat previous theories as a subset of a larger picture.

Only a century ago it was suggested that the physics of the day could explain all basic physical phenomena. Within twenty years, the discovery of features within the atom itself and the observance of activities taking place at close to the speed of light showed that classical mechanics and electromagnetism did not apply at the atomic level or at very high speeds. Einstein's Special Theory of Relativity thus superseded Newtonian Mechanics, not making it wrong, but limiting it to objects of ordinary size and speeds. Fundamental mechanisms still beg the question of why they are there in the first place. Newton's law of universal gravitation does not really explain what gravity is but just how it acts.

An even more subtle illusion is hidden in the almost religious belief that the methods of science will answer all life's questions and eventually allow for a more stable and satisfying life on the planet. Many of the noted physicists of the twentieth century were essentially mystics. They allowed the possibility of a dimension to human life experience that was not accessible by the methods of their science. That doesn't mean they invoked God or some outside mystical force to explain the problems of their science. But neither did they expect science to explain the mystical elements of their unique life experience. Science seeks only to illuminate the mechanisms of repeatable phenomena in all domains of our universe. As for ultimate questions about the meaning of life, science may provide clues but no answers.

The Illusion of Certainty

Organic life, we are told, has developed gradually from the protozoan to the philosopher, and this development, we are assured, is indubitably an advance. Unfortunately it is the philosopher, not the protozoan, who gives us this assurance.

Bertrand Russell

What men really want is not knowledge but certainty.

Bertrand Russell

Limits of the Possible

Douglas Shenson

Cardiac intensive-care units are paradoxes. They are filled with the tools to delay dying but they keep the language of death at a distance. As an intern, I worked in such a place: a small, brightly lit area, partitioned into eight cubicles and filled with an overwhelming array of electronic equipment. Watching the nurses fit a patient into one of the cubicles was like watching an astronaut slip into a space capsule, engulfed and diminished by the machinery. But such thoughts did not immediately occur to me. My job was to work hard, attend to my patients, and leave the deeper problems of philosophy for later. Those were my priorities on the first day of my intensive-care rotation.

It was also the day we admitted a man I'll call Mr. Strap to the hospital. He came to us with an extraordinarily long and complicated history of heart ailments: three attacks, one bypass operation, and one heart-valve replacement. Now he had returned, complaining of chest pain—brought in by the paramedics when his wife suspected he was having another heart attack.

I met him in the emergency room. He was sitting up on a gurney, breathing slowly through an oxygen mask; he wore a patient's pajama top, but had on his trousers, shoes and socks. Like a minotaur, I would later kid him, neither man nor patient.

In his late seventies, Mr. Strap had the false robustness of a chronic smoker, and tired, apprehensive eyes. He spoke with the anxiousness and impatience of one who has met too many doctors, each seeking an understanding of his illness, which he himself had not yet found.

We talked about his previous hospitalization, his medications, his smoking. I examined him carefully, and told him I would be taking care of any day-to-day problems in consultation with more senior physicians. I communicated with that combination of signs doctors use when brought to a patient by crisis: the well-chosen word, the reassuring touch, the articulation of friendship, all mixed to support a sense of self, which, in parallel with his heart might also be collapsing.

It was not possible to assess how sick he was simply from his symptoms, I told him. It would be the laboratory that would indicate whether he had suffered another heart attack.

"I don't need a lab to tell me my chest hurts," he snapped, "I'm telling you, I'm having another bad one."

His family doctor soon arrived to evaluate his condition. After speaking at length to Mr. and Mrs. Strap, he moved away so we could discuss our initial therapeutic approach. I wrote the orders for Mr. Strap's medication and the family doctor rejoined the couple—only to be interrupted by the paging operator. Shortly, with a harried, fraternal look, he left for another patient.

I introduced myself to Mrs. Strap, who scrutinized me as we talked about the next steps in her husband's hospitalization. She spoke quietly, bracing herself for the unwanted intimacy inescapable in such encounters. We covered what must have been familiar material. I ordered medication and said he needs sleep now—that morning would be a better time to visit.

She turned to squeeze his hand and utter a few words before leaving; there was talk between them only of the magazines and family snapshots she would bring in—the soothing vocabulary of ordinary life, which she used instinctively to reduce their fright.

When she had left, he looked at me again.

"A kid like you really knows what he's doing?"

I smiled and assured him I had my medical school debt to prove it. Eventually he relaxed, and through the verbal jockeying I made myself a doctor in his eyes, as his disease had made him a patient in mine.

We came to know each other slowly. I was at first preoccupied with exploring his illness through the conventional prisms of medicine: evaluating the results of his blood tests and analyzing subtle changes in his X-rays and electrocardiograms. Every morning I checked his blood pressure, listened to his heart and lungs and watched for changes. I would in all likelihood be the first to detect it if he started to deteriorate.

Initially, the news was good: he had not had another heart attack. Yet the bouts of chest pain continued, only sometimes relieved by tablets of nitroglycerin. There were also episodes of difficulty in breathing. I was called repeatedly in the early hours to help him through these times. At one point, I found him struggling, sitting up in his darkened cubicle, neighboured by sleeping cardiac patients, a look of terrible fear in his eyes, nearly drowning as fluid seeped back in his lungs—the burden of a heart unable to pump blood through his arteries. An injection of medicine promised to bring back his breath to retrieve him from the disarray of his panic. As moments passed and the drug worked its way, I calmed him with explanations of how his heart was contracting more easily, of how his blood pressure was returning to normal, plying him softly with the reassurances of science, words in a kind of medical lullaby.

Soon it was over and we spoke again, like victorious confederates, conspiring now to exploit the coming day: there would be his wife's visit, family gossip, and reports of his young grandson's Little League accomplishments (there was greatness in this natural outfielder—he just knew it!). Before long, his energy dissipated and he fell asleep.

In time, we became chums. He seemed to depend on me more and more as his drug regimen was adjusted and readjusted. When a conference was called between his cardiologist and his family physician, he naively turned for my opinion first. With halting success, the team tried new approaches, investing him with our own sense of the possible. He clung fiercely to my medical powers, to my expert knowledge, to my white coat.

"You'll see me through, Doc. You're a magician," he would say.

•

Perhaps I could—my pride swelled and I told him that, with the right medicines, he'd soon be feeling much better. But by believing in the power I became a magician who had eaten his own rabbit; swallowing the illusion was simply the last possible trick, and nothing was left up my sleeve. The chest pain continued, exacerbated by his dread of each coming night and the fear of a body over which he had lost control.

Exacerbated—made worse.

More specialists met to consider therapies. Experimental drugs were proposed and other diagnostic tests were performed. As he was too old for a heart transplant and had already undergone extensive surgery, we searched for a successful pharmacologic approach. The cardiologist began his analysis by drawing graphs of a normal cardiac output: the contractility of muscles, the size and internal pressures of the heart chambers, the rates of cardiac contractions, all playing their parts. Then, superimposed upon these orderly studies, he drew in the distortions of Mr. Strap's cardiovascular machinery. Our goal was to find the ways to get it running properly again.

But as we concentrated on the mechanics, we became captives of our own metaphors. We had persuaded ourselves that his sick heart was simply a pump in disrepair, and had forgotten that his body, despite our exertions, would tell its own story. When his wife visited, she saw things we did not: his wilting posture, the altered resolution in his voice, a different look in his face.

"Just do what you can," she said.

Her conversation had a premature sadness in it, coming—I thought then—from her lack of knowledge rather than her wisdom. She, better than we, understood the evanescent source of his deterioration.

Evanescent—fading.

As we turned more toward our pharmacopeia, I watched his faith in the scientific arsenal ebb. And as the algorithms of the medical textbooks that guided our decisions failed him, so did the roles that went with them. Our relationship transformed itself again—I went subtly from doctor and saviour to friend and son. It was as if he had forgiven me for something he had known all along I could not do.

In this transformation our customary discourse dissolved with the inability of the machinery and the drugs to fulfill their promise. Each layer of formality faded away, and the two of us were left surrounded and unhindered by the equipment, simply as witnesses to a repeating, timeless process: a young man watching an old man die. And this teaching hospital, with its complex hierarchy and its ambitious science, became in that moment merely a place where young men and women, with titles of maturity and profession, oversee the dying of their elders.

Soon our conversations were punctuated by the empty dance of doctors confronting terminal illness. The pace of these activities quickened, and I worked to manipulate his failing blood pressure

~ Review ~

Limits of the Possible

This article, which originally appeared in the *New York Times,* is about an interning doctor's first days in a cardiac intensive-care ward. In particular, it is about the nature of the relationship that develops between himself as "doctor" and the elderly, seriously ill "patient," named Mr. Strap.

At first, Mr. Strap responds well to various forms of treatment, and increasingly regards the novice medicine man as a kind of magician, seemingly able to correct any health problems with pills and machinery.

Over the next few days, the patient survives one medical crisis after another, and his faith in medical science grows. However, his wife seems to understand, even before the doctors, that her husband is dying and their reassurance that medicine can save him is their illusion.

Mr. Strap's condition deteriorates and the doctor-patient relationship is transformed; the doctor becomes "a young man watching an old man die" as he realizes the limitations of the discipline of medical science.

and improve his breathing. But Mr. Strap's death occurred while I was not in the hospital, and he seemed to leave me without transition. His last breath and heartbeat were caught immediately by the intensive-care nurse, and I was told that a long and energetic cardiac arrest code was performed on an unresponsive patient. I must have looked as though I was going to cry when they told me, because the resident on duty placed his hand on my shoulder and said it would be different next time. I wasn't sure.

QUESTIONS

1. Explain why Shenson calls his words "a kind of medical lullaby."

2. Explain what Shenson meant when he said that the doctors became "captives of our own metaphors" and why this resulted in the man's wife seeing, before the doctors did, that the man was dying.

Acid Rain

Michael Badyk

Acid rain is a term that is now in common use by us all, including most of the people involved in the study of this problem, such as biologists, ecologists and chemists. In reality, the problem includes not only acid rain but also acid snow, acid fog, acid dew, acid frost and dry fallout that occurs on perfectly sunny days. It is reaching the earth all day, all year and all over the planet.

The source of this problem is the technology that we have used over the last few hundred years. Acid rain is not new to the last 20 or so years. There is some evidence from illustrations made from carved wooden stamps and also from paintings originating in Germany in the late 1700s that suggests that acid has been damaging trees for some time. The main aspects of our technology that have contributed to these acids are: first, the refining and burning of fossil fuels (including the production of petrochemical based materials such as plastics); and second, the refining and manufacture of metals.

Our global economy is tied to these activities. Our technology often is measured by what we can produce from metal or plastic, and by using power contained in the carbon of the fossil fuels we can accomplish fantastic things. The burning of coal over the last few hundred years greatly improved life for all humanity, and the more recent use of oil and gasoline has changed our society forever. Automobiles and aircraft that we really can't do without any longer are perfect examples of the application of these technologies. The use of metal and the acquisition of the means to do things with it is woven through our past. It can be seen in such terms as the "Bronze Age" and the "Iron Age," used as labels for time periods based on the metallic achievements of the times. These two terms are used to denote our increasing sophistication in the application of technology over time.

ACID RAIN

Acid rain is a term that is now in common use. In reality, the problem includes not only acid rain but also acid snow, acid fog, acid dew, acid frost and dry fallout that occurs on perfectly sunny days.

Impurity as a Normal State

There is one aspect of the fossil fuels and metals that is not evident to most people—what we pull from the ground to use is seldom pure. Sulphur is commonly contained in coal, oil and natural gas. There are exceptions of course. In Pennsylvania, some of the oil is so pure that you could take it out of the ground and pour it right into your car. Normally, though, if you tried this with most crude oil, you would destroy the engine. The purer the oil or coal or natural gas is, the more its value increases. The less pure is known as dirty coal, or sour gas, and there are many different types of oil quality. Something like iron or nickel doesn't occur very often in purities that would allow us to use it directly out of the ground. Again, there are some exceptions. On the south shore of Lake Superior in what is now the State of Michigan there are deposits of copper that are almost pure. The aboriginal peoples who inhabited the area discovered it and were able to fashion useful items from it (which were traded all over the Great Lakes region). Again, normally what we get is the metal contained in something called an ore. Iron ore, for example, has lots of iron but also impurities, including other metals, silica, and most likely sulphur.

By-Products: The Result When Impurity Changes to Purity

These impurities are removed by refining. Most of the sulphur can be removed from the fossil fuels by chemical treatment. One of the common sights around a petrochemical refinery is a flame. This flame is fuelled by the sulphur waste being burned off. The same thing is true with natural gas. Further, more often than not, we don't even try to remove the impurities from coal—we just burn it as is. The product of this burning is a chemical compound known as sulphur dioxide.

An oxide is produced when a substance reacts with oxygen in the atmosphere to form a compound. Iron oxide, which we call rust, is a simple example. Sulphur dioxide denotes that there are two oxygen molecules linked with one sulphur molecule. When we turn on our automobiles we burn the gasoline and any sulphur that still may be in it, once again producing sulphur dioxide. We purify metals by heating them to liquify the solid ore. We can then separate the part we want. The only thing wrong with this procedure is that the sulphur in the ore burns off rather than liquifying. And once again, this produces sulphur dioxides that enter the air. And, unfortunately it isn't just sulphur dioxides. There are oxides of nitrogen contained in there, too. There is also a range of other materials released into the atmosphere. They might not necessarily form acids, but their production goes hand in hand with acidic materials.

Basically, anywhere on earth where we refine fossil fuels or purify metals, we will be creating pollutants. You could look at the Tar Sands project in Alberta, the iron factories of Hamilton, the metal refining of Rouyn and Noranda in Quebec for Canadian examples. Everywhere that you can find an automobile you can find another source of pollutants.

From a chemical standpoint, the problem is that sulphur dioxide combines with water to form an acid. Nitrous oxides do the same thing. The water can be in a cloud (where the compounds of sulphur and nitrogen combine with the water) and then subsequently fall to earth. Or, the compounds can fall in a dry form (dry fallout), and when they encounter water they form an acid just as easily as the acids form in the clouds.

Acids and Bases

Acids carry the connotation of something harmful. However, we use acids quite often in our everyday lives. Lemon juice is an acid, and so is vinegar. Coffee and tea are acids. We also use acids to power batteries, thus creating the term "battery acid."

Almost everyone knows that acids are reactive—in other words they act upon whatever they come in contact with to form a new substance, which obviously alters the old substance permanently. That is, if an acid is poured on an object, then something is going to happen (e.g., if you pour acid on your hand and your hand dissolves). But there is a range of substances that are reactive that are not called acids; they are known as alkaloids or bases or antacids (the opposite of acids). This would include such things as hydrogen peroxide and ammonia.

There are two substances that make things reactive. For acids it is hydrogen ions (H), and for bases it is hydroxides (OH). If you combine the two of them in equal strengths and quantities you end up with something un-reactive that is very familiar: H_2O (water). Pure water is said to be neutral. If this is true, then we can use it as a means of comparing the other substances that may be acidic or basic.

In order to make comparisons between substances, chemists have devised a scale known as the *pH*, or *potential hydrogen scale*. It has values that run from 0 for the strongly acidic, to 7 for the pure water, and finally to 14 for those that are strongly alkaline. Vinegar would have a value of about 3.1 and ammonia would have a value around 11. Lemon juice comes in at around 2.2 and battery acid is about 1.8. You might ask how we can drink lemon juice with a *pH* value not too far from battery acid when we know what would happen to us if we drank the battery acid. The way in which the *pH* scale has been constructed is on a logarithmic basis. That implies that, for example, if the *pH* value went from 5 to 4, then the actual acidity of the substance increases 10 times. So the difference of 0.4 *pH* units between lemon juice and battery acid is very significant.

The Neutralizing Process

If acids can be so damaging, how can we get rid of them? To neutralize the acids a base of equal strength would have to be added. If you have ever had a bitter cup of tea or coffee you would normally add milk or cream to it to reduce the bitterness. The bitterness comes from the acids that are contained in the beverage. The milk or cream contains a reasonable amount of calcium carbonate, which is the base. By combining the two of them, you approach the neutral value. If you have ever had an acidic stomach, then you have probably taken an antacid such as Rolaids or Tums, which contain calcium carbonate, just like the milk.

The Buffering Capacity of Rock

Lakes, rivers and the soil have a built-in neutralizer, similar to Rolaids. This usually comes from the type of rock that the body of water or the soil sits upon. This ability to neutralize an acid is referred to as the *buffering capacity*. This capacity is extremely variable on both a global and local basis. In southern Ontario the rock is mostly limestone, which is high in calcium carbonate. A lake that sits on this limestone will be able to neutralize a good deal of acid that falls into it because the soft and easily dissolved rock will enrich the water with minerals. The exact opposite is true of the area in central and northern Ontario, which is dominated by the type of rock known as the Canadian Shield. It is very different from the limestone. It is infinitely harder and is usually lacking in calcium carbonate. In fact, it is so hard that very few minerals ever dissolve into the water. This makes the buffering capacity very low. Unfortunately, both areas receive precipitation that has to be considered acidic.

Normal precipitation has a value between 5.5 and 7.0 on the *pH* scale. Ontario quite regularly receives precipitation with values around 4. While the lakes in southern Ontario are still in good condition, and the soil and the vegetation seem to be reasonably good, on the Canadian Shield it is a very different story. Some of the trees seem to be dying and some of the lakes are dead.

What Makes a Lake Live

The death of the lakes is really what has attracted public attention. You have to understand how a lake lives before you can understand how it dies.

To make a lake you first of all need water. Then you need some sort of basin to put it in. That is a start, but it still doesn't make it suitable for life. You need certain dissolved minerals to feed the plants (mineral nutrients) and you also need sunlight and warm temperatures over a reasonable period of time. These variables mean that there can be many types of lakes and also a great variety in both the amount and type of life that a lake will have.

Just from this you could probably tell that a lake on the limestone of southern Ontario will potentially have more life in it than a lake on the Canadian Shield, based on the amount of dissolved minerals and the latitude. You might have noticed this on your own. The lakes of the tourism area of the Canadian Shield are noted for their clarity, while most lakes on the limestone turn into green soup by the end of the summer. The presence of all those mineral nutrients will feed a wide variety of aquatic plants. The plants in turn will feed a variety of plant-eaters (herbivores) and subsequently a variety of meat-eaters (carnivores). This interconnection is known as the food chain. The water and minerals of the lake make life possible for a wealth of plants and animals both in and around the lakes.

The Death of a Lake: How "Wet Deserts" Are Created

Acid affects the lakes in a number of ways. The first thing that happens is that the mineral nutrients that would normally feed the plants are used up in the neutralization of the acid. This, of course, implies that less is available for the plants, so the number of plants in the lakes decreases. This then lessens the herbivore and the carnivore population which affects the animal life directly. The acid in their systems forces dramatic chemical changes, the most insidious of which is that the animals' reproductive organs are slowly destroyed. This means that the existing animals are the last of their kind in the lake—they will not produce offspring. The overall effect on the lake is that life slowly winds down. It is a slow, gradual fade to oblivion over 20 years or even longer. The strangest thing is that the water looks to be in perfect health. It is absolutely crystal clear. That extreme clarity is achieved because there are no algae or bacteria or anything in there that would cloud the water—it has been called a "wet desert." Perhaps that is why we have not reacted to it until recently—the water is clear so it has to be healthy.

That is the scientific, objective, quantified assessment of this problem. We used chemistry, geology, geography and biology to assess the acidification of our lakes. You may not have understood all of the technical information, but you will understand the implication. Canada is dominated by the Canadian Shield geology. We have millions of lakes on this type of rock and they are all potentially threatened.

Human Losses: Where Science Ends

Science is able to illustrate the chemical and biological loss. However, it is unable to illustrate the losses to humanity. These losses are many and varied.

Psychological Losses

It is not possible to list these losses in any sort of hierarchy, or order of importance; that is up to the individual person to determine. But let us look at some of them. There is definitely a psychological loss. It is very common for people, even those in urban areas, to think that there are or should be areas on this planet where the hand of humanity has not reached. It is stressful to think that there are many remote lakes that are dead. Killarney Provincial Park, south-west of Sudbury, is officially designated as a wilderness park and is often called the "Crown Jewel" of the province's parks. It has magnificent high ridges of startling white quartzite rock, almost pure silica, and on a bright day it gives the illusion of snow on top of these high rounded ridges. These high ridges look down on brilliant blue lakes, but most of the lakes are dead. One can describe this but it is difficult to convey the profound feeling one gets when standing beside this clear lake knowing that it is dead. Or, what it feels like to cup your hand and drink some water from the lake and taste aluminum that has been pulled out of the rock by the acidic water. That impact is far greater than reading that there are so many parts per million of aluminum in the water or that the *pH* is at a certain level. It is a profound sense that something is dreadfully and painfully wrong.

Social Losses

There is a social loss here as well. The native people of the area are now living with lakes that are not in the same condition as they were for thousands of years. We might not be able to appreciate this. The ridges of Killarney are holy places to these first peoples and are regarded as a source of great spiritual power. Natives today still seek the solitude and power emanating from nature in these ridges. To be on a ridge top and look down on a lake and know that it is now dead must be unbelievably sad to them. Or possibly it is maddening. Someone not from their culture can identify with their anguish and anger.

In non-Native society there is a loss as well. The people that would go to the north, the wilderness, and the solitude, are now faced with an altered world. We can't escape the hand of humanity even in the Canadian north. That hand is there in the lakes in which we fish, on which we canoe, in which we swim and by which we live. It may never be the same. Throughout this text, we have discussed the fact that societies do change, but are we prepared to see our world and that of Native peoples change so dramatically in this way?

Economic Losses

An economic loss is present here as well. Many of the communities of the north owe their existence to the recreation that occurs on the lakes around them. The small community of Killarney just outside of the park is a perfect example. Although it is not evident as yet, it is inevitable that people will stop coming to an area where all the lakes are poisoned and polluted. The loss of the tourism dollars will lead to the end of the community, a fact already appreciated by the people of the north. Their livelihood could disappear very soon. Their economic well-being will fall into our hands through unemployment insurance and welfare payments. We may even have to pay to have water brought into the community because the residents can no longer drink it. Acidic water can dissolve the copper in the plumbing of homes and businesses and poison people with copper sulphate, which can affect their liver and kidneys. Once again, the rest of society will have to pay for the health care costs to these victims of acid rain pollution. As our taxes will probably have to be increased to pay for all this, the standard of living of all Canadians will be directly affected.

Cultural Loss

In one sense, the greatest loss is a cultural one. The one thing that is deeply engrained in the Canadian mind is a sense that this great and untouched wilderness is just over the next hill. The sense of wilderness turns up in our art. Musicians such as Gordon Lightfoot, CANO, and Bruce Cockburn have composed lyrics and ideas based on these images. Writers such as Farley Mowat, Pierre Berton and Gabriel Roy craft pictures of wilderness which once read are never forgotten.

Probably the most distinctive appreciation of this wilderness is the paintings of the Group of Seven. The abstract landscapes of these artists are part of the Canadian identity. They are found in all of our museums and art galleries, and many of them are found as reproductions in our homes. They are part of our culture, and they are painted at Killarney. There is an A.Y. Jackson Lake in the park; there is also an O.S.A. Lake, standing for the Ontario Society of Artists which is the official working name for the Group of Seven. Most of us have seen paintings of the Killarney area in their art and not even known it. They depict rugged hills and lone gnarled pine trees. They are almost a stereotype of what the north should be. And those lakes in those paintings are now dead. We, as Canadians, have lost something here.

The Role of the Subjective Self

We may now be at the limits of what science can do. It is not to say that we should abandon the science, it is just that science needs to be motivated by a profound sense of humanity and human emotion. To solve the problem of these dead lakes will take human emotion more than it will take a scientific solution. We will have to become concerned or angry enough to become involved with the solution. Science can supply us with the tools, but our emotions and our feelings will be a vital part of the solution. It might require a deep involvement in our economic or political system to say to the people in charge that the losses that have been detailed in this short essay are no longer acceptable, and those prepared to sacrifice our environment in the name of profit or science or both should be stopped.

Adding more science is not the answer. Science is sometimes seen as a way of automatically solving the problem that it has created. This is a false sense of security. It has been suggested that we could dump concentrated calcium carbonate, lime, in the lakes and then restock them with plants and fish, but this is only a band-aid solution that looks at the symptom but not the cure. We have to look at ourselves. We are the cause because of our demand for energy and consumer products. That point has to change before the problem is solved.

Ultimately our lives depend on the solution. If the food chains of our planet, both on land and in the water, fail, then the life-support system for us will also have failed. Are we, as a technically advanced society, prepared to die by our own hand? We can't ignore what we have done to this planet. We have to be aware of all this because "all this" is us—we are dependant on the whole variety of plants and animals that exist here. The tool we have in science is very powerful. With this power comes great responsibility. One can only hope we are responsible enough to make the right decision.

Our life depends on it.

Farewell Address to the Los Alamos Scientists

J. Robert Oppenheimer

J. Robert Oppenheimer is often described as the "father" of the atomic bomb. He was responsible for bringing together some of the greatest scientific minds of the time to work on the development of a nuclear weapon. The work was carried out in great secrecy in the isolation of Los Alamos, New Mexico. The Second World War was at its peak, and there was some concern that Nazi Germany would develop the bomb before the Allies. After the war, the Los Alamos facility was closed and the scientists who had gathered there went on to other pursuits.

Oppenheimer had mixed feelings about the development of the atomic bomb. In his farewell address he poses several questions to his colleagues. He was proud of the accomplishment, but he was concerned that it had been used against fellow human beings. He did not like the secrecy that had been attached to the project because he was convinced that science should include sharing and learning. He also worried about the future use of atomic energy. He challenged his colleagues to consider the moral implications of what they had achieved. Individual humans had unleashed tremendous forces—but who was going to take responsibility for the consequences?

In considering what the situation of science is, it may be helpful to think a little of what people said and felt of their motives in coming into this job. One always has to worry that what people say of their motives is not adequate. Many people said different things, and most of them, I think, had some validity. There was in the first place the great concern that our enemy might develop these weapons before we did, and the feeling—at least, in the early days, the very strong feeling—that without atomic weapons it might be very difficult, it might be an impossible, it might be an incredibly long thing to win the war. These things wore off a little as it became clear that the war would be won in any case. Some people, I think, were motivated by curiosity, and rightly so; and some by a sense of adventure, and rightly so. Others had more political arguments and said, "Well, we know that atomic weapons are in principle possible, and it is not right that the threat of their unrealized possibility should hang over the world. [It is] right that the world should know what can be done in their field and deal with it." And the people added to that that it was a time when all over the world men would be particularly ripe and open for dealing with this problem because of the immediacy of the evils of war, because of the universal cry from everyone that one could not go through this thing again, even a war without atomic bombs. And there was finally, and I think rightly, the feeling that there was probably no place in the world where the development of atomic weapons would have a better chance of leading to a reasonable solution, and a smaller chance of leading to disaster, than within the United States. I believe all these things that people said are true, and I think I said them all myself at one time or another.

But when you come right down to it the reason that we did this job is because it was an organic necessity. If you are a scientist you cannot stop such a thing. If you are a scientist you believe that it is good to find out how the world works; that it is good to find out what the realities are; that it is good to turn over to mankind at large the greatest possible power to control the world and to deal with it according to its lights and its values.

There has been a lot of talk about the evil of secrecy, of concealment, of control, of security. Some of that talk has been on a rather low plane, limited really to saying that it is difficult or inconvenient to work in a world where you are not free to do what you want. I think that the talk has been justified, and that the almost unanimous resistance of scientists to the imposition of control and secrecy is a justified position, but I think that the reason for it may lie a little deeper. I think that it comes from the fact that secrecy strikes at the very root of what science is, and what it is for. It is not possible to be a scientist unless you believe that it is good to learn. It is not good to be a scientist, and it is not possible, unless you think that it is of the highest value to share your knowledge, to share it with anyone who is interested. It is not possible to be a scientist unless you believe that the knowledge of the world, and the power which this gives, is a thing which is of intrinsic value to humanity, and that you are using it to help in the spread of knowledge, and are willing to take the consequences. And, therefore, I think that this resistance which we feel and see all around us to anything which is an attempt to treat science of the future as though it were rather a dangerous thing, a thing that must be watched and managed, is resisted not because of its inconvenience—I think we are in a position where we must be willing to take any inconvenience—but resisted because it is based on a philosophy incompatible with that by which we live, and have learned to live in the past.

There are many people who try to wiggle out of this. They say the real importance of atomic energy does not lie in the weapons that have been made; the real importance lies in all the great benefits which atomic energy, which the various radiations, will bring to mankind. There may be some truth in this. I am sure that there is truth in it, because there has never in the past been a new field opened up where the real fruits of it have not been invisible at the beginning. I have a very high confidence that the fruits—the so-called peacetime applications—of atomic energy will have in them all that we think, and more. There are others who try to escape the immediacy of this situation by saying that, after all, war has always been very terrible; after all, weapons have always gotten worse and worse; that this is just another weapon and it doesn't create a great change; that they are not so bad; bombings have been bad in this war and this is not a change in that—it just adds a little to the effectiveness of bombing; that some sort of protection will be found. I think that these efforts to diffuse and weaken the nature of the crisis make it only more dangerous. I think it is for us to accept it as a very grave crisis, to realize that these atomic weapons which we have started to make are very terrible, that they involve a change, that they are not just a slight modification: to accept this, and to accept with it the necessity for those transformations in the world which will make it possible to integrate these developments into human life.

As scientists I think we have perhaps a little greater ability to accept change, and accept radical change, because of our experiences in the pursuit of science. And that may help us—that, and the

~ Review ~

Farewell Address to the Los Alamos Scientists

Scientists are obliged to find out as much as they can about how the world works. That is their job according to physicist J. Robert Oppenheimer, who asserts that our discovered knowledge about the world is of intrinsic benefit to humanity. Scientists should not operate under a partisan veil of secrecy but should share their findings with all branches of humanity.

Developing the world's first atomic bomb was an "organic necessity,"

Oppenheimer told the scientists who had helped him do just that. In his address to departing colleagues after the job had been successfully completed, Oppenheimer discussed the profound effects atomic weapons had on civilization, and the moral and social responsibility of scientists towards their work and its implications.

Oppenheimer objects to the view that modern science is dangerous, arguing that rather than suppress our pursuit of knowledge, we must deal openly with its moral consequences.

He acknowledges the "grave crisis" that atomic weaponry has instigated, however, and says that those who prefer to minimize or deny this crisis inevitably deepen it. He urges his fellow scientists to stick scrupulously to the truth, expressing his conviction that they must continue their pursuit of knowledge without hesitation.

Finally, he reminds his listeners that they are humans as well as scientists, and deeply bound to protect the interest of humankind.

fact that we have lived with it—to be of some use in understanding these problems…

•

There are a few things which scientists perhaps should remember, that I don't think I need to remind us of; but I will, anyway. One is that they are very often called upon to give technical information in one way or another, and I think one cannot be too careful to be honest. And it is very difficult, not because one tells lies, but because so often questions are put in a form which makes it very hard to give an answer which is not misleading. I think we will be in a very weak position unless we maintain at its highest the scrupulousness which is traditional for us in sticking to the truth, and in distinguishing between what we know to be true from what we hope may be true.

The second thing I think it right to speak of is this: it is everywhere felt that the fraternity between us and scientists in other countries may be one of the most helpful things for the future; yet it is apparent that even in this country not all of us who are scientists are in agreement. There is no harm in that; such disagreement is healthy.

But we must not lose the sense of fraternity because of it; we must not lose our fundamental confidence in our fellow scientists.

I think that we have no hope at all if we yield in our belief in the value of science, in the good that it can be to the world to know about reality, about nature, to attain a gradually greater and greater control of nature, to learn, to teach, to understand. I think that if we lose our faith in this we stop being scientists, we sell out our heritage, we lose what we have most of value for this time of crisis.

But there is another thing: we are not only scientists; we are men, too. We cannot forget our dependence on our fellow men. I mean not only our material dependence, without which no science would be possible, and without which we could not work; I mean also our deep moral dependence, in that the value of science must lie in the world of men, that all our roots lie there. These are the strongest bonds in the world, stronger than those even that bind us to one another, these are the deepest bonds—that bind us to our fellow men.

QUESTIONS

1. List the three reasons Oppenheimer gives for saying that "secrecy strikes at the very root of what science is and what it is for."

2. Oppenheimer felt it was very important that scientists accept responsibility for the "very great crisis" that came with the development of atomic weapons. State what the two beliefs are that he felt people used to "wiggle out" of this responsibility.

3. List the three things that Oppenheimer believed scientists should be reminded of.

UNIT 5

ARTS AND CULTURE

■ **ISSUE 1:**
  The Role of the Arts

■ **ISSUE 2:**
  Objective vs. Subjective Responses to Art

ISSUE 1

The Role of the Arts

A capitalist society requires a culture based on images. It needs to furnish vast amounts of entertainment in order to stimulate buying and anaesthetize the injuries of class, race, and sex. And it needs to gather unlimited amounts of information, the better to exploit natural resources, increase productivity, keep order, make war, give jobs to bureaucrats. ... The production of images also furnishes a ruling ideology. Social change is replaced by a change in images. The freedom to consume a plurality of images and goods is equated with freedom itself. The narrowing of free political choice to free economic consumption requires the unlimited production and consumption of images.

Susan Sontag

The purpose of art is the lifelong construction of a state of wonder.

Glenn Gould

The Role of the Arts

Clive Cockerton

Think about the sports hero, after scoring a touchdown or a goal. Picture the athlete in uninhibited self-expression, the little dance that celebrates the moment, the moment when for once the event planned for and visualized actually takes place. Most of us share in the athlete's joy (unless we have a big stake on the other team) but a few people are embarrassed by this exuberance, and can be heard muttering words like "hot dog" or "grandstanding" that clearly indicate disapproval. For these people victory should be savoured quietly, with a certain decorum that might suggest that nothing unusual (goal/TD) has happened.

There's another moment, probably a great deal more important than the athlete's dance, and that's the moment of the Saturday night dance. Whether it takes place at a prom, a club or somebody's recreation room, the moment requires careful preparation. There's all the body prep, the showering and the hair, and the crucial choosing of clothes to achieve *the look*. There's the rehearsal in front of a mirror, not just the look, but the right *moves*. Some thought is given to the right music and where you can go to get it (do you have to bring it with you or can you request it?). And when you're finally dancing with someone important, and the right song comes on, you really *listen* as you move, because you want it to be perfect, no mis-steps, no awkwardness. Sometimes life then smiles, and says to both of you, "OK truehearts, you've prepared for this, you deserve it, you can have your moment." And then you can't believe it as you both surrender to the music and the mood, you can't put a foot wrong, you move in harmony, you pulse in rhythm AND you achieve insight, not really as a thought or an idea, something much more fleshy and salty, a strange union of perception and pleasure, that tells you that life is MAGICAL after all.

Of course, this is why many belief systems discourage dancing. It offers a competitive view of the world, one devoted to pleasure, the senses, the here and now. Parents, even liberal ones who want you to have a good time, want to be sure you've got your algebra homework done first. Their voice says, get the work done before you play. Dancing, fooling around, the pursuit of pleasure are dangerous because they can distract us from our reality goals—getting our homework done, passing our courses, achieving a good education, getting a good job, getting ahead in life. Our reality goals demand that priorities be established, schedules be followed and discipline and order become a habit. In extreme form, this point of view is sceptical about pleasure itself, and seems to believe that anything pleasurable can't be serious. As anti-life as this view seems to be, the flip side, that anything serious can't be pleasurable appears thin and trivial to the same degree. This last notion reduces the idea of seriousness to a draggy sombreness, the domain of the long-faced and the stuffy. Perhaps both pleasure and seriousness need to be rescued from this debate.

At the very least, the reality instructors have convinced many of us that our success depends on the mind controlling the body and all its instincts for comfort, release and pleasure. Yet we are haunted by that moment on Saturday night, that perception that there's something else even more important than the progress we make in overcoming life's barriers.

These objections made to dancing are also voiced (in more muted tones, perhaps) about other arts (film, novels, music, etc.). In many people's eyes, the arts are the toy department of life, occasionally amusing perhaps but in the long run a waste of time for men and women of action and purpose. The Greek philosopher Plato (427–347 B.C.) argued that art was a distraction that someone looking for reality or truth would be better off without. According to Plato, art was a distraction because:

- art deals with images not truth; it doesn't advance knowledge, it doesn't discover anything, it only *seems* to understand.

- art imitates reality; to learn about reality it is much better to study reality itself rather than the pale imitation.

- art is sensual and distracts us from the more important quests (spiritual quests for instance). In its arousal of basic instincts, in its stimulation/simulation of violence and lust, it is anarchic, a force for disorder in the community.

Since Plato, many moralists have branched off of these arguments and have (less eloquently than Plato) argued, at various times, that bright colour and decoration is immoral because it calls attention to the self instead of singing the praises of God, or that "realistic" novels were too shocking for the delicate sensibilities of young women, or that rock'n roll would corrupt and deprave youth with its jungle rhythms. At a much less passionate level, business people, the folks of the bottom line, are sceptical of the arts, except where they can be trained to serve the purpose of promoting consumption of goods and services in advertising. Politicians of the small view frequently see the arts as frills, and in time of recession the artistic community is the first to feel the cuts of government spending and support. All of these views, whether held by philosophers, moralists, business people or politicians, have in common the conviction that art is not serious.

Television Fiction

Let's begin to look at the notion of seriousness by examining the art form most people spend the most time with (on average 24 hours per week)—television fiction. Television fiction, whether in the form of situation comedy, action adventure, or police drama *doesn't share* one very important ingredient with all other forms of fiction—suspense. The "what is going to happen next" question that accelerates into page-turning concentration in a novel or the laser-eyed excitement in the movie audience doesn't happen on TV. Only on rare occasions does suspense occur, such as the "who shot JR" question on *Dallas* or the "who killed Laura Palmer" question on *Twin Peaks*. So predictable are TV formulas, that having seen one it is usually possible to predict what will happen (in general terms at least) next week.

We keep watching for a number of reasons, one of them being the charm/presence/relationship of the main characters. TV is a small intimate medium and spends a lot of time focusing on the faces of main characters. If we find these characters attractive they become like family, invited into our homes every week, and the series becomes a success. It is interesting to note, however, that characters rarely change or develop. But if the plots are predictable and the characters don't develop, how does TV hold our attention? The main method is by multiple storylines, so that before we become bored with the plot, predicament, or character's reaction we are whisked off to another dimension (usually parallel) of the plot. Our interest is therefore spread over a larger field, reducing the chances of our becoming bored with any one aspect of the story. A look at a typical episode of the popular show *Magnum P.I.*, "Old Acquaintance," illustrates this process.

The program begins by showing the theft of a dolphin from an outdoor aquarium. Next we see Magnum at his home with T.C. and Rick. Magnum is preparing to meet an old acquaintance. Goldie Morris had been a friend of his in high school and had tutored him to help him pass English. T.C. and Rick tease Magnum about Goldie's unattractiveness in her high school photo. (At this point, the alert viewer is put on notice that this sexist fooling around will be rebuked by the now stunning presence of Goldie. This is as angry a rebuke as a TV series usually allow.) As Magnum is about to leave, Higgins enters, asking Magnum to drop off his credentials at the yacht of a visiting president of a mythical African nation. Higgins is planning to attend the meeting of the International Human Rights Advisory Council on this yacht as an unofficial representative of the British government which wants to keep its distance from President Kole and his record of atrocities towards his people. So, in the first three minutes, three storylines are set in motion:

1. The theft of the dolphin. Who took it and why? Will it be recovered?

2. Magnum and Goldie's relationship. When it turns out that she's become quite pretty, will their friendship change to romance?

   and

3. Higgins meeting with President Kole. Should he go? What is to be done about Kole's crimes?

It turns out, however, that these three storylines are intimately interconnected: Goldie was involved in the theft of the dolphin (out of over-zealous concern for animal rights), but her politically extreme cohorts have actually kidnapped the dolphin to use it to carry a bomb to blow up Kole and all those aboard his yacht. Magnum recovers the dolphin, saves everyone's lives (assassination is not the answer to dealing with dictators) and affectionately, but paternally, extricates Goldie from her difficulties (thereby paying her back for past kindnesses and reasserting his superiority). (From Sarah Ruth Kozloff, *Channels of Discourse*.)

Perhaps the hard-nosed critics of the arts can be forgiven for thinking of the arts as the toy department. The storylines interconnect in ways that are incredible and Magnum navigates his way through the maze without ever really being in great danger.

Episodes conclude at the same place they begin—with the unchanging hero ready to resolve new predicaments next week. Think of *Miami Vice*. Over four seasons of being spectacularly under-cover, the audience was expected to wonder if Crockett and Tubbs would be (a) exposed or (b) corrupted. Miraculously, the Miami drug barons never figured out that the chicly-dressed pair in the Ferrari were always involved when one of their number went down. Towards the end of the run, the producers began to flirt with the notion of (b), Sonny being corrupted and going over to the other side. As soon as that happened, the air went out of the Mi-Vi balloon. These ultimate questions that lurk behind the action should only be implicitly present, like an ominous shadow, and never explicitly dealt with. Much better to return the heros to the police station, safe and secure, ready for next week's villains.

OK. The world of TV fiction is a fantasyland. But what happens when fantasyland tries to deal with serious issues from the real world? Issues of gender are usually presented as a "fun battle of the sexes," as in *Designing Women*. Single-parent families also share in a life that can be described as a *Kate and Alie* laugh riot. Being black in America becomes the cozy, comfortable *Cosby Show* or the loony *Fresh Prince of Bel-Air*. Homosexuality is the latest "issue" to surface on TV. *Hooperman* had a gay cop. *L.A. Law* has a lesbian lawyer; *thirtysomething* featured a homosexual relationship in which two men were seen in bed together, enjoying the afterglow but not actually touching. Despite the noble attempts of *thirtysomething* to present a real situation involving gay men, most TV dramas play up the "gayness" as a gag, focusing on the alarmed and frustrated reactions of parents and peers.

As irritating as this downsizing of their dilemmas may be to women, single parents, blacks and homosexuals, TV does take away the threat to the status quo implicit in any political cause or vocal minority. It's a trade-off; something is lost and something won. When a group or cause makes it to TV, television domesticates the dilemma, reducing it to manageable proportions suitable for the living room. Still, something has been gained from this understandably annoying process. Television reduces fear, encourages tolerance if not acceptance, and most importantly confers normalcy on what had previously been regarded as aberrant and threatening.

Television Fact

Many people rely on television news/documentary as their chief source of information. By and large, Canadian news teams do a creditable job of providing and interpreting information. However, an awareness of the limitations of the medium is essential if the audience is not to be deceived.

The first and most obvious limitation is that television must photograph something. When a story is relatively difficult to film, such as inflation, the producers may try to illustrate the falling purchasing power of the dollar graphically by showing $100 worth of groceries in two shopping carts. Shopping cart no. 1 contains $100 worth of groceries in 1975; shopping cart no. 2 contains $100 worth of groceries in 1991. See the difference. Yes, it's a neat visual summary of inflation, but once you've done this once, it's hard to keep repeating it. What in fact happens is that the non-visual story gets less air-time; it is devalued as a news item because of the presentation difficulties, however important it may remain to the economy and the viewer.

The second major limitation comes from the news/documentary team's goal to entertain as well as inform. What's the matter with entertainment? Who wants a stuffy, dry presentation of events that may seem very distant to the average viewer? As much as I agree with the spirit of those questions, it is also true that in practice the efforts of producers/directors and writers are bent towards telling a compelling story. The real world is chaotic, with events sometimes happening at random, without satisfactory explanation. However, a news story that can't make up its mind, that tells us that country X could go to war with country Y, or maybe country Y would align itself with Z, making war unlikely, or that internal dissension in country X could prevent any action—well, that is a news story fast on the way to losing our attention. We don't look for nuances on TV. We want to know—war or peace? Which is it? The producers are well aware of this need for a clear and dramatic answer and they're prepared to find it. And if finding it at times seems a little difficult, perhaps they can invent a thesis and hope their educated judgment stands them in good stead. All too frequently a camera crew is let loose on a situation, not to make discoveries, but to search for preconceived moments that support a satisfying interpretation.

The temptation to use television techniques (such as skilful editing of opposing views, or excessively tight close-ups of the "villain" in the piece) to colour the story, is enormous. In a now famous dispute between the head of the American Army in Viet Nam, General Westmoreland, and the CBS network, the program *60 Minutes* implied that General Westmoreland set out to conceal estimates of enemy strength from the President of the United States, Lyndon Johnson. Although there were plenty of knowledgeable people prepared to support the General, many were not approached for interview. Of those interviewed, those in favour of the *60 Minutes* thesis outnumbered those against by 9–2. Of course, they had to include *some* contrary views, to avoid charges of bias, but by following the statements of support for the General with, for instance, shots of the interviewer in mouth-opened disbelief, it can be very easy to undermine what has just been said. As much as many people are inclined to believe ill of the U.S. military in Viet Nam, when they ran up against the might and technique of CBS, they became the victims of reporting. The American military has learned much about dealing with the media, and during the recent Gulf War, managed to control the news of the war and to shape the debate over the war. What was permitted to be shown were neat images of high-tech weapons searching out the door of a bunker. We marvelled at the stunt, the techno-wizardry of it all, and didn't much think about the human misery that is attendant to all wars.

Because television shows us real people in real situations we tend to believe it too much. Since television interprets the world for so many people, it is crucial that they are not innocent of the warp that television brings to the world.

Television Propaganda (Commercials, Advertising)

Now, who takes commercials seriously? Well, the average Canadian spends 32½ working days per year watching them (according to the Bureau of Broadcast Measurement, 1989 figures). Commercials underwrite everything you see on TV—fiction and news/documentary programming. Without commercials our present system of programming would collapse. Business people take commercials very seriously indeed, spending large portions of their budgets to advertise and promote their products. And, of course, the commercials are the best made element in TV. The budget for a 30-second commercial can exceed the budget for the half-hour or even hour-long program. Commercials present their messages with a dazzling display of technique.

Of course they have to be dazzling for they are meant to be viewed over and over again, sometimes within the same hour. If suspense is absent to a surprising degree from most of television fiction, it is totally absent from commercials after the first viewing. The rapid succession of images (sometimes faster than 1 image per second) sets up a visual rhythm, the soundtrack an aural rhythm, and the narration punches us silly with the slogan.

Commercials adopt one of three basic approaches. They can present their case in a visual essay, a mini-documentary, arguing that Brand X really is preferred by most doctors over Brand Y. (Pain relief ads seem particularly fond of this approach.) The lyrical, image-laden car/beer commercial presents another approach, full of vitality, sex and adventure. The third and perhaps most often used approach is the mini-story. Part 1: Your laundry powder doesn't seem to get things clean any more, your drains are plugged, your hands are chapped, your muffler falls off. Part 2: Someone suggests you try new Sunlight, Liquid Plumber, Vaseline Intensive Care, or Speedy. Part 3: Your whites are whiter now, your drain sucks water, your hands are touchable again, and not only is your car fixed, you're a Somebody, too. It is the pattern of the faery-tale. The problem is stated, the magic wand appears, the problem not only vanishes but also the very quality of one's life has been enhanced.

But it doesn't stop at just the small vexatious problems of everyday life. The world of the commercial is a world where most women have now become airline pilots, bank managers and entrepreneurs. It is a world where racial tension is replaced by harmony and mutual understanding (think of the Bennetton ads). It is a world where everybody behaves with great respect for Nature, and sees in the communication of wolves or whales an organic system worthy of being copied. It is a world of our fondest wish and the message is that it can be ours, here and now. It is a vision of great innocence and attractiveness, despite its lack of any clues as to how to achieve this world. You have to remind yourself that it is a vision bent to the task of selling—soap, mufflers and hand cream. Those thirty-second visions are important because they create urgency around a purchase and complacency around a world.

Film

Television is like someone you know who's "nice enough" but who you have no desire to know further; film is like someone who breaks through your social reserve, someone who has a hold on you, someone to be passionate about. They are very different media as anyone who has studied them will tell you. As television domesticates issues and renders people predictable and safe, film casts a magic light, transforming events into crises and people into heroes. Partly it has something to do with scale; the size of the image in film is heroic. Partly it has to do with the intensity of the image; it's so much brighter, sharper, you can see much more than you can see with current TV technology. Partly it has to do with technique; in film the camera explores its subject with imagination, from a variety of angles, with dramatic lighting falling on the subject. As well, the camera *moves through* a situation, a crowd, a landscape, which psychologically creates the illusion that you, the viewer, are in the scene, surrounded by action. This seductive camera movement is in stark contrast to the more static point of view of television, which imitates the point of view of the tennis spectator, "thwack"—look left, "thwack"—look right. The images change (on average every 3½ seconds) but they are seen from a relatively unchanging perspective. On film it is possible to leap onto the court, to visually both serve the ball and return it. It is a more complex, more varied and more intense experience.

Film is also a bigger adventure. There are bigger risks, the heroes sometimes die, the lovers sometimes end tragically. The predictability that we find on TV is available only on certain types of film (those starring Sylvester Stallone, for instance) and even in these films there lies the compensation of truly spectacular effects. But generally in film the question "What is going to happen next?" carries some force; far more options, both happy and sad await. We watch the story unfold, acted by recognizable if heroic people, told by a dynamic and fluid camera, and for the two hours of watching, the film reality can be almost as strongly experienced as any other reality. As we face the dilemmas with the characters in the film, our sense of what drives, disturbs and delights other people is deepened.

The Novel

Deepened by film, but if we want to get to the source of all human understanding, that quivering voice within us all, we have to go to novels. For in novels we can not only see behaviour as we do in film, but we can follow the contents of the mind as it responds and reacts to the world around it. We are not just limited to experience another's external behaviour, but, by crawling into the fictional character's mind, we can experience another's experience as well. It is this ability that makes literature the most intimate of the arts, able to explore the faintest shadows of thought and the most powerful of emotions.

We experience novels as we do the world—from a perspective, a point of view that is both emotional and rational. Despite the major role that the scientific process has played in expanding our understanding, we generally don't experience life as detached observers. Instead we grope about through our lives, using bits of knowledge and lots of emotion in a constantly shifting understanding—as we do in novels. When we persevere through a novel, we may come to know a situation or a character very intimately; indeed, we may know all the significant details about a person's life (thoughts as well as actions). It's possible to know fictional characters better than our close friends. By providing us with all the information we need and by coming to a conclusion, novels present a complete vision. This completeness necessarily lacks some of life's random quality. Novels conclude, life goes on. By concluding, novels ask us to stop and think. By focusing on some of the most fundamental issues (growth, independence, love, pain, death) that we encounter in the real world, novels ask us to reflect on our own lives. But they don't just ask, they seduce us with pleasure, with worlds spun from word-magic; they seduce us with intimacy, they leave us with insight.

If you've ever seen a film adapted from a favourite book, you know the two media have very different insights, very different strengths. To put it in simple terms, the film paints a physical landscape, shows us physical action. The novel gives us an interior landscape, lets us hear the deepest voice. Of course, films are not satisfied with telling just physical tales; actors speak and gesture and through these techniques suggest interior emotion. Lighting and camera work can create an emotional atmosphere. Voice-over narration can tell us (usually in an awkward fashion) what a character is thinking. Still, despite film-makers' efforts to stretch the structure of their medium it is generally true that they do not succeed in going as clearly, completely inside the individual as do novelists. However, this fact doesn't mean that novels are always more serious than the films that get made from them. Some novels (*The Godfather*, for instance) don't exploit the structural advantages available to a novel, while the film version does stretch the structural limitations of film resulting in a great and serious film based on an inconsequential and superficial book.

Literature is the most intellectual art form. Ideas are produced by scientists, philosophers, academics, teachers, journalists but it is in literature that the ideas are given flesh, tested not in debate, but in a re-creation of life. Through this process we find what ideas are useful, not just as ideas but as guiding principles. We learn what works, what is credible, what plays. The pages of literature contain a great sifting and a great pleasure.

It is unfortunate that seemingly fewer and fewer people partake of this great pleasure. A few years ago, parents were concerned that if their children weren't computer literate, that somehow they would be condemned to a powerless position in society. Computers were brought into the home, computer courses introduced into the curriculum. Now everyone computes, but only the powerful still read. It is a pity, for its pleasure and insight should be shared by all.

Conclusion

In the rest of this unit other arts, such as photography and rock music, will be discussed. Susan Sontag in her sometimes difficult but rewarding essay "On Photography" points to the role that photography plays in family life, as validation and verification that various family experiences (birthdays, holidays, graduations, weddings) have indeed taken place. As well, Sontag argues that photography is conservative in spirit, on the side of the status quo, for in order for a photograph to be justified, the events (even tragic ones) have to take place. Given a choice to intervene or photograph a suicide, the true photographer's instinct is to get the picture. Although many photographers have used their art on the side of social change (war photographers especially), it remains undeniable that they must first record the gruesome reality before they can secondarily work to change it.

Another article, "Leftist Causes: Rock Seconds Those Emotions" looks at the power of rock'n roll to voice anger over injuries of class and age. Unlike pop music, which papers over the cracks of our differences with its over-produced, cholesterol-rich sound, rock music forcefully articulates the frustration of those who will inherit a world not of their own making. The music from the other side of the tracks isn't safe; it has the power to focus the anger of the young and the under-valued, to urge defiance of the old order. Its politics may be rebellion, its pleasure is manic delight in the body.

Which reminds me of that moment at the Saturday night dance where we began—that strange union of perception and pleasure that is as fundamental to the arts as to a dancing couple. Many cold winds blow through an individual's life, but the arts tell you that you're not alone, that others have cried as hard, laughed as loud, and loved as deeply. There's pleasure in that—in the community with others that the arts magically bring to us. Serious pleasure.

On Photography

Susan Sontag

Photographs furnish evidence. Something we hear about, but doubt, seems proven when we're shown a photograph of it. In one version of its utility, the camera record incriminates. Starting with their use by the Paris police in the murderous roundup of communards in June 1871, photographs became a useful tool of modern states in the surveillance and control of their increasingly mobile populations. In another version of its utility, the camera record justifies. A photograph passes for incontrovertible proof that a given thing happened. The picture may distort; but there is always a presumption that something exists, or did exist, which is like what's in the picture. Whatever the limitations (through amateurism) or pretensions (through artistry) of the individual photographer, a photograph—any photograph—seems to have a more innocent, and therefore more accurate, relation to visible reality than do other mimetic objects. Virtuosi of the noble image like Alfred Stieglitz and Paul Strand, composing mighty, unforgettable photographs decade after decade, still want, first of all, to show something "out there," just like the Polaroid owner for whom photographs are a handy, fast form of note-taking, or the shutterbug with a Brownie who takes snapshots as souvenirs of daily life.

Mimetic—imitative.

Virtuosi—people of great skill in the arts.

•

Recently, photography has become almost as widely practised an amusement as sex and dancing—which means that, like every mass art form, photography is not practised by most people as an art. It is mainly a social rite, a defense against anxiety, and a tool of power.

Memorializing the achievements of individuals considered as members of families (as well as of other groups) is the earliest popular use of photography. For at least a century, the wedding photograph has been as much a part of the ceremony as the prescribed verbal formulas. Cameras go with family life. According to a sociological study done in France, most households have a camera, but a household with children is twice as likely to have at least one camera as a household in which there are no children. Not to take pictures of one's children, particularly when they are small, is a sign of parental indifference, just as not turning up for one's graduation picture is a gesture of adolescent rebellion.

Through photographs, each family constructs a portrait-chronicle of itself—a portable kit of images that bears witness to its connectedness. It hardly matters what activities are photographed so long as photographs get taken and are cherished. Photography becomes a rite of family life just when, in the industrializing countries of Europe and America, the very institution of the family starts undergoing radical surgery. As that claustrophobic unit, the nuclear family, was being carved out of a much larger family aggregate, photography came along to memorialize, to restate symbolically, the imperiled continuity and vanishing extendedness of family life. Those ghostly traces, photographs, supply the token presence of the dispersed relatives. A family's photograph album is generally about the extended family—and, often, is all that remains of it.

As photographs give people an imaginary possession of a past that is unreal, they also help people to take possession of space in which they are insecure. Thus, photography develops in tandem with one of the most characteristic of modern activities: tourism. For the first time in history, large numbers of people regularly travel out of their habitual environments for short periods of time. It seems positively unnatural to travel for pleasure without taking a camera along. Photographs will offer indisputable evidence that the trip was made, that the program was carried out, that fun was had. Photographs document sequences of consumption carried on outside the view of family, friends, neighbours. But dependence on the camera, as the device that makes real what one is experiencing, doesn't fade when people travel more. Taking photographs fills the same need for the cosmopolitans accumulating photograph-trophies of their boat trip up the Albert Nile or their fourteen days in China as it does for lower-middle-class vacationers taking snapshots of the Eiffel Tower or Niagara Falls.

A way of certifying experience, taking photographs is also a way of refusing it—by limiting experience to a search for the photogenic, by converting experience into an image, a souvenir. Travel becomes a strategy for accumulating photographs. The very activity of taking

Assauges—makes milder or less severe.

Exacerbated—made worse.

pictures is soothing, and assuages general feelings of disorientation that are likely to be exacerbated by travel. Most tourists feel compelled to put the camera between themselves and whatever is remarkable that they encounter. Unsure of other responses, they take a picture. This gives shape to experience: stop, take a photograph, and move on. The method especially appeals to people handicapped by a ruthless work ethic—Germans, Japanese, and Americans. Using a camera appeases the anxiety which the work-driven feel about not working when they are on vacation and supposed to be having fun. They have something to do that is like a friendly imitation of work: they can take pictures.

People robbed of their past seem to make the most fervent picture takers, at home and abroad. Everyone who lives in an industrialized society is obliged gradually to give up the past, but in certain countries, such as the United States and Japan, the break with the past has been particularly traumatic. In the early 1970s, the fable of the brash American tourist of the 1950s and 1960s, rich with dollars and Babbittry, was replaced by the mystery of the group-minded Japanese tourist, newly released from his island prison by the miracle of overvalued yen, who is generally armed with two cameras, one on each hip.

Babbittry—a self-satisfied, middle-class conformist (from the character in the novel *Babbitt* by Sinclair Lewis).

Peremptory—absolute, dictatorial.

●

A photograph is not just the result of an encounter between an event and a photographer; picture-taking is an event in itself, and one with ever more peremptory rights—to interfere with, to invade, or to ignore whatever is going on. Our very sense of situation is now articulated by the camera's interventions. The omnipresence of cameras persuasively suggests that time consists of interesting events, events worth photographing. This, in turn, makes it easy to feel that any event, once underway, and whatever its moral character, should be allowed to complete itself—so that something else can be brought into the world, the photograph. After the event has ended, the picture will still exist, conferring on the event a kind of immortality (and importance) it would never otherwise have enjoyed. While real people are out there killing themselves or other real people, the photographer stays behind his or her camera, creating a tiny element of another world: the image-world that bids to outlast us all.

Photographing is essentially an act of non-intervention ... how plausible it has become, in situations where the photographer has

~ Review ~

On Photography

In this thoughtful essay, the author studies the camera and the role the related practice of photography plays in our lives.

As Sontag suggests, photographs are regarded as such an accurate representation of what lies "out there" that they are commonly admissible as evidence in a court of law. We "take" wedding, baby and other pictures to chronicle important events.

And we use the camera, Sontag argues, as a defense against our anxieties and fears to make us feel comfortable in foreign spaces. "Most tourists feel compelled to put the camera between themselves and whatever is remarkable that they encounter," she observes. "Unsure of other responses, they take a picture."

So, when encountering amazing works of nature or humans, like Niagara Falls or the Great Wall of China, the Grand Canyon or the Parthenon, the tourist aims, frames and clicks the shutter. The camera shapes the experience and by default establishes a passive role for the tourist, who by seeing the world through a viewfinder becomes a chronic voyeur, a spectator, an observer instead of a participant. The tourist denies his own awe and sense of wonder, capturing though diluting the power of the moment.

According to Sontag, the camera, and thereby the person using it, takes a morally neutral position towards the photographic subject. Taking a photograph, she writes, is "an act of non-intervention." The media show astonishing, even shocking photographs related to natural and human-made disasters and tragedies, floods, famines, assassinations and other events focusing on human suffering that are repetitiously the central component. By snapping the picture, the photographer preserves the unfortunate situation on film before attempting to improve it. And so, says Sontag, the picture taker may end up prolonging the suffering for as long as it takes to get a "good" picture.

the choice between a photograph and a life, to choose the photograph. The person who intervenes cannot record; the person who is recording cannot intervene. … Even if incompatible with intervention in a physical sense, using a camera is still a form of participation. Although the camera is an observation station, the act of photographing is more than passive observing. Like sexual voyeurism, it is a way of at least tacitly, often explicitly, encouraging whatever is going on to keep on happening. To take a picture is to have an interest in things as they are, in the status quo remaining unchanged (at least for as long as it takes to get a "good" picture), to be in complicity with whatever makes a subject interesting, worth photographing—including, when that is the interest, another person's pain or misfortune.

Status quo—things as they are at present.

Complicity—involvement in wrong-doings.

Leftist Causes? Rock Seconds Those Emotions

John Rockwell

Inherent—existing in something.

I s there an inherent leftist political bias, or even component, to rock-and-roll? The issue came to mind recently when Richard Taruskin, a musicologist writing in *The New Republic*, called into question similar assumptions about classical-music modernists of earlier in the century by citing right-wing opinions of various sorts held by such icons as Stravinsky, Schoenberg and Webern.

Icons—greatly admired thing or person.

The leftism linked with rock is most immediately visible in the periodic political benefits and tours undertaken by such leading rock performers as U2, Sting and Bruce Springsteen. Be it anti-nuclear protest or anti-apartheid or anti-political oppression or anti-poverty, likely as not your favourite rock stars are raising money for it or contributing their own money to it or writing songs about it.

Rock's leftist bias arose from its origins as a music by outsiders— by blacks in a white society, by rural whites in a rapidly urbanizing economy, by regional performers in a pop-music industry dominated by New York, by youth lashing out against the settled assumptions of pre-rock pop-music professionals.

Plethora—overabundance.

That bias was solidified by the 1960s, with its plethora of causes and concerns. For a few years, it looked as if society really were changing in some profound way. (In a sense, it has indeed changed, but we don't think about that so much in this time of conservative reaction.) Rock music was the anthem of that change—racial, with the civil-rights movement, and also social, sexual and political.

But a closer look at rock and politics reveals a more complex, or perhaps just a more muddled, picture. First of all, as rock has spread from an outsider protest to the mainstream, it has been embraced by nearly every constituency, from neo-Nazi skinheads and their head-banging speed metal to the Christian right to Reagan-style populists to leftists of every stripe.

Most rock is not about specific political positions, after all, but more generally (vaguely? deeply?—it depends on whether you're an artist or an idealogue) about basic human emotions. Likely as not, that emotion is love, to which no political faction has yet established a convincing claim.

Idealogue—propagandist for a particular cause.

Even when Mr. Springsteen writes of embittered Vietnam veterans in "Born in the U.S.A."—his most controversially political song—he doesn't make it a point-by-point political broadsheet. His meaning seems clear to anyone who listens closely. But his lyrics are not so explicit as to purge his song of deep emotion—or, if you want to be cynical about it (and lots of Springsteen-bashers want just that these days) to alienate any portion of his potential market.

There is another reason that rock sideslips away from neat ideological categorization. Words may have political meaning, more or less explicit. But music operates on its own more powerful, more primordial agenda. People loved "Born in the U.S.A." because of the catchy title/choral refrain, to be sure, but also because the music, huge and powerful and booming through a stadium sound system, galvanized them to a mass communal response.

Primordial—fundamental.

It is just that power to motivate the masses that has attracted totalitarian manipulators to popular music, not least Joseph Goebbels at the Nazi Nuremberg party rallies. Understandably nervous highbrow critics have often denounced rock not just for its real or imagined sexual licentiousness (the usual complaint) but also for its hypnotic, brutalizing power.

Joseph Goebbels—Adolf Hitler's Minister of Propaganda.

Licentiousness—a lack of sexual restraint.

These critics have been on the left as well as the right. British Communists have been hip enough to invite rock bands to play for party functions. But traditionally, Eastern European Communists have been suspicious of rock, seeing it as an example of commercialized Western decadence. (Now, however, they seem to be lightening up a bit.)

More significantly than as a symbol of capitalism, rock has the power to unsettle any repressive regime: it can inspire a rage or an exhilaration unrelated to any precise political agenda. In Marxist terms, it can become the anthem not of the proletariat but of the Lumpenproletariat, those debased members of the underclass just as

Proletariat—working class.
Lumpenproletariat—unskilled workers.

Fascism—extreme
right-wing political beliefs.

Liturgical—a form of public
worship.

Connotations—associations.

likely to become the footsoldiers of Fascism as the standard bearers of a Marxist revolution. It was John Cage, of all supposedly open-minded, tolerant souls, who provoked a controversy at a New Music America panel discussion in Chicago a few years ago by branding the instrumental avant-garde rock of Glenn Branca as "Fascist."

The current popularity of Christian rock, from the blander pop of Amy Grant to the tougher stuff purveyed by Stryper, recalls the controversies that have surrounded religious music as far back as Luther, or even Plato. It was Plato who, in *The Republic*, remained stoutly suspicious of all art, especially music, as inherently untrustworthy within the rational moral order. Luther, who championed a powerful liturgical tradition in his church, was combatting those deeply suspicious of anything so potent that was not certifiably holy.

With Christian music, whatever the outwardly pious correctness of the lyrics, the music swelling those lyrics into emotional significance is less easily controlled. And with Christian rock, whose inherent connotations seem to evoke sexual excitement and political unrest, one can understand the hesitations of those within the more straitlaced Christian community who remain suspicious of any and all Christian rockers. U2 is a Christian band, after all, in that most of its members are avowed Christians and the band's songs sometimes make use of overt Christian imagery. But U2 resolutely refuses to associate itself with any of the approved Christian denominations.

To this taste, the overt leftism of present-day rockers is partly a matter of fashion, however sincere any individual performer may be. Deeper down, true rock (as opposed to the "product" of all-purpose contemporary electronic pop music, which has hardly any ideas at all, let alone political ideas) remains inescapably a music of protest.

That protest is likely to express itself in leftist terms in the West because our basic political and social system (especially in the Reagan-Thatcher climate of the last decade) is conservative, in the face of third-world and underclass unrest. But art has its own meanings that don't always neatly correlate with political programs. For those of us profoundly moved by art, it is art's bedrock significance that is more likely to effect meaningful change in human society than mere party politics.

Objective vs. Subjective Responses to Art

The whole of art is an appeal to a reality which is not without us but in our minds.

Desmond MacCarthy

Art is ruled uniquely by the imagination. Images are its only wealth. It does not classify objects, it does not pronounce them real or imaginary, does not qualify them, does not define them; it feels and presents them—nothing more.

Benedetto Croce

Introduction

Clive Cockerton

When we attempt to choose a movie for Saturday night, we might begin by poring over the newspaper, scanning the listings, reading the reviews. We might weigh and balance the fact that Costner is "one prince of a thief" in *Robin Hood*, whereas Anthony Hopkins' performance is "chilling and brilliant" in *Silence of the Lambs. Jungle Fever* is mercilessly funny while *Thelma and Louise* is one of the best films of the year. This film is an "absolute delight," that film is "irresistible," this one "touching and sensitive." Choices, choices. How does one sort the good from the bad from such a list? Add to the questions of the intrinsic worth of the film the problem of the individual's mood. Sometimes "touching and sensitive" just doesn't stand a chance against "frivolous and fun."

In fact, most of the decisions regarding choosing a film are subjective. After all, how can one effectively compare a musical to a thriller except on the basis of how one feels at the moment? In choosing a film we make decisions based on content that is suitable to our mood and a faith that the form of the film will measure up to its content. Once we have seen the film, however, we usually wish to weigh the success of our choice. Our conclusions usually fall into two categories:

1. "I really like the film because … "
2. "That is a good film because … "

These statements are really very different from each other, with the first statement recording a subjective preference while the second attempts an objective evaluation. Preference tends to be more content-oriented as in "I really liked the ending," or "It was a great love story," while attempts to prove the worth of the film tend to be more form-oriented as in, "The photography was beautiful" or "The pace was exciting."

For most of us, whether or not we like a film is much more important than whether the film is any good. As well, it is clearly possible to like a film we know we cannot defend as a good film. Our preference may be formed because of the presence of a favourite actor, a locale such as Africa or New York that fascinates us, or moments such as steamy love scenes or violent car chases that we find irresistible. The presence of these elements in no way forms a criterion for excellence, and the absence of these elements does not indicate a bad film. Indeed, our preference for these elements declares a lot about ourselves and our own feelings but says virtually nothing about the film. As well, it is quite possible to dislike a film that we know to fulfill all the requirements of a good film, again for strictly personal reasons such as the fact that the film reminds us of unpleasant or painful moments in our own lives.

Although there is clearly no possibility of argument or contradiction about personal feelings on an art object (they just simply are what they are), it is also clear that we can change our minds about works of art. A painting can look shapeless and disorganized to us until someone more expert reveals a previously overlooked organizing principle. A novel can sometimes seem obscure and difficult until we become familiar with its language and world view. We might condemn a film as confusing and subsequently read an interview with the director where he states that he wants his audience to feel confused. If the film achieves its aim, how can we condemn it? These examples happen frequently and point to the fact that proper artistic evaluation is more than just a subjective statement about our perspective at the moment. It is not simply a case of thinking one thing on Monday and another on Friday. We replace the first view with the second because we think that the second view more accurately and objectively describes the art. It is as if at first glance we perceive a frog, but after consultation with experts we begin to discern the prince hiding within. Of course, there are many more frogs than princes, and we are more frequently deceived by art works that initially seem good but over time don't stand up to close examination.

Experts attempt to engage our minds in the task of analyzing the aesthetic emotion. They teach us to analyze the art work, to look separately at its elements, and to establish standards or criteria to evaluate the elements. The use of this largely mental process can help us to understand more about the art work independent from our own subjective bias. Aristotle identified three criteria based on his study of Greek poetry and drama: unity, clarity, and integrity. Unity (of mood, of time and place among others) as a criterion didn't have the longevity of the other two: Aristotle couldn't anticipate the successful mixing of comic and tragic mood that would take place in Shakespeare's plays and other later works. However, clarity of expression seems as useful a standard by which to judge as any. Integrity, in the relationship of the parts of the play/poem to the whole and in the relationship of the whole to reality, forms the basis of much critical judgment. If we substitute simplicity of design, or perhaps more appropriately, focus for the concept of unity, we have a starting point in our discussions of criteria.

However, in our search for objective criteria by which to judge art objects, it must be admitted that no criteria work universally for all art objects. We praise the playful fantasy in the paintings of Henri Rousseau yet we do not condemn the paintings of Eduoard Munch for lacking that quality; indeed we praise Munch for his graphic rendering of inner torment. We appreciate one novel's realistic depiction of character and delight in another's cartoon-like parodies. We appreciate the grim honesty of films like *Full Metal Jacket* and at the same time are charmed by the simple beauty of films like *The Black Stallion*. Yet on occasion films displaying "simple beauty" or "grim honesty" lack other qualities and we find them unsatisfactory. The fact that no one criterion or element guarantees a work's value makes the job of appraisal that much more difficult. One thing is clear: on different occasions we judge by different criteria. Moreover, the skilled and open-minded consumer of art lets the individual work of art dictate by which criteria it is to be judged.

Banality—dreary, predictable, worn-out quality.

Some contemporary critics suggest that in a modern consumer society we are so overwhelmed with artistic experiences and images that the task of sorting them into piles of good and bad is a hopeless one. These critics see a rough equality of banality in all objects, and find that wit and beauty come from the perspective of the audience, and are not necessarily contained in the art. It is how you see a TV program, for instance, not the TV program itself that makes the experience lively and intelligent or dull and stupid. Some of these critics would go so far as to say that a book has no meaning by itself, that an unread book is a vacuum, and that the reader is the one who provides the meaning. Since every reader's experience is shaped by their gender, their class and cultural background, there can be no universal objective meaning, only a collection of diverse and subjective impressions. As one recent critic, Frank Lentricchia, has written of his relationship to literature:

> I come to the text with specific hangups, obsessions, worries, and I remake the text, in a sense, for me, for my times. ... The moment you start talking about it, you have injected interpretation. The text is not speaking; you are speaking for the text. You activate the text.

Still other critics focus on the possibility of consensus (among informed observers) operating as a kind of objectivity. This agreement by experts operates as a kind of "rough guide" to truth. However, these "agreements by experts" do not always have the shelf life that one would expect. It is clear that some art work does not seem to travel well from one historical period to the next. The novels of Sir Walter Scott (*Ivanhoe, The Heart of Midlothian*) were extremely popular in the nineteenth century, and are hardly read today. In our own twentieth century, the literary reputation of Ernest Hemingway was extraordinarily high in the '20s and '30s but today Hemingway is more often seen as an interesting but minor writer.

One historical period may form an aesthetic preference for certain artistic qualities, preferring, for instance, clean and simple elegance to the previous generation's taste for exuberant and stylized decoration. When watching old films on television, we can be initially struck by what now seems bizarre fashion and style. Our experience of these films can be even more seriously undermined by outmoded attitudes, particularly sexist and racist ones. Everything that has happened to form our present consciousness stands as an obstacle to the appreciation of these films.

Even within an historical period critics sometimes disagree about the value of an individual work. Recently, films such as *The Prince of Tides, Pretty Woman,* and *Ghandi* have received very diverse reviews. All the critics may agree for instance, that pace in editing and structure is a very important element in a film's success. They may all agree that pace is a problem in a film such as *Ghandi*. But some critics will find that the other elements of the film compensate for the weakness in pace and will give the film an overall high evaluation. Some of the disagreement can be explained by the fact that, despite agreement *in theory* on the importance of pace, *in practice* many critics habitually weigh some criteria more than others. Therefore those critics who regard editing as the most essential creative act in film will habitually favour films that possess skilful editing in spite of other problems that may exist in the film. Other critics may habitually value elements of script, acting or cinematography more highly than editing and refuse to accept that the obvious virtues in editing make up for the perceived weakness in acting. When a preference is habitual, we can be pretty sure that its origin is rooted deeply in our own personality and experience.

In spite of the effort of art critics to focus on the art rather than themselves, to analyze and evaluate the elements of art rather than narrate and describe their own experiences, it remains obvious that elements of personality can't always be overcome or transcended. Perhaps the relationship between art and our experience of art is circular. The more we possess the inner experience, the more we grow curious about that external art object. The more we learn about art, the more we learn about what makes us who we are. That moment on Saturday night when the theatre goes dark, we watch the slowly brightening screen and wonder what this film world will be like. At the end of the film, if we have been moved by the film, the natural instinct is to be quiet, to digest our own experience before surfacing to the workaday world. But watching movies is a social activity, and it's irresistible to turn to our friends and ask "What do you think? Wasn't it good? I really liked the part where …" We share our delight, and we compare experiences. Our view becomes larger.

* * *

Ultimately, the question is much larger than whether our statements about art are objective or not. The question applies not only to art. It's about the world. It's just that art is a convenient place to begin the argument. If we cannot agree on the meaning of a single art object, with its known borders, its beginning, middle and end, with its human author, how can we make statements about a limitless universe—a universe not divided into neat stages of development, ending in closure, but a universe (caused/uncaused) constantly evolving, stretching out to infinity and a universe whose author is either unknown or not available to interview.

Is the external world totally independent of us or as the Greek philosopher Protagoras held, is it us, and our perceptions that are the measure of all things? Even if we grant the existence of the external world, it doesn't seem possible to get beyond our perceptions of it. Scientists have their protocol, the scientific method, that is meant to banish subjective interpretation. In the search for the underlying principles of things as they are (remember Tom Olien's article) science took over from religion the chief role of establishing truth. And what a magnificent job science has done. In revealing the structure of subatomic particles, in predicting the location and timing of an earthquake or volcano, in isolating a deadly virus and developing vaccines and in improving the quality of life for millions, science can lay claim to being humanity's most successful enterprise.

Think of the surgeon holding a human heart in his or her hands, repairing a faulty valve and placing it back into the person's chest, giving them twenty years more of life. All of the knowledge, the complex theory and practical skill that go into a successful operation rest on a physician's informed judgment that an operation is called for. That judgment is fallible, as are all human judgments. For the history of science is full of examples of misreadings, of scientists finding only what they were looking for, and not finding what they weren't, of finding solutions to problems that not only fit the hypothesis but also the prevailing ideology. Ultimately, scientists too must depend on their very fallible senses (or their high tech extensions) to draw conclusions. As well the role of the scientist confers no immunity to normal human pressures, the ego needs, the economic necessity to succeed, the political compulsion to research in certain directions. Scientists may be the most objective amongst us, but even in this highly trained class of people, subjective considerations colour many perceptions.

The truth about the world, the final objective Truth, is getting harder to find, yet meaning, subjective meaning is everywhere. A single rational explanation for the universe and all it contains may no longer be possible. Our knowledge (scientific and otherwise) has grown and grown until it has reached a point beyond where any one individual can comprehend the whole. To see the whole domain of our knowledge we need to climb a very high mountain; we haven't found the mountain yet (although on several occasions we thought we had) and are beginning to doubt if it exists.

Instead of the overview from the mountain, what we have is the micro-view of the specialist. What we have are fragments of the whole, knowledge and insight from the physicist, the philosopher, the biologist, the historian, the psychologist, the literary critic, the political economist. The fragments don't cohere into one magnificent interpretation of the universe. They exist as beams of light that illuminate the darkness for a certain time, as probes that reveal something about the world, and as a point of view.

We both rely on and are suspicious of experts. We rely on them, for their fragmentary understanding of the world is the best insight that we've got. But in a deeper sense we know them to be fallible. No political thinker predicted the collapse of communism in Eastern Europe, yet we continue to tune into the TV to hear what they have to say. Young parents read everything they can get their hands on about child rearing, yet are highly selective in what ideas they apply to their own children. We may listen with interest to the reasoned arguments of the nuclear power experts, but when they tell us that we have nothing to fear the shadow of Chernobyl falls over the discussion.

Every discipline of study is currently racked with conflict, with dissenting voices. If even the experts can't agree, are the rest of us just gambling on what and who we choose to believe? It becomes so difficult to judge the worth of arguments that quickly threaten to go beyond our expertise. The difficulty causes many of us to give up the task of sifting through the ideas, adopting instead a weary and cynical assumption that all views are equal. Many of us come from school systems that value self-expression as the highest good. It doesn't so much matter what gets expressed (all views are roughly equal anyway); just so long as a view gets expressed, the system will applaud. This emphasis involves a radical turning away from the searching after truth that has so long inspired our education. If there's no truth to search for, why struggle so hard?

If there's no truth, then what we have left is competing views, subjective perceptions. My view becomes as valuable as yours because there's no way to successfully weigh and measure them against each other. On the surface, there's an increase in tolerance as we all recognize that what may be true for me may not be true for you. But beneath the surface lurks the urge for dominance, the recognition that the prevailing view belongs to the loudest, most powerful voice.

And so we have the competition of interests and perspectives: Quebec, the West, free trade, feminists, unionists, native peoples, blacks, environmentalists. The competition is healthy, the diversity of views enriching. But without truth as a goal, the contest of ideas has no referee; it's too easy for reason to become a weapon to beat your opponent, not a tool to dig for understanding. Still, we're in the middle of a huge process in our relationship to the world and each other. If fragmentation into competing perspectives and specialized bits of knowledge is the current mode, perhaps all we need to do is wait for the emergence of new and better ideas that might reconcile some of the conflicts and satisfy our yearning for something to believe in. The competition of ideas has been evident throughout this text: are we free or determined in Unit One; what changes and what remains the same in Unit Two; do we have the sense to co-operate with each other or are we doomed to conflict in Unit Three; can science provide the solutions to the problems it creates in Unit Four? Do we have to make a choice? Do we have to run to the comfort of certainty? Or do we have to learn to love the paradox—to see in contradiction the breathing in, the breathing out of ideas?

The arts, particularly narrative arts such as film and the novel, may have a role to play in helping us to reconcile apparent contradiction. By successfully creating a fictional world that re-creates the real world, the author/artist sets artificial boundaries to what is included in the story, how many characters, subplots and themes. Fictionalizing the world tells us everything we need to know; the author/artist creates a vision of life that is remarkable in its completeness. The sharing of this vision creates a sense of community between artist and audience and holds out the possibility of consensus. We are not alone; others see the same world, sometimes with great clarity and undeniable insight. It's as if the film or novel creates a fictional mountain, from which we can finally see the human truth stretched out below, in all its complexity and contradiction. It is just a glimpse, but reassuring. In the midst of the darkest night-time thunderstorm, the lightning can suddenly illuminate our world in a flash of brilliant light, letting us know that the world is still there, under the cover of darkness.

The Search for Form

Clive Cockerton

It is clear that the Canadian government, through its body of experts, believes that objective evaluations can be made about works of art and about what they can contribute to a culture. The experts reward the good art with government money and discourage the bad by withholding funding. Each of the experts from the different artistic areas brings criteria drawn from years of experience to judging art. As well as the criteria for good art, they also bring some sense of what might contribute to the broader Canadian culture, what might serve as Canadian cultural self-expression. The problem occurs when certain themes or styles become identified as officially Canadian, that is, promoting a standardized Canadian vision. It has been frequently said that our best Canadian film director, David Cronenberg, seems somehow un-Canadian. His stories of sophisticated people in urban settings confronted with physical horrors don't address the "official" themes of Canadian culture. His films may be about victims, but they are not victims of the cold or of loneliness. They do not endure long and hard trials; rather, they explode in intense and horrific ways. How un-Canadian. Yet he is a director who has lived all his life in Toronto and who has made all his films in Canada. If he is not Canadian, it is because we have an overly rigid expectation of what constitutes a Canadian vision. Organizations like the Canada Council naturally tend to promote works that express a coherent view of ourselves, but this coherence can sometimes become conformity, conformity to an official version of ourselves.

More fundamentally, many people have difficulty accepting the notion that a body of experts can come to valid conclusions about works of art. We can probably all recall moments when a teacher seemed to drone on about the monumental significance of a short story that made us ache with boredom, or the deeper levels of meaning in a poem whose message totally eluded us. It is always right to be skeptical about the experts, but our challenges to authority should also be matched by a willingness to apply the rules of evidence to any work of art. Just as we must always question the officially proclaimed ideas, we must also discover that some work is simply better than others.

Take the following two sentences, containing roughly the same content, and try to rank them according to merit.

> *Version 1:* Generally speaking, there are a lot more unhappy moments in life than there are happy ones.

> *Version 2:* Happiness was but an occasional episode in a general drama of pain.

As subjectively attached as I am to Version 1 (I wrote it), it must be admitted that while it has a conversational matter-of-fact quality about its grim message, it lacks the complexity and power of Version 2. When we look at Version 2, we notice the precision of the language and the tightness of the structure. Notice how key words are twinned to heighten the contrast: occasional and general, episode and drama, and, most importantly, happiness and pain beginning and ending the sentence. You might also notice that the sounds of the first half of the sentence are softly melancholic, while the second half has a leaden heaviness and finality. No doubt about it, once you examine closely, it is easy to see that in Version 2 the content has found its clearest and most forceful expression.

Let's look at two versions of another grim sentiment.

> *Version A:* Days go by one after the other in a monotonous way. This trivial parade of time ends in death. Life doesn't mean anything; it is just full of noise and anger, ultimately meaningless.

> *Version B:* Tomorrow and tomorrow and tomorrow creep in this petty pace from day to day, lighting the way for fools to dusty death. Life is a tale told by an idiot, full of sound and fury, signifying nothing.

Version B is probably the most famous statement of thoroughgoing pessimism in the English language. It is full of wonderful images, days lighting the passage to ultimate darkness, the ranting idiot's tale, while Version A will never be read anywhere beyond these pages, and even then quickly forgotten.

In literary terms, having the right (write) stuff has its base in the author's ability to create magical effects with language. These effects can be achieved through precise use of words, through an ability to manipulate the sound and rhythm of language, and through an ability to create haunting images.

Look at the following paragraph and notice how it begins in relaxed but precise observation of an ordinary occurrence. Where and how does it turn into something monstrous?

> Four men were at the table next to mine. Their collars were open, their ties loose, and their jackets hung on the wall. One man poured dressing on the salad, another tossed the leaves. Another filled the plates and served. One tore bread, another poured wine, another ladled soup. The table was small and square. The men were cramped, but efficient nonetheless, apparently practised at eating here, this way, hunched over food, heads striking to suck at spoons, tear at forks, then pulling back into studious, invincible mastication. Their lower faces slid and chopped; they didn't talk once. All their eyes, like birds on a wire, perched on a horizontal line above the action. Swallowing muscles flickered in jaws and necks. Had I touched a shoulder and asked for the time, there would have been snarling, a flash of teeth.

D. H. Lawrence in his novel, *The Rainbow*, wrote the following description of horses bunching around a woman walking in the fields. The woman has broken off with her fiancé and has subsequently discovered that she is pregnant. She walks the fields in extreme anguish when she confronts a herd of horses.

> But the horses had burst before her. In a sort of lightning of knowledge their movement travelled through her, the quiver and strain and thrust of their powerful flanks, as they burst before her and drew on, beyond.

> She knew they had not gone, she knew they awaited her still. But she went on over the log bridge that their hoofs had churned and drummed, she went on, knowing things about them. She was aware of their breasts gripped, clenched narrow in a hold that never relaxed, she was aware of their red nostrils flaming with long endurance, and of their haunches, so rounded, so massive, pressing, pressing, pressing to burst the grip upon their breasts, pressing forever till they went mad, running against the walls of time, and never

bursting free. Their great haunches were smoothed and darkened with rain. But the darkness and wetness of rain could not put out the hard, urgent, massive fire that was locked within these flanks, never, never.

She went on, drawing near. She was aware of the great flash of hoofs, a bluish, iridescent flash surrounding a hollow of darkness. Large, large seemed the bluish, incandescent flash of the hoof-iron, large as a halo of lightning round the knotted darkness of the flanks. Like circles of lightning came the flash of hoofs from out of the powerful flanks.

Why the horses seem menacing is mysterious, but we're sure that we're seeing them with the eyes of the Ursula, the heroine. Literature can often startle us with this kind of experience, with being inside the head of another (if fictional) person. But it's the *form* of the language that opens the door to this experience.

Michael Herr, in his book *Dispatches*, a chronicle of the Vietnam war, attempts to capture the emotional texture of combat in this paragraph.

Fear and motion, fear and standstill, no preferred cut there, no way even to be clear about which was really worse, the wait or the delivery. Combat spared far more men than it wasted, but everyone suffered the time between contact, especially when they were going out every day looking for it; bad going on foot, terrible in trucks and APC's, awful in helicopters, the worst, travelling so fast toward something so frightening. I can remember times when I went half dead with my fear of the motion, the speed and direction already fixed and pointed one way. It was painful enough just flying "safe" hops between firebases and lz's; if you were ever on a helicopter that had been hit by ground fire your deep, perpetual chopper anxiety was guaranteed. At least actual contact when it was happening would draw long ragged strands of energy out of you, it was juicy, fast and refining, and travelling toward it was hollow, dry, cold and steady, it never let you alone. All you could do was look around at the other people on board and see if they were as scared and numbed out as you were. If it looked like they weren't you thought they were insane, if it looked like they were it made you feel a lot worse.

This is a writer writing at the top of his game, taking the reader on a roller-coaster ride, using his craft to capture the subtle ways terror can grip.

•

There is a deep satisfaction that comes from an appreciation of form. An arrangement of words, images, colours or notes can illuminate a moment, create powerful emotion, and so change our perceptions that we never look at life or art in quite the same way again. Art can be more than form, and to be sure it can be full of ideas, archetypes and moral discriminations. But while it can be more than form, without form it is nothing; it loses its magical hold on us.

Outside of the realm of art, that perfect arrangement is harder to find in human relationships. Many of us find a sense of energy and harmony in nature, and discover a solace in contemplation of the beauties of nature. Perhaps this respect for nature explains our sense of the violation we experience when confronted with massive pollution, and explains why acid rain, the lead in the air, the depletion of ozone, the poisoning of our water, seem obscene. We have become so sensitive to this tampering with natural form that intentional pollution with toxic substances is now considered a criminal and not merely a civil offense. Companies such as Exxon become associated in the public mind with ecological disaster and do so at their peril. The public's tolerance of irresponsible and negligent behaviour on the part of private companies is slowly becoming a thing of the past, and the so-called "green movement" is emerging as a powerful political force.

In Unit IV Tom Olien talked of the search for an underlying principle as the great creative urge of scientists. Toby Fletcher's article in Unit III looks for a new world order to deal with global problems.

> When we transcend sovereign nation thinking, we become citizens of the world, loyal members of humanity. Global interdependence requires new definitions. Our personal and national interests can only be served through a more sophisticated, cooperative and collaborative relationship among nations.

Clearly, this relationship among nations can only be achieved by providing the institutions (the form) which will guarantee enough safety and security for sovereign nations to surrender some portion of their power to a world body.

This global view is evidenced in the way we look far beyond our national borders, the way we appreciate the inter-connectedness of nations. We listen with keen interest to reports from the former Soviet Union hoping for a better life for the average Russian and a more secure future for us all. If we accept the good things of interdepend-ence, however, it is also true that we feel more keenly the tragic disappointment of hopes in China, as the tanks and boots of the army attempt to crush the democratic spirit of the young students. It is an event that takes place far away, yet it touches us because we share the same urge for freedom as the Chinese students—our freedom already won, theirs in the process of a fierce and bloody struggle with a repressive government.

Whenever new ideas clash with an existing form, there is some dislocation, something lost as well as gained. Unit II of this text looked at what happens when the old values are challenged by new technologies and new ideas. People cannot see what is happening to them and vainly try to deny the impact of the change. Some societies can be aware of the process of change in varying degrees, but the task of integrating new forms with old always challenges our best efforts.

Finally, it is in our own lives that form has the greatest significance, as we attempt to find shape and meaning in the daily flow of our existence. The facts, the contents of our lives, are distressingly similar, as a comparative glance at any number of résumés shows. We are born, go to school, make friends, take part-time jobs, go to college and then on to a career. Along the way, we may form romantic attachments, get married, have children, grow older, watch children leave us, retire from our jobs and grow older still. But this sameness doesn't tell the whole story. As the old jazz lyric goes: "It ain't what you do, but how you do it." Some people's lives are tragic, while others with the same observable facts seem heroic. After we bury some people, all we can hear, after our own tears subside, is the sound of their laughter. What makes this life comic and that life pathetic? Clearly, it has something to do with perception, the percep-tion of the individual who lives it as he or she contemplates the moment and discovers the pattern in the flow of daily experience. These moments of perception are often struggled for, but sustain the idea of a conscious life. To be conscious, to understand what is happening to you, and to others, here and now, is a large part of the urgency and energy of human life.

Printed in Canada